D0993873

Sold

TESS STEVENS

Sold

HODDER

First published in Great Britain in 2008 by Hodder & Stoughton
An Hachette Livre UK company

First published in paperback in 2008

2

Copyright © Tess Stevens 2008

The right of Tess Stevens to be identified as the Author
of the Work has been asserted by her in accordance
with the Copyright, Designs and Patents Act 1988.

All rights reserved. No part of this publication may be reproduced,
stored in a retrieval system, or transmitted, in any form or by any
means without the prior written permission of the publisher, nor be
otherwise circulated in any form of binding or cover other than that
in which it is published and without a similar condition being
imposed on the subsequent purchaser.

A CIP catalogue record for this title
is available from the British Library

ISBN 978 0 340 96085 1

Typeset by Hewer Text UK Ltd, Edinburgh
Printed and bound in the UK by CPI Mackays, Chatham ME5 8TD

Hodder & Stoughton policy is to use papers that are natural, renewable
and recyclable products and made from wood grown in sustainable
forests. The logging and manufacturing processes are expected to
conform to the environmental regulations of the country of origin.

Hodder & Stoughton Ltd
338 Euston Road
London NW1 3BH

www.hodder.co.uk

To my dear daughter, with thanks
for just loving me, warts and all.

Acknowledgements

I'd like to thank all my wonderful friends who've encouraged me to write the story of my life, most of all Carol, who's stuck with me through thick and thin, and helped me cope when the memories got too much. Shirley and Babs, too, cheered me on, and so did Nickie and Greg – I'll never forget their note that arrived one time when I had my doubts: 'Go for it, girl!'

The book would never have got off the ground without my agent, Sheila Ableman. Not knowing anything about the publishing world, I picked her name at random, and as fate would have it I couldn't have made a better choice. She had faith in me from the very start. She introduced me to her professional writer, Chris King, who sat with me for hours and hours, recording my words, and worked with me to put the whole story together. Heartfelt thanks to both of them.

And thanks to the team at Hodder, especially Helen Coyle for her belief that I had a story worth telling.

Contents

I

Listen to Mother

Mother burst into the kitchen and made us jump. 'Right, you kids,' she said sharply, 'finish your tea and get out of here. I want you in bed in ten minutes flat.'

Ten minutes? We've only just sat down, I thought to myself. But there's no arguing with Mother. As she whirled out through the door again, us kids just gobbled down the banana sandwiches and doughnuts in front of us. I was sorry about the doughnuts. When you eat them fast, you can't taste them properly, and I especially liked the jam.

I finished first, and watched my little brothers and sisters cramming their mouths and dropping crumbs on the table. I automatically brushed up the crumbs in my hand, so Mother wouldn't tell us off for being untidy. Then I realised Andy, the youngest, had stopped eating. He was sitting quite still, holding the remains of a sandwich in one hand, and staring straight ahead. His mouth was closed, and his eyes were going glassy. He started to lean forward like a little rag doll.

'Mum!' I yelled. 'Andy's at it again!'

In an instant Mother was back in the kitchen, standing in the doorway, a duster in her hand. 'Oh, he is, is he?' she snapped. Her eyes were blazing blue, and patches of red suddenly appeared on her cheeks. 'Well, I haven't got time for this – I've just about had it up to here.'

She stalked over to Andy and yanked his head back by the hair.

'D'you hear me?' she yelled into his face. 'You've pulled this stunt one time too many, you little cunt. You hold your breath if you want, 'cos I don't give a shit. I've had enough. If you're gonna fucking die – well, die. The sooner the better. No one's gonna blackmail me, specially not a fucking child.'

And with that she slammed Andy's head against the chair back. He was blinking with shock, his mouth open. He started gasping in short sharp bursts.

Mother was grinning. 'Well, what d'you know,' she said. 'You can breathe after all. Making us run around like blue-arsed flies.' And she slapped him hard on his arm.

She turned to the rest of us. We were sitting frozen in our seats, gaping at her, while she glared at us. She flicked me on my face with the end of her duster. 'You, Ginger Cunt, make yourself useful for once. Your little brother will be sleeping with all of you – buggered if I'll have him back in my room. Clean him up with the rest of them.'

I nodded, and she stomped out of the room, saying over her shoulder, 'Ten minutes, or else.' I was hurt that she said 'for once'. I was always trying to be useful. What with the hurt and the way she'd had a go at Andy, I felt like crying, but stood up and said, 'Come on. We'd better hurry up.' As the oldest, at ten years of age, I was expected to keep the others in line.

Kath, Jess and Buddy whizzed into the scullery, and ran cold water into the sink. I went and knelt by Andy. He was still sitting in his chair, still clutching the half-eaten sandwich.

He was sobbing quietly, tears running from his eyes, his lovely dark eyes with their long curling lashes. I felt sorry for him. He wasn't used to Mother in one of her rages.

'Don't worry,' I said. 'You'll come in with us, you'll be all right.' I stroked his arm where Mother had slapped him, till the others came out of the scullery and headed down the passage to the toilet. I prised open Andy's hand and threw the squashed sandwich into the bin, then led him into the scullery. I wiped both our faces with the old flannel, then crouched down in front of him. I spoke slowly and clearly, so he would understand me. It was important for him to understand me, and he was only two and a half.

'Do you want a wee?' I asked him.

He nodded.

'Then go to the toilet now,' I said. 'You won't have another chance for ages.'

I saw him to the toilet, and he managed by himself. He was a smart little lad. If he was coming in with us, thank goodness he was out of nappies. Then I told him to go to the big front room while I used the toilet myself. Time was ticking by, so I hurried up the hall and joined the others. We all stripped down to our vests and pants, me helping Andy, and put our clothes on the wooden chair by the door. Kath and Jess hopped into the top end of the big old bed. Buddy as usual got in the bottom end.

I helped Andy on to the bed. 'You'd better go next to Buddy,' I told him. So there we were lying top to toe, three girls at the top, two boys at the bottom, our feet meeting in the middle. We all lay there quietly, not daring to move. Sunlight streamed through the large bay window – but not for long.

Mother appeared in the room, saying, 'Good job you haven't kept me waiting.' She walked quickly to the window, which had full-length shutters, old-fashioned wooden ones that folded out like doors to meet in the middle. She pulled them across with a bang, and fastened them with a metal bolt that sat in a kind of bracket. Then she headed back to the door, scooping up the clothes we'd left on the chair. She paused in the doorway, the light from the hall illuminating her red curly hair like a halo.

'Remember, you kids,' she said. 'One peep out of you and you know what you'll get.'

Then she shut the door behind her and turned the key in the lock. Now we were in almost complete darkness. Just a few thin streaks of sunlight came through the cracks in the shutters, and where they didn't fit properly.

We stayed silent for a while, not daring to speak. We heard Mother bustling up and down the hall, and into the other big front room. That must be where she was holding her party. Then she was back down the hall, into the kitchen.

'She won't be able to hear us now,' I whispered, sitting up and looking at my brothers and sisters. My eyes had adjusted to the low light and I could make out their shapes, though I couldn't see their faces. 'Want to play a game?'

'Can't be bothered.' That was Jess. Kath didn't speak. The boys seemed to be asleep already, but they were only little. They needed more sleep.

I was disappointed. I was hoping for a game of I Spy, at least. It didn't matter that we couldn't actually see much in the room. We simply remembered what was in there. Still, nobody wanted to play, so I lay down again. I wished I could make myself sleep, so I wouldn't have to put up with hours and hours of just lying there.

At least there were noises I could listen to. Kids were playing out in the street, shouting and laughing. Sounded like they were kicking a ball around, or playing tag. Some girls must have been playing Two Balls, as I could hear the steady beat of the balls being bounced on a nearby wall. I really envied those kids. I would have given anything to be out there with them. It was such a lovely day, the sun shining, not a cloud in the sky – I'd been hoping Mother would let us go out and play in the park this afternoon. Or maybe she would have turned us out of the house in the evening to go to the pictures. But no chance today.

Lying there in the darkness, I could hear other reminders of the outside world going about its business. Every half-hour or so the local train steamed by, blowing its whistle with a loud 'Wheeep!' Our house was on a bus route, and the red double-decker came to a shuddering halt right outside our garden wall. While people got off and on, the engine throbbed loudly. Then there were the rumbling coal lorries, working out of the yard just up the road. Once I heard a different kind of truck, and the sound of mooing and men shouting. I knew what that meant. These were the days before Croydon was all built up into a concrete jungle, and there was still a slaughterhouse across the street. I felt very sorry for those poor cows.

I must have eventually drifted off to sleep because I was suddenly awake, eyes wide open, the shrill sound of crying filling my ears. It was Andy, bawling his heart out.

My own heart thudding, I pushed back the sheet and moved down to Andy. I held him in my arms and desperately tried to soothe him. 'Sshh, sshh, it's all right,' I whispered. 'You've gotta be quiet, Mum will hear you. Sshh . . .' The other kids moved restlessly. They'd be awake themselves in a minute. I realised that there was no sunlight streaming in through the cracks in the shutters, just the faint orange glow of the streetlamp outside. It must be late evening. Mother's party would be in full swing.

Just then I heard the sound I'd been dreading. The key turned in the lock. I looked up just as Mother came through the door. By the light of the hall lamp I could see she was wearing one of her party frocks, a green one with a wide skirt, and was carrying a long-handled broom in one hand. Before I could think anything else, she'd grabbed Andy from my arms and flung him back down on the bed. His crying stopped dead. Pushing her head close to his, she hissed, 'If you don't shut up I'll give you something to cry for!' Then she lashed out at me, but I'd whizzed back to the top of the bed and had pulled the sheet up to my chin.

'Why didn't you keep the little bastard quiet?' she said in an angry whisper.

I started to say, 'I couldn't help it—' when she slammed the broom down across the full width of the bed, again and again, on our legs. 'I – told – you – to – be – quiet!' The thin sheet didn't do much to cushion the impact, and the other kids woke up in shock, and in pain. It took only seconds for them to realise that Mother was on the warpath again. We all huddled down, trying to make ourselves as small as possible, drawing up our legs to avoid the broom.

When she'd finished, Mother snapped, 'Look at me!'

We immediately did as we were told.

She spoke in a soft voice, which made the back of my neck prickle. 'What have I done to deserve such disobedient children?' she said. 'What have I done to make God punish me like this?'

She glared at each of us in turn.

'When I say be quiet, you'd better be quiet. If you're not, I won't be responsible for the consequences. Understand?'

We nodded, all except Andy, who was still lying huddled up.

'Good.'

And keeping her eyes on us, still holding the broom, Mother stepped backwards out of the room and closed the door. The key turned in the lock.

We kids lay still, just our chests heaving as we tried to stop crying. Buddy suddenly said, 'I need a wee.'

He clambered out of the bed and reached underneath for the chamber pot.

'Be careful,' I whispered. 'Make sure it goes in the pot.' I hated it when the wee splashed out – or, worse still, when everybody used it and it overflowed. It was always me who had to clean up next morning.

Buddy did his business and pushed the pot under the bed. He hopped back in under the sheet, and we all settled down.

As usual on one of Mother's special nights, we stayed in the room for about eighteen hours all told. Children should be seen and not heard, that's what people said in those days. But as far as Mother was concerned, us kids shouldn't even be seen, let alone heard. And we tried, we really did – me more than anyone. I only ever wanted to please Mother, to make her love me as much I loved her. I'd do whatever she wanted.

2

Mother's Little Ways

'Open the door! Please open the door!'

I was beating on our bedroom door with my fists and yelling out to anyone who might be around to hear. It was morning – I could tell by the light coming through the old shutters. I didn't have a watch, so I wasn't sure exactly what time it was, but I could just hear the sound of the wireless floating back down the hall. Someone must be up. One of Mother's visitors, maybe. It wasn't likely to be Mother herself. She was never one for early rising.

I hammered on the door again, desperately keeping my legs crossed. I was dying for a wee, but no way would I use that pot unless I absolutely had to. I hated using it at the best of times, and this morning it was impossible, overflowing with wee. It made me sick to my stomach.

'Hey! Open the door!'

I didn't care if I woke up my brothers and sisters. I had to get out. To my relief I could hear footsteps in the hall. Even if it was Mother, up early for once, it would be worth having a slap just to reach the toilet in time. As it happened, it was Don who turned the key in the lock, saying, 'Keep the noise down, can't you?'

I whizzed out, overtaking Don, who was making his way back to the kitchen, fag in hand. I was just in time, whacking myself down on the toilet as the heavens opened. I sat there, heart thudding in relief. That was the worst thing about being kept locked in, even worse than feeling as if I was buried alive.

Now to wash my hands. Mother was always very particular about hygiene. I wandered into the kitchen, where Don was sitting at the table, reading his paper, a cup of tea beside him. I went through into the scullery and washed my hands under the tap, using the stick of red carbolic soap. The clock in the kitchen said eight o'clock. That was early for Don to be up on a Saturday. He must be working an extra shift at the factory. Might as well stay up now I'm up, I thought to myself, and washed my face too. I picked up a clean vest, socks and knickers from the wooden clothes horse, and made my way back down the hall to the bedroom. Don ignored me as usual.

The other kids seemed to be fast asleep. That disturbance with Andy had broken up the night, of course. It was always hard to go back to sleep after an upset. I walked over to the chest of drawers where our clothes were kept, and pulled out a light dress. It looked like it was going to be another fine day. I dressed quickly, looking over at Andy. His face was flushed, and his thumb was in his mouth.

Poor little boy. No wonder he cried last night. When he woke up he must have wondered where he was. Ever since he was born, he'd slept in Mother's room, which she shared with Don. Don was Andy's father, so that made the bond more special. Don wasn't my father. He wasn't Kath's, Jess's or Buddy's, either. Just Andy's. Me, Kath and Jess had the same father, but to us he was just a name. Which was one up on Buddy: he didn't even know his father's name.

There was another reason for Andy sharing Mother and Don's bedroom. When he was born, he was what's called a blue baby. At the time I didn't know what that meant, exactly, except that it was something to do with his blood, and it was dangerous. For a while it was touch and go whether he'd make it. But make it he did, and he was everyone's darling, a beautiful child. Don especially thought the sun shone out of his bum. Nobody could understand why Andy suddenly started holding his breath, when he turned two. We all thought he'd die, and we'd go into a mad panic. It happened time and time again – until, obviously, Mother had had enough. She put Andy straight, right enough, and since yesterday he knew where he stood.

He stood like the rest of us kids, exactly where Mother wanted us.

As I leaned over Andy, I caught an unmistakable whiff.

'Have you wet yourself?' I muttered, checking the sheet underneath him. Sure enough, there was a big damp patch. That's all we need, I thought. Mother'll go mad. I wasn't sure what to do. I could get him a clean pair of pants, but there was no way I could take the bottom sheet off the bed without disturbing everyone.

Oh, well, just have to wait. Might as well get myself some breakfast.

I picked up my old vest and knickers and took them to the bagwash in the scullery. We had three pillowcases for the bagwash, two for whites and one for coloureds. What with the dirty sheet, it was a good job it was washday today. Mother would be sending someone to the bagwash place later on. When I came back out into the kitchen, I wondered if I should tell Don about Andy. He was his father's darling after all, maybe he'd help him. But looking at Don's scowling face, I thought better of it. He'd only blame me. So I set about cutting myself a couple of slices from the big white loaf in the bin, and spreading them with dripping from the basin on the table. Lovely stuff, thick white fat and dark juices from the meat. I shook a little salt over, put the slices on a plate, and sat down at the other end of the table from Don. He glanced up at me, then looked at my breakfast.

'Fat for the fat,' he sneered, shaking out his paper and folding it up. He slurped down the rest of his tea, then, clutching his paper, walked out of the kitchen.

'I'm off, Grace!' he called to Mother. 'See you dinnertime.'

Then the noise of the front door bolt being drawn, and a bang as he left the house.

I sat chewing my bread and dripping. I was used to Don calling me names. They were always about me being fat, like a pig. I tried telling myself that it didn't matter what he said, only Mother mattered in this house, but they still hurt a bit. I could understand that he didn't like me, I wasn't his daughter. Then again, Kath and Jess weren't his daughters either, and Buddy wasn't his son, but he wasn't so horrible to them. I shook my head. Just something I had to put up with, like a lot of other things in my life.

Don had finished all the tea in the pot, so I put the kettle on for a fresh one. Would Mother like one? Bit early for her, so I'd get her one later. I measured out a bare teaspoon of tea from the caddy, and poured in the boiling water.

'Never make more than you need!' Mother always said. 'Tea costs money.'

With a bit of luck she wouldn't know I'd sneaked myself an early cup. For a while I just relaxed, enjoyed the quietness in the kitchen. I could hear birds in the garden, singing away. They seemed happy. I gazed out of the window, smiling at the sight of the big plum tree just outside. When the fruit was ripe, you could reach out through the window and pick some. I looked forward to that every year. It was about the only thing worth looking at in the garden. There were no flowers, just weeds straggling about, and no grass to speak of, only patches of dust and dirt.

'You think I've got time to work in the fucking garden?' Mother had once said to Don when he asked about putting something nice out there. 'As if I haven't got my hands full, working my fingers to the bone with this house, and the kids, and the business?'

Don just sighed and said nothing. So the garden stayed how it was. I did wonder why Mother had bothered to make the garden bigger if she wasn't interested in it. Part of it was once fenced off, long before I remember. It belonged to the little old sweets factory that used to be in the basement of our house. When us kids heard about it, we wished it was still in business! We fancied that – sweets on the doorstep, so to speak.

'I had that fence down before you could say knife!' Mother would say, her eyes flashing. 'No one's gonna put a fucking fence in my garden!'

But, as I say, the garden was hardly used at all. Mother forbade us kids to go out there, unless she gave special permission. It was somewhere to kick a ball, if we were lucky. As I was standing at the window, teacup in hand, my eye was caught by the old wooden shed at the back of the garden.

Filth must still be asleep, I thought. A bit early for him. I hoped he wouldn't appear. He always gave me the willies, ever since I saw him for the first time. One morning, a few years ago, I happened to be standing at the kitchen window and saw the shed door opening. A scarecrow had walked out!

'Mum!' I'd screamed in fear. 'There's a scarecrow in the garden and it's walking about!' I was only little at the time, after all.

Before I could draw breath Mother was slapping me round the head. 'You silly cow,' she snapped. 'That's no scarecrow.'

'What is it then?' I asked, fear making me bold. 'And what's it doing in the garden?'

Another slap. 'Did I say it was any of your fucking business?' Mother demanded. 'As it happens, that's Filth out there, and that's where he belongs!'

'Filth?' I asked. As he got nearer, I could see the figure was a man. He was quite short, on the chubby side, with thin grey hair plastered over his head. He was filthy all right. His battered, shapeless old jacket and trousers were stained and torn. He was wearing big boots, with no laces, so they slipped up and down as he walked.

'He looks horrible!'

Mother slapped me again, this time with a big grin on her face. 'That's no way to talk about your father!' she cackled.

My father? How could he be my father? Mother had talked about my father. She always said he'd gone back to a place called Ireland. Surely he couldn't be this broken-down old man?

I had no more time to wonder, as Mother pushed me out of the kitchen. 'Go to your room,' she snapped.

In the big front room, I sat with the door shut, hearing Mother's heels tapping on the wooden floor of the hall. There was another sound, a shuffling.

'Come on, Filth,' Mother said, opening the front door. 'Time and tide wait for no man, and neither does the post office.'

So they were going out to the post office . . . Well, all a mystery to me.

As I stood in the kitchen now and looked at the shed, I thought about that old man. Did he actually live in the shed? I certainly caught sight of him now and then, shuffling about in the garden. Surely Mother must have been joking about him being my father? Whatever, I hadn't dared mention him again.

Just then I heard a voice behind me.

'Any more tea?'

I spun round and nearly dropped my cup – but it was only Jess, looking around in that vague way she had. A right Dolly Daydream.

'You'll do me in,' I said, 'creeping up on me like that.'

But I was so relieved she wasn't Mother that I squeezed out a cup for her.

'Is anybody else up?' I asked.

'Yeah,' murmured Jess, sitting down and holding her cup with both hands. Right. A chance for me to strip the bed. If I got things sorted before Mother got up, she might not be so angry. But first, I had Andy to attend to.

The other kids were just coming out of the bedroom. I caught hold of Andy and crouched beside him.

'I know you've done a wee,' I said. 'I'll have to clean you up. Come on, we'd better hurry.'

While the others used the toilet, I took Andy into the scullery and stripped off his wet clothes, which I put in the bagwash. I washed him quickly with the flannel and a little soap, and dried him with the old towel. Finally I dressed him in clean vest and pants off the airer.

'Go and sit at the table,' I said, 'and I'll get breakfast. Bread and dripping or bread and jam?'

He smiled, his little face lighting up. 'Jam.'

I cut enough slices for everybody to help themselves, then went back to the bedroom with a bucket and mop. I cleaned the floor first, the smell of the pot making me gag. I emptied the pot down the toilet, then saw to the bed. I pulled off the top sheet – only a faint patch of wet from touching the bottom sheet. That'd soon dry. I bundled up the bottom sheet to put in the whites bagwash. Meanwhile, what to do about the stain on the mattress? I'd have to ask Mother. I simply didn't know how to wash the mattress without soaking it.

Talking of Mother, what was the time? Getting on for ten. Maybe she'd like a cup of tea now. I made a fresh pot, waited for it to brew as Mother liked it strong, and poured out a cup. Milk and two sugars, that's the way she liked it.

I tapped on her door and went in. She was lying sprawled on the double bed she shared with Don.

'Cup of tea, Mum?' I asked, putting it down on the bedside cabinet.

She opened one eye. 'What's the time?'

'Nearly ten.'

'Nearly ten?' she snapped, sitting bolt upright. 'You little cunt – what do you mean waking me up so early?' She flung a pillow at me and flopped down again.

I crept out of the room and closed the door quietly, thinking, One day I'll get it right!

*   *   *

When Mother emerged an hour or so later, she chased us out of the kitchen where we'd been sitting, just hanging about and chatting.

'Get back to your room, you little bastards – can't I have any peace and quiet round here?'

I hesitated in the doorway. 'Mum—'

'What! What is it? If it's not bad enough you robbing me of my beauty sleep—'

It all came out in a rush. 'Andy wet the bed but I changed him and I've stripped off the sheets and put the dirty one in the bagwash and the mattress is wet how do you dry the mattress?'

Mother sat at the table looking at me. She lit a cigarette and blew the smoke towards me.

'You've done what?' she said in the soft voice that always made my blood run cold.

'Andy wet the bed,' I said miserably. 'I changed him—'

'I heard you!'

Mother stood up and stepped towards me. I braced myself.

'So you took it on yourself to change Andy, did you? You took it on yourself to get the sheets off the bed, did you? You put the sheet in the bagwash without telling me and left the mattress to dry off, did you?'

I nodded. As her arm rose I dodged out through the door. 'I wanted to help!' I cried.

'Help!' Mother's look would have curdled milk. 'Help? You helped all right. Just gave me another fucking load of work to do.'

I was desperate. 'But, Mum, I couldn't leave Andy—'

And then Mother laughed. 'Of course you couldn't,' she said, in something more like her normal voice when she wasn't angry. 'I know you did your best, Tess. You're a good girl. You can help me finish off later, before dinner.'

I stood outside the door, stunned, my heart swelling. I'm a good girl. Mother said I'm a good girl.

'Piss off now,' said Mother more sharply. 'I want to finish my fag in peace.'

I could have flown up the hall, I was so happy. Mother might scream and shout sometimes, but she knew when I was trying to help. As I joined my brothers and sisters in our darkened room, my heart sang.

My mood didn't even wear off as I helped her sort out the bed. 'Nothing like Dettol!' declared Mother, as she opened the shutters and light flooded the room. Dettol was her solution to everything. She wiped over the stain on the mattress and said, 'That'll dry in no time. If it doesn't, Andy can just bloody well lie on it.'

Then while she was at it, she hauled the mattress off the bed entirely. 'Might as well do a proper job,' she said. The mattress was so heavy I had to help her. Then she made up another solution of Dettol, and we both wiped down every bit of metalwork, every single spring. Mother was always so thorough. That was her idea of changing a bed.

By the time we'd finished, Don had come back.

'You've been busy,' he said to Mother.

'When am I ever anything else?' she said. 'Well, I don't know about you lot but I could do with my dinner. Tess, run to the chippie, will you? Don, give her the dosh.'

Don handed me some coins, making sure his fingers didn't touch mine. I lost no time whizzing out of the door and down the street, round the corner. There wasn't much of a queue, and it didn't take long for the lady to serve me. Clutching hot bundles wrapped in newspaper against my chest, I ran back home as fast as I could.

I loved fish and chips. It was our Saturday treat, the same every week. One portion of cod and chips for Mother, and one for Don. Two portions between us girls, and one between the boys. Always enough for everyone. What with salt and vinegar – a feast. I looked forward to it every week.

As I sat in the kitchen with the other kids, I relished every mouthful. The batter was perfect today, crisp not soggy. I ate every last bit, with my fingers, leaving not a flake of fish or a speck of batter on my plate. It looked like Andy and Buddy were leaving some chips.

'Do you want those?' I asked them, nodding at their plates.

They shook their heads, mouths full, so I grabbed the chips and stuffed them down too. If only this meal would go on for ever, I thought, trying not to think what was waiting for us.

'Piss off out of it and don't come back till four o'clock,' said Mother. 'I want you in the bath, then tea, then bed by five.'

That was it. Bath. Put a dampener on the day, all right. Meanwhile, I took the kids to the local park, where we played on the swings. You could see the church clock from the park, and I kept an eye on it. When Mother said four o'clock, she meant four o'clock.

It was quite a walk to the park, so at half past three I said, 'Come on, you lot. Time to go home.' They'd all been playing happily on the swings, the slide, the seesaw and the big roundabout we called the umbrella. It looked a bit like an umbrella, with seats going all the way round, and a tall metal framework forming a point above. We all trooped home, quiet now, knowing what was to come.

Even before we got home, Mother was waiting in the doorway. 'You're late,' she snapped. 'I said four o'clock.' And as each one of us went up the stairs she slapped us round the head.

I was first for the bath, as the eldest. That was lucky for me, as there was only one lot of water for us all. That water could get pretty mucky by the end. It was heated up in the copper in the scullery and ladled out with a big jug into the bath. When it wasn't in use, the bath was covered with a lid made of wooden boards, so it made a kind of table. It wasn't the bathing I dreaded – in fact I liked being clean – but it was Mother's day of reckoning for us. It was when she totted up what we'd done wrong all week and got away with, and then we'd cop it.

I took off my clothes and put them in the bagwash. Then I sat in the water, waiting for Mother. She bustled in, holding a couple of large towels. As she poured water over me, scrubbing with the carbolic soap, I was thinking, What did I do? What's coming? It was when she was pouring water over my hair that she started.

'That's for Monday,' she said, whacking me across the head. 'That's for Tuesday' – punch on the arm. 'That's for Wednesday' – slap round the face. The slaps hurt more on wet skin. By the time she got to today, Saturday, I was really hurting, and my tears were mixing with the bathwater. She pulled my hair sharply. 'And that's for today. I'll give you waking me up at the crack of dawn.'

Was that the end? Surely I hadn't done anything else wrong? She usually managed to collar me at the time when I was annoying her, answering back or not being quick enough to do what she wanted. Then I'd get a good hiding. Otherwise, during the week when you were in trouble with Mother, you quickly had to make up your mind. Get hit now, when she was angry and might be heavier with her hands, or take a chance on her being in a better mood by Saturday? I usually took pot luck. If any of us did manage to dodge out of reach, Mother often couldn't be bothered to chase us. Then she'd say, 'Please yourself – have it now or Saturday, no skin off my nose. I'm not chasing you, but by God you're gonna fucking get it.' And we did.

But that seemed to be it for now. Mother had washed my hair and was rinsing it with a jug of water. As usual, she'd added Dettol to the water. Good old Dettol. 'No nits on you,' Mother would say. As it happened, none of us ever got nits at school. In fact when the nit nurse heard our name, whichever one of us it was, she'd say, 'Oh, that's a Stevens, no need to check them.'

Mind you, we never had close friends at school, when our heads might have touched, so that might have had more to do with it.

Anyway, it looked like my turn in the bath today was done. Thank goodness for that.

'Get out and get dry,' Mother said briskly.

I towelled myself as fast as I could, rubbing my hair as well. I was shivering. The scullery always seemed cold, even on a warm day like today. There was an open fire, like every other room in the house, but it was only lit when the weather was really cold. Even then, it never gave off much heat.

Mother handed me my clean vest and knickers. 'Here, put these on.'

As I did so, she said, 'Get the tea ready while I'm busy in here. Bread in the bin, and there's some bananas left. Slice them up. And Battenburg in the cake tin.'

Battenburg? That cheered me up. I was very fond of Battenburg, with its pink and yellow sponge squares and thick white icing. I got busy in the kitchen as Mother called, 'Kath!' And one by one my brothers and sisters went into the scullery. As I cut bread, spread it with marge, sliced the bananas and put the sandwiches on plates, I heard a steady stream of 'That's for Monday . . . that's for Tuesday . . .'

Rough with the smooth, that's what we had. When Mother was in a good mood, everyone was happy. When she was angry – well, the world went dark. But whatever she did, she was the centre of our lives and made them the way she wanted. We would no more have questioned her than we would have asked the sun why it was shining, or the rain why it was wet. Mother was Mother. It was only later, when I was older, that I ever began to wonder what made her the way she was, and why she did the things she did.

3

Don't Leave Us!

After that first broken night, Andy soon got used to sleeping with the rest of us. Before long, it was like he'd always been there. And to tell the truth, I liked us to be together. We were very close. It probably helped that we were all pretty close in age. After me – I was born in May 1943 – Mother had had a kid every eighteen months: Kath, then Jess, then Buddy and finally Andy. 'Like an assembly line!' Don would joke. But there'd been a bigger gap after Andy. He was already eighteen months old, about a year earlier, when Mother fell pregnant again – and something terrible happened that haunted me for all my childhood. Something that showed me just what my mother meant to me.

She was taken away from us.

People didn't talk much in those days about pregnancy and babies, and us kids were never told exactly what was wrong with Mother. All I knew was that one winter afternoon we came back from school to find Don at home, holding Andy, who was crying.

'Your mammy's poorly,' he told us. He always called her Mammy to us, even though Mother protested: 'Makes me sound like a fucking nigger!' Don went on to explain that she'd gone to hospital and would be away for some weeks.

I was stunned. Mother had seemed invincible to me. I'd heard talk of a baby, but she'd had babies before, hadn't she? Much later, of course, I realised she must have had an ectopic pregnancy, where the baby develops in the fallopian tube and not the womb – very dangerous, even now with all the medical advances.

There was another shock in store.

'You're going to have to go off and stay somewhere else,' said Don. 'I can manage Andy here, but the rest of you will have to go into care.'

We all burst into tears. This was too much. Not only had our mother been taken away from us, but we were being sent away to a strange place ourselves.

'Don't carry on, now,' said Don. 'Go along and pack up your stuff. Tess, you help the little ones. I've put a bag in your room. The car'll be here in a minute.'

I walked into the bedroom, hardly able to see for the tears streaming down my face. As I automatically picked out our clothes and packed them into the bag, I thought to myself, Will I ever see her again? What if she dies? This was too much. I just sat on the big bed and wept. Until Don came in and spoke sharply.

'Look lively, girl, the Social's here.'

I tried to dry my eyes, and picked up the bag. I joined Kath, Jess and Buddy on the doorstep, where Don was saying hello to a nice-looking middle-aged lady. She had short curly brown hair, and wore a smart costume of fitted grey jacket and A-line skirt.

'This way, children,' said the lady, and led us down the path to a big car parked by the kerb. We didn't have a car ourselves – not many people did in those days – and usually I would have loved being taken for a ride. But that day I couldn't appreciate the novelty. We all sat silently as she drove us off. I looked back at our house but Don had already closed the front door.

As she drove through the streets of Croydon, I tried to get my spirits up. No point being a wet blanket. Mum was in the right place to get better, and it was just a matter of time. This new place mightn't be so bad.

In the event, it was worse.

If memory serves me right, the council home was some-where in Beulah Heights. But as far as I was concerned it could have been an ogre's castle in the bad bit of fairyland. It was getting dark when we arrived, and cold rain was lashing down. The house was enormous, all crooked shapes and bits sticking out. I'd later know this sort of house was called gothic, a popular style in Victorian times. Probably worth a million quid now. At the time it just struck me as very dark and sinister, not at all homely. Things didn't improve when the nice lady knocked on the door, and it opened to a woman who straight away didn't seem so nice.

She was tall and thin, and looked old to me, though she was probably only in her forties. She wore a long black dress, very plain, and I remember a bunch of keys attached to the belt at her waist. I can't remember her real name, but to me she's always Mrs Danvers. The minute I saw Judith Anderson playing that part in the film of *Rebecca*, I thought of the woman in the council home. The same flat dark hair, stern face and scary eyes.

The nice lady waved us goodbye, and we were on our own.

'Come with me,' said Mrs Danvers.

We followed her up two flights of stairs, and she opened the door of a long, narrow room. There were eight beds in it, four either side. Each bed had a little cupboard-cum-wardrobe next to it. The room looked clean and smelled of disinfectant.

'This is the girls' dormitory,' Mrs Danvers announced.

We must have looked blank, as she explained, 'This is where the girls sleep.'

Girls?

'Where's Buddy going then?' I asked.

Mrs Danvers raised an eyebrow. 'Buddy?' she said, looking like she was sucking on a lemon. '*David* will of course be in the boys' dormitory.'

'We always call him Buddy,' I told her, trying to keep my end up.

'While he is here, he will be called by his proper name. Now, you girls will have those beds.' She nodded at three that weren't made up. 'Unpack your things while I take David to his room.'

'But I've got his stuff,' I said, indicating the bag I'd brought.

She sighed. 'Well, kindly take it out.'

I fumbled around, sorting out Buddy's clothes while she stood there tapping her foot. I wrapped them into a bundle and handed them to her, then she turned on her heel, saying, 'Come down to the living room when you're finished.' Then to Buddy, 'This way.'

It hurt my heart to see Buddy looking so miserable. Of all my brothers and sisters, I've always had the softest spot for Buddy. He was the gentlest soul, who wouldn't hurt a fly. And here he was now, having to go away all by himself. At least us girls had each other. I followed Buddy with my eyes as he trailed after Mrs Danvers, looking wistfully back at us.

None of us had ever spent a night alone in a bed. Well, I suppose I had, when I was very little, before Kath was born. But certainly all any of us could remember was being together in the one big old bed. The night was going to be very lonely for Buddy.

We unpacked, and found our way downstairs. This place was huge. Where was the living room? We heard voices, and followed them to a big room furnished with hard wooden chairs and a table. Some other kids were there, and they stared at us. We stared back. We sat and waited in silence.

After about ten minutes Mrs Danvers reappeared, leading Buddy by the hand. I could see he'd been crying, and I jumped up to go to him.

'What's the matter?' I asked.

'Nothing is the matter,' said Mrs Danvers in a voice like ice. 'David must learn to behave himself.'

Buddy? He always behaved himself. I looked at Mrs Danvers. That woman was going to be trouble. How much trouble I was going to find out that very evening.

First we had tea, what she called supper – and it wasn't bad, bangers and mash, and gravy. We had to stand behind our chairs at a long table while she said grace. Not the sort of thing we did at home! Afterwards she came up to me and said, 'Your brother needs new shoes. Bring him upstairs.'

New shoes? What was wrong with the ones he was wearing? Nothing that I could see. Still, I took his hand and followed Mrs Danvers up the stairs and into a small room that had a big cupboard against one wall. She opened it and a whole load of shoes fell out, piles of them. I could see they weren't even new, quite battered and smelly, in fact.

Mrs Danvers grabbed a small pair and said to Buddy, 'Here, put these on.'

He sat on the floor and I sat beside him to tie the laces. When he stood up, he winced. 'Hurt, Tessie, hurt.'

They were obviously too small, so I said to Mrs Danvers, 'These shoes don't fit.'

'Don't fit?' she said.

'They're too small,' I explained.

And without warning she whacked Buddy round the face, sent him flying. For just one shocked moment I couldn't move. Then I thought, This cow isn't gonna get away with hurting my Buddy, so I stood up and went for her. But she got in first and whacked me too. Both me and Buddy were crying our eyes out. She was a strong woman, and that was the first of the good hidings we all got while we were there.

It's not that we weren't used to being hit; Mother of course could let fly on many an occasion, only not so much around the face. And anyway, that was different. As Mother always said, she hit us with love. It was for our own good. A stranger hitting us was another matter entirely. In bed at night I'd lie there trying to keep back the tears. I could hear Kath and Jess sniffling too.

'Put a sock in it!' one of the other girls would say, but we didn't. When we were together we just put our arms around each other and said, 'I wish Mum was here. Oh, I do miss her.' We even wondered if she'd decide she could do without us, if we were so bad she wouldn't want us back. I'd send up many a silent prayer: 'Please, God, make her remember the good things about us, not the bad things.'

We'd been in the home for about two weeks and were having breakfast. We weren't used to cereal and milk, and it made a change, though given a choice I'd always go for bread and dripping.

'You Stevens children will be going home this afternoon,' Mrs Danvers announced.

Home! We were over the moon. We hadn't heard a thing since we'd been here, how Mother was, not a peep from anyone. But it didn't matter now – we were going home and we cheered.

Mrs Danvers said, 'Is it asking too much for you to behave?'

Well, who cared what the old bag thought?

I don't know how I got through that day. We had to go to school – we'd been going as usual as it wasn't too far away – and every lesson dragged. I normally enjoyed school, but I couldn't wait for the day to end. At last we were called for, by the same nice lady who'd driven us there, and we went back home.

Mother was sitting in the front room, Don beside her with Andy on his lap. She looked much the same as usual, maybe a bit paler, a bit thinner. She smiled when we trooped in and said, 'Kids!' And she actually opened her arms. All four of us fell into them, overcome with relief at seeing her again. I can honestly say I don't remember a single other time that she held us, cuddled us. Just that one time. No kisses, though, that would have been too much.

For a time life at home was blissful. I was the happiest I'd ever been. Mother still couldn't do a lot, so us girls did more chores than usual. We told her time and time again how much we'd missed her, how awful it was to be in care, how horrible the home was, and how nasty the woman in charge was. Mother said more than once she'd missed us, and that was music to my ears.

I didn't notice things getting back to normal. It must have happened gradually as Mother got her strength back. Anyway, after a while it was business as usual and us kids learned all over again to be careful of Mother. Not that we always succeeded. One day, when we'd been home for some months, there was big trouble.

Somehow Mother had got hold of a baby grand piano, and it stood proudly in the big front room, which was on the other side of the hall from the room with the shutters where we usually slept. Mother called the front room the best room, and it was where she held her parties. It was furnished with a three-piece suite, a round table with some wooden chairs, and an old sideboard. The floor was just covered with lino, which I had to polish every Sunday. Mother added an artistic touch to the room with the curtains. They looked like red plush velvet, hanging in pin pleats either side of the window. It was only when you got nearer you realised they were made out of crepe paper, the pleats held together by drawing pins. Still, they looked perfect from the outside, and not too bad from the inside.

Now there was a piano in the room, I must say it all looked pretty classy, like something out of a film, and us kids were very impressed.

'Don't you go touching that piano!' Mother said to us. 'It's not for you to get your sticky fingers on!'

On the day I'm talking about, we were in the kitchen having our tea when Mother said, 'I'm off to the shop for some fags. No messing while I'm out.'

We sat there obediently, eating our sandwiches. When we'd finished, we looked at each other. I can't swear who first suggested it – well, all right, it was me. 'Let's have a go on the piano.'

'Mum said we mustn't touch it!' said Kath, always the goody two-shoes.

But Jess was keen. She followed me to the front room, and watched as I lifted the lid. All those black and white keys: it looked like magic, just like in the films. I tapped one key down, and a sweet musical note sounded. Then another, and another. I'd no idea how to play tunes, but just the sound was good enough. Then Jess had a go, crashing the keys at the deep end. Trust her to be dramatic! The noise reverberated in the room, and we both laughed with the fun of it. Kath, Buddy and Andy were hovering in the doorway.

'You'll catch it if Mum hears you,' said Kath.

'If she hears me,' I said, getting carried away.

Buddy was fascinated, and inched towards the piano.

'Have a go,' I said, and he wiggled his little fingers over the keys.

Suddenly Kath said, 'Mum's coming!' She must have heard the key in the lock. She whizzed back down the hall to the kitchen, followed at a trot by Andy.

I slammed the lid down and we headed for the door – to be met by Mother standing in front of us, arms crossed, staring at us.

For a moment you could have heard a pin drop. Then in that soft voice that made me shiver Mother said, 'I heard you. I heard you from outside. You were touching the piano when I'd told you not to. I told you not to, didn't I?'

We stood there frozen.

Then Mother exploded. 'You're gonna pay for this, you little bastards. Touching my things behind my back. Get to your room!'

I tried to be brave. 'It was my fault,' I whimpered. Mother just whacked me across the head, then pulled me by the hair into the bedroom. Jess and Buddy followed, looking as scared as I felt.

Well, Mother walloped us up hill and down dale till we were lying on the floor and she had no more strength in her arms. Then she left us, saying, 'And you can stay here for the rest of the day.' She turned the key in the door, and we had nothing to do but cry and nurse our bruises. That'd teach me.

Next day at teatime we were still very subdued. Kath and Andy had been spared, but they knew Mother was still in a bad mood. As we finished our food, Mother came into the kitchen, and said, 'I have something very important to show you. Get your coats.'

This was unusual, but we did as we were told and followed her out of the house. We walked down our road and turned into another. Across the road was a big detached house, with a fence round the garden. Mother pointed at it.

'Do you know what that place is?' she asked us.

We shook our heads.

'Well,' said Mother, looking very serious, 'it used to be an ordinary house, but the council have bought it. They've turned it into a home for naughty children, really naughty children. It's not like that home you stayed in when I was in hospital. When naughty children are sent here, they can never go home again.'

We looked at the house, horrified. What had this house got to do with us?

'Now, I want you all to stay here while I go and talk to the woman who runs the home. I'm asking her to take you in, as you have been very naughty children.'

She stepped across the road while we reeled back in shock. Was this my fault? Was it the piano? What had I done? Nobody said anything. Andy was shaking his head. He didn't seem to understand what was going on.

Mother was knocking on the front door. It opened, and a young woman came out. They spoke to each other. We watched from over the street. By now we were huddled together, full of fear and trembling, crying our eyes out. We couldn't hear what they were saying, but now and then Mother turned to us and pointed, and the young woman nodded. Were they deciding who was going to be taken first?

Mother came back and looked sternly down at us, hands on hips.

'It's all arranged,' she said. 'You're going into care on Monday.'

The world was falling about our ears, there on the street.

'Unless,' she added – and we clutched at straws, 'unless you promise to be extra specially quiet the whole weekend. Not a peep.'

What a relief! 'Yes, Mum, of course, Mum, whatever you say.'

We crept home, and from then on, all weekend, we went about on tiptoe, speaking in whispers. Any job we were told to do, we did it double quick. Mother locked us in the room for most of a day, and you'd never know we were in there. Could we be quiet enough, though?

Monday morning arrived, by which time we were all in a state, breathless and quivering. Had we been quiet enough, or would the Social carry us off?

Mother gathered us together. For once she was up at the same time as us.

'Well,' she said, looking at each of us in turn. 'I must say you have been quiet, so you won't be going into care today.'

Gasps of relief all round. A narrow escape.

'But watch it,' she said. 'Next time you're naughty and noisy you mightn't be so lucky.'

We took the lesson to heart. Do as you're told, don't make trouble, don't make noise. Otherwise, terrible things would happen.

It took me years to put two and two together. It couldn't be a coincidence that Mother only started going on about putting us into care after we'd actually been in the council home. She knew we hated it, feared it. What a handy weapon to put the fear of God in us. Every time I found myself near that dreaded house I'd run past as fast as I could, scared that somehow it would catch me, and once I was in there, that was it. I'd never be let out.

Of course, we didn't know at the time that the house was actually a dance studio, and Mother was pretending to the woman that we wanted to take some classes.

4

Keeping Me in My Place

If I'd known that so-called care home was really a dance
studio, wouldn't that have made me dream! I would have
loved the chance to dance. Of course it would never have been
on the cards that I'd go there. Quite apart from the expense,
us kids just never went anywhere, did anything. No classes
outside school. But that was my cherished ambition.

When we were locked in our room for hours on end, us girls
would often pass the time talking about this and that. (The
boys would usually be asleep long before us.) Or playing the
Film Star game. I might say, 'DD. *Calamity Jane*.' And Kath
or Jess would say, 'Doris Day!' We three loved going to the
pictures, a real treat, even if we did have to drag our little
brothers along with us. When Mother allowed us to go, we
knew it was to get us out of the way, but still, no one
complained. Sitting in the dark of the cinema or lying in
the dark of the bedroom? No contest!

But what I really liked talking about was the future. What
we'd do when we grew up, when we could choose what we
wanted to do. Whenever I heard those poor cows mooing on
their way to the slaughterhouse over the road, I'd feel a bit like
them. Herded about, pushed around, no say in the matter, do

as you're told. It was wonderful to imagine a time when I'd be free. Kath always knew what she wanted to do. She was mad on animals, and wanted to look after them, even be a vet. Jess – well, for a long time Jess wanted to be a nun, of all things. God knows where she got that idea from, so to speak. But she was always a strange girl, dreamy and not with it half the time. At least Kath had a fighting chance of achieving her ambition.

As for me, ever since I was little I'd wanted to be a ballerina. I'd seen pictures and the odd film and bits on telly, and to my mind there was nothing more beautiful and graceful. Even in black and white on the small screen those lovely dancers were pure magic; they made my heart sing. One evening we were all watching a performance in a variety show on telly and I made the mistake of announcing, 'I want to do that. I want to be a ballerina.'

At once Mother and Don burst out laughing.

'News to me they've got elephants in the chorus!' That was from Don.

My mother added, 'You – a ballerina! Come off it! You're not called Tess for nothing, are you?'

Oh, yes, my name. Which wasn't my real name. I've been calling myself Tess all along, just as everybody always has, but it's a nickname. When I was little, people started calling me Tess after Two-Ton Tessie O'Shea. For anybody too young to remember, she was a very popular music-hall entertainer, a singer and comedian. As you'd expect from her nickname, she was on the large side, all right – larger than life, in fact. What with me being chubby, to put it mildly, and according to my mother always wanting attention, you can see the resemblance. And to be honest, if I couldn't be a ballerina then I would have given anything to be a performer myself, like the film stars I idolised: Debbie Reynolds, Jane Powell and Doris Day of course . . . They were my heroines, and now and then I had a chance to play-act just like them.

That was when we were locked in our room, but knew that Mother was going out. She was a keen dancer herself, though ballroom rather than ballet, and she was very good at it. When we heard her talking about going out in the evening, we knew we'd have some time safe from her. As soon as we heard the front door slam, we were out of bed. We loved acting out scenes from a film we'd seen, draping ourselves in the bed-clothes and trying to remember the words. I was always the heroine. Or we'd sing songs – us girls loved musicals. The little boys weren't that keen, but they had to go along with it. Of course, if we were in the room with the shutters we couldn't see very well. There was no point even thinking about putting the light on – we'd done that once and Mother had noticed and removed the bulb. But we'd do our best. Fortunately the room was pretty bare, just the old chest of drawers and the wooden chair as well as the bed, so there wasn't much to bump into. We played that game for hours, till we heard the front door bang and Mother was home. Then it was straight back to bed, lying rigidly, the bedclothes back in place, as Mother was known to make a lightning inspection when the fancy took her.

Anyway, my real name, as far as I knew at the time, was Sandra – but even this, as I was to discover, wasn't my real name, any more than the father's name on my birth certificate was my real father's. Meanwhile, except at school, which didn't allow nicknames, I was Tess. Or Ginger Cunt to my mother if I was out of favour. My hair was ginger all right, not red like hers, and straight, not curly. With my round face and freckles, I was not the prettiest girl on the block. With all my heart I wished I was, then life would be better. I so envied my sister Kath, who was very pretty with lovely long wavy hair. When Mum took us both out, people would stop in the street and look at Kath and say, 'Oh, what a lovely girl! You must be so proud of her.' Then they'd catch sight of me and add, 'Well, she's a right Tessie O'Shea that one, and no mistake.'

As if to sweeten the pill, they might add, 'She's a laugh, though, got a right little personality.' I guess I tried to make up for not being attractive by being jolly, cracking jokes, making people laugh. Two-Ten Tessie coming out, a performer. But let me tell you, as far as I was concerned, you could stuff personality. I wanted to walk into a room and have people look at me and say, 'Wow! She's drop dead gorgeous!' I wanted to knock 'em in the aisles with my looks, like a film star.

Well, I could still dream of a time when I wouldn't be fat and ugly, and people would love me, want to be with me. Meanwhile, like my brothers and sisters, I was haunted by the fear of not being good enough, of losing Mother, of being sent away. Knowing there was that home for very naughty children just nearby, waiting for us to slip . . .

It was a relief to bump into Mrs Hodge now and then. She was our upstairs neighbour in the Croydon house. She and her family lived in the two top floors. They needed all the room they could get, seeing as how there were seven kids all told. Mrs Hodge, a plump, motherly lady, took a shine to me. At least, she was always friendly when she saw me, and smiled and gave me a sweet. She invited me to drop in whenever I liked. I just adored being around her, in her big, homely kitchen full of delicious cooking smells. I felt myself relaxing, not looking over my shoulder. So any time I wasn't locked in or sent out of the house, I was forever popping upstairs.

Then one day, when I was chatting to Mrs Hodge in her kitchen, telling her things about school that my mother would never have wanted to know, there was a tap on the door. It was Maureen, one of Mother's friends who often dropped round. Maureen was usually very bright and sparky, but this time she looked serious.

'Tess,' she said in a low voice, 'I've got some bad news. It's your mum. She's very ill – you'd better come down straight away.'

I felt like my heart stopped, and scrambled off my chair. Mrs Hodge didn't say anything, she just frowned at Maureen.

I dashed downstairs, beside myself with fear and panic. Mother was in the living room, lying on the settee with her leg up. A white bandage was wound round her leg, but lots of blood had obviously leaked through – there was red everywhere.

'Mum, what is it?' I cried. 'What's wrong with your leg?'

Mother looked at Maureen, who'd followed me down.

'It's a sign from God,' she said faintly. 'He's made my leg bleed because I'm such a bad mother—'

'You're not a bad mother!' I cut in, desperately afraid.

'I must be a bad mother, because you don't love me any more, do you? You're always upstairs with the Hodge woman. You love her more than you love me, so it must be my fault. God is punishing me.'

I was speechless, shaking my head as the tears started.

'My leg will bleed and bleed,' Mother went on. 'It'll bleed until I've got no more blood in me and I'll die.'

As I was sobbing, Mother added, 'There is something you can do to help me, though.'

That brought me up short. 'What?' I asked excitedly. 'Anything, I'll do anything!'

'Well,' said Mother slowly. 'If you promise never to go upstairs again, and only love me and not Mrs Hodge, God will think I'm a good mother again and will make my leg better.'

'I swear to God!' I cried. 'I love you more than anyone else in the world, Mum.' And I meant it from the bottom of my heart. 'I'll never go upstairs again!'

I saw Mother glance at Maureen, who must have been very upset as she was holding a hankie over her mouth, and her shoulders were shaking.

'Let's hope God has heard you,' said Mother. She stretched her leg and sat up. 'Do you know, I reckon it feels better,' she said in a stronger voice. 'I'm cured!'

I clapped my hands in relief, as Maureen said, 'Yeah, all that blood's been changed to lipstick – look, Tess.'

I looked and just gave thanks for a miracle. I was filled with joy that God had saved my mother's life.

Other times, she terrified not just me but all the other kids too. One night, I think we must have got carried away by one of our games, laughing too much maybe. All of a sudden the key turned in the lock and the door opened. The light in the hall illuminated a figure standing in the doorway. Us kids looked up – and screamed. It was a monster. It would have looked like our mother, only the face was hideous, a strange green colour, all lumpy and scaly like the skin of a crocodile.

Then the monster spoke, its lips moving stiffly but the voice unmistakable.

'See what you've done, you little bleeders? You won't do what I say so God has punished me.'

'Mum!' we chorused. Andy and Buddy dived under the covers, while us girls were rigid with shock.

'Mum?' I whispered. 'What's happened to you?'

'Can't you see, you dozy cow?' came our mother's voice again. 'God has seen that I can't control my children so he's sent me this punishment.'

Oh no! What had we done? I remembered bits in the Bible I'd read at school about lepers. Leprosy was a terrible disease, bits of you fell off – was this what God had given our mother? Was she going to die?

As us girls started to cry, Mother spoke.

'There's one thing you can do to help me,' she said.

'What, Mum, what? We'll do anything.'

'You can all keep quiet for the next hour. Then God might take pity on me.'

'Yes, Mum,' we cried. 'We'll do that, we promise!'

Then the light was off and the door was shut and locked again. We all lay in bed in the dark clutching each other. We'd done this to our mother?

For what seemed like ages we lay there, afraid to move. Then suddenly there was the sound of the key in the lock and the door opened. Mother was standing in the doorway – and God had lifted the curse! Her face was back to normal. In fact her skin looked clearer than ever, positively glowing.

We were flooded with relief. Our mother was safe again.

'This time God forgave me,' she told us. 'He might not do it another time, so you be careful.'

'Yes, Mum,' we said together, as the door closed and cut off the light. We could sleep soundly now.

Mother worked that one on us every so often, and we never twigged. Well, we didn't know anything about face packs in those days.

I reckoned God was an even more powerful threat than the Social, though it was a close-run thing. If us kids did anything wrong, two things could happen. First, Mother would punish us – straight away if she could catch us, or later, on Saturday, when we'd get a week's worth. If we were really bad, then we would be sent away to the home for naughty children. This hadn't happened yet, but it was a distinct possibility and we had to keep on our toes.

Second, it wasn't us who would be punished, but Mother. And that's where God came in. He would punish her for being a bad mother who couldn't control her children, who was so bad that her children didn't love her.

And that would be the unkindest cut of all. It was our mother who mattered, to all of us, especially me. We lived in terror that something would happen to her. We owed everything to Mother. After all, as she told us time and time again, 'I gave you the greatest gift anyone can give another person – I gave you life. But for me, you wouldn't be here.' That was so true. And, as she drilled it into us every day, 'You owe me, you owe me big-time.'

Of course, as a child I had no idea that what she was doing to her kids was nothing less than brainwashing. I reckon she could have given the KGB a run for its money. She was living proof of that old saying, 'Give me a child at the age of seven and I will give you the adult.' Except that knowing Mother, she would have done the job in half the time. No hanging about.

So when Mother asked me to jump, I'd jump without question. There was one time, though, when I found it really difficult. I had to tell a lie, a barefaced lie.

Mother gave me a shopping list and said, 'I want you to take this to the grocer's. Get your bag filled up before you take out your purse. Shake it out so they can see there's nothing in it, then turn on the waterworks. "Oh dear, I've lost my money, what will Mummy say? I'll get into trouble! Boo-hoo!" Then the stupid bastards will let you off and give you the stuff for nothing.'

Would they? I was terrified by this. I had to tell a lie. How could I say I'd lost my money when there was nothing in the purse in the first place? So wasn't it like stealing? From what I was told at school, stealing was wrong . . .

Mother was obviously annoyed by my reluctance to jump to her bidding.

'Don't you get it, you little cow? I want you to do this. If you don't, God will punish me for being a bad mother. I must be a bad mother if my own child won't do what I want.'

No contest, then. I crept along the streets clutching the shopping bag. The purse was in my coat pocket, most definitely empty. I pushed open the door of the grocer's, the bell jangling madly over my head, and made my way to the counter.

'What can I do for you, little girl?' asked the grocer, a big man with a round red face. He seemed kind. At least, he added, 'And aren't you a good girl to be shopping for your mother!'

I could only nod, and handed him the shopping list. He piled up the tea, the sugar and all the other stuff on the counter and I put it into my bag.

'That'll be six and eight, please.'

And out came the empty purse. I was so upset that the tears came naturally. There was a real break in my voice when I wailed, 'I've lost my money! I'm gonna get into trouble!'

Sure enough, the grocer tut-tutted, and said, 'Never you mind, dear, just be more careful next time.'

Still blubbing, I left the shop feeling like a criminal. I could only cling to the knowledge that Mother wanted me to do this, so there must be a good reason for it that I couldn't understand. When I got home, Mother took the bag and grinned.

'Worked a treat,' she said. Then she looked thoughtful.

'Better watch it, though, Tess. You don't want to work the same shop more than once or they'll wise up . . .'

Mother didn't mind sending me to the coal yard more than once. The first time was the winter between my tenth and eleventh birthdays. 'You're getting to be a big strong girl now,' Mother said, and I was filling out, no question.

Though the only source of heat in our house in winter was the open fires, in the four main rooms, the kitchen and the scullery, Mother hardly ever bought any coal. She'd get someone to go up to the nearby coal yard on a Sunday, when it was deserted, nip over the fence and help themselves from the heaps lying around. Now that someone would be me.

'Just one load, Tess,' she said, and I trundled off with the old pram now used just for ferrying stuff, not kids. It was an old-fashioned one with big wheels, not that easy for me to manoeuvre. I wheeled it past the slaughterhouse and reached the fence of the coal yard up the road. I parked the pram right by it, then stood on the pram to get over into the yard. I'd brought an empty sack with me, which I had to fill with my bare hands. On a freezing cold day that was hard work. Then I lugged the sack across to the fence, stood on a handy bunker, and hauled the sack up and over into the pram below, before clambering back over the fence. I wheeled the pram home, and poured the coal into the big old dustbin out the back we used as a bunker.

Mother greeted me with thanks, and, 'Will you just nip out and get another sackful, Tess? There's a good girl.' Seeing my face, she added, 'I'll make up the fire nice and bright for when you get home, and you can sit right by it and get lovely and warm.'

That was a tempting prospect, so off I went again, filling another sack. I got back home, to find Mother and the other kids clustered by the fire. Mother said, 'Can you get just one more, Tess? It's gonna have to last us through the week.'

I stood there, shivering with cold, and Mother added the sweetener. 'This time when you get back the fire is gonna be up the chimney, and there's gonna be a spot there just for you. And I tell you what, you're gonna sit down and I'm gonna make you a nice hot cup of tea and you can have your favourite, bread and dripping or whatever you want. How about that?'

My mouth watered at the prospect. As further encouragement Mother added, 'You're a good girl, Tess. I don't know what I'd do without you.'

That worked. I went back to the yard, my heart swelling with pride and self-importance, my arms and legs aching with effort, my hands so cold I could hardly feel them on the pram handle. I staggered home, proud and pleased to be helping Mother, but longing for rest and the treats waiting for me. Only to find Mother bustling about in the kitchen.

'Go and get ready for bed,' she said sharply.

'What? Oh, Mum, you said you'd make the fire up for me and bring me a cup of tea and some bread and dripping—'

'Stop whining. No time for that now, you shouldn't have taken so long. Don'll be back from his football in a minute and he'll want his tea. Now shift yourself.'

Gloomily, I washed in cold water, and got ready for bed. All right for Don, coming back from the game at Crystal Palace. Bread and dripping for him, all right, and probably even cake.

My brothers and sisters hadn't been in bed long and the sheets were still cold. I slid down between them, next to Kath as usual, and hugged myself to get some warmth. Could I ever do enough to please Mother? I just prayed that day would come.

I look back now and can hardly credit how gullible I was. I was like a little puppet being jerked around on strings. And Mother was the puppet-master.

5

Mother's Little Helper

I could help Mother in a lot of routine ways too, especially with the other kids. When Andy joined Buddy at nursery, I could take them all out with me in the morning. This was a great help for Mother as she usually got up late, especially after one of her parties. Nursery was over before school, so Mother herself would pick up the boys, or send one of her friends if she was busy.

Getting the kids ready was a bit of a mad scramble, me chivvying everyone like a bossy big sister. Which is what I was, I suppose. First I had to make sure they all washed their hands and faces, then put on the clean socks and underclothes hanging on the airer in the scullery. Mother usually washed those out every night, and they weren't always perfectly dry in the morning. Us girls, with similar-sized feet, would tussle over who got the driest socks. Next I had to get their breakfast down them, usually bread and jam or dripping.

Then out of the door, walk up the street, drop off the boys at nursery, and go on to school, where me, Kath and Jess would go our separate ways. After all that activity, it was always a relief to get to the classroom and sit down quietly.

If I hadn't had time to eat breakfast myself, I'd grab some bread and dripping, wrap it in newspaper, and take it with me to eat in morning break. Once I saw one of the girls in my class looking at my snack, then at her own. She didn't say anything, but I realised hers wasn't wrapped in newspaper, but in greaseproof, very clean and tidy. We never had greaseproof. It seemed very posh to me, and there and then I thought, Right, one day all my snacks will be wrapped in greaseproof.

Still, the food was the important thing, and I always enjoyed it. I loved school dinners. I can't remember whether they were free for everybody when I was little, in the early 1950s, or whether they were free to us as we were hard up. Whatever they cost, they were cheap at twice the price. A proper meal, with spuds and meat and veg, even gravy. And afters, usually custard and some kind of sponge pudding. I specially liked treacle stodge, which was sweet and really filling. I even liked tapioca, which other kids called frogspawn. When anybody said, 'Yuck! This is disgusting,' I couldn't understand why. All food was good. I even liked those little bottles of milk we had every day at school. I'd down mine in one go, and keep an eye on the crate to see if any were left over, in which case I'd grab another, even if it was warm and a bit off by then.

Mind you, almost anything would taste good compared to what Mother gave us, which was usually sandwiches and cheap cake, anything to fill us up. We never dreamed of complaining – you ate what was on your plate and that was that. She only made an effort on Sundays. If we were lucky there'd be a cooked breakfast, with egg, bacon and tomatoes, but if Mother wasn't up, we'd have the usual bread and stuff.

We nearly always had a proper Sunday dinner, with roast leg of lamb, two roast potatoes each and vegetables. It wasn't bad at all, in fact it was my second favourite meal of the week after fish and chips on Saturdays. We'd sit in the kitchen wolfing it down, usually accompanied by *Two-Way Family Favourites* on the radio. There was quite a mixture of music, I remember. I'd always keep an ear out for any ballet music I recognised, like *Swan Lake* or *The Sleeping Beauty*.

One dinnertime, Don complained about the vegetables.

'Why do we always have the same veg every week?' he asked. 'Bloody peas and carrots. And always out of a tin – can't we have anything fresh?'

''Course they're fucking fresh,' Mother shot back. 'I've only just opened the bloody tins!'

Don persevered. 'I mean, what about cauliflower, or runner beans? You know all those blokes in the market – why can't you get some of them?'

'You want it, you get it,' said Mother, in a voice that threatened thunder.

I knew she was often round our local market, which was in Surrey Street, a walk away. But the market was packed with stalls selling all kinds of stuff, so maybe she went to those rather than the fruit and veg places.

After Sunday dinner there was afters to look forward to. We often had tinned pears or tinned peaches, nearly always with Libby's evaporated milk. Sometimes there'd be con- densed milk, which was deliciously thick and sweet. Or Ambrosia creamed rice. Nobody would have complained about having those tins!

When we were on holiday from school, I really missed school dinners. For our main meal of the day we had to make do with whatever Mother threw together. Otherwise it was just more and more sandwiches. More than ever, we couldn't wait for Saturday's fish and chips and Sunday's roast!

It wasn't only the food I liked at school: I liked the lessons too. I was quick at reading and writing, and loved books. We never had any books at home, at least not any meant for children. I looked forward to Friday afternoons when we could choose a book from the classroom shelves and read on our own. I'd lose myself in a story. Most of the other kids made a beeline for Enid Blyton's adventures, and though I quite liked them I really preferred the old classics: *Black Beauty*, *Anne of Green Gables*, *Little Women*. I especially loved Marmee, the mother, in *Little Women*. I'd find myself thinking, I wish my mother was like that, so loving, so caring. Then I'd feel guilty, as if I was betraying my own mother. Of course Mother was loving and caring. It was just that she didn't always show it. I happily identified with all the March sisters, though. One time I'd be a sweet-natured would-be homemaker like Meg, another time a tomboy like Jo, or, when I was feeling sorry for myself, poor suffering Beth who everybody loved. In my heart of hearts I really wanted to be Amy, the beauty, who everyone admired, but one look in the mirror would put the kibosh on that.

So reading was a doddle for me. There was a bit of a problem when it came to writing our own stories, though, especially after a weekend or a holiday.

The first time the teacher said, 'Now, children, I'd like you to write a story all about something you did with your family,' I was stumped. Joan could write about going to the zoo, Valerie could write about going to the seaside, Douglas could write about going to a museum (he was a swot), but what could I write about? Mother never took us anywhere. I had a dim memory of being with her at a fairground once, with those big swing boats, and wearing a blue coat with a velvet collar. Somehow I got it dirty, and she gave me a slap. I suppose I was about three, as I remember a baby in a pram, who must have been Kath. Other than that, she never took us to a zoo, a circus, the seaside, anywhere. I had to use my imagination. I thought of a story I'd read recently, and put me and my family into it. 'Last Saturday our mother took us on a picnic in the park. She made lots of sandwiches and took bottles of lemonade . . .' I got good marks too!

There was another reason why I was happy at school. Unlike some of the children, I never had a problem with discipline and I never misbehaved. And in those days it was much stricter than it is now, and teachers were allowed to use the cane or a slipper. What I really liked was how predictable it was. If you did as you were told, did your best, you were fine. If you didn't, then you were in trouble. I couldn't have put it into words at the time, but I felt safe. At home, Mother would punish us if we did wrong – but she would punish us if we hadn't done anything too. You were always on tenterhooks with Mother.

And recently she'd been making me more uneasy than usual.

She'd started keeping me off school every so often. 'I need you to help me,' she said.

I didn't like being off, but of course I didn't argue. I don't know what tale she spun for the school, but no one ever mentioned my odd absences.

I had tried saying, 'What about getting the kids to school?'

But Mother had just said, 'Oh, Kath's old enough now. Don't you worry about that.'

So I'd get the kids ready, and off they'd go. The house was very quiet after they'd left.

It was a Thursday, the first time. I was wiping down the kitchen table, and Mother was standing by the window.

'Look out there,' she said.

And in the back garden was Filth, making his way to the house, wearing an old cap that was as dirty and ragged as the rest of his clothes. I'd never met him to talk to. Us kids just saw him occasionally in the garden and simply took him for granted.

'Do you know his name?' Mother asked me.

'Er . . . no. You call him Filth.'

'That's right. Filth by name and Filth by nature!' Mother laughed. 'Well,' she went on. 'Guess what his surname is.'

I hadn't a clue. 'I give up,' I said.

'Well, you'd never guess,' said Mother. She paused, then added dramatically, 'It's Stevens!'

Stevens? I thought. 'That's the same as us,' I said, wondering what on earth she was getting at.

'Well, it would be,' said Mother. 'Seeing as how his name is on your birth certificate!'

'My what?'

'Oh, it's the bit of paper you get when you're born. It says who your mother and father are, where you were born, that sort of thing.'

I was gazing at the figure shambling towards the back door. Mother had said before that he was my father, and I'd hoped she was joking. Now I could only look at her, bewildered.

'Stevens,' said Mother. 'He gave you his name. Kath and Jess too.'

At least that made sense. I'd always known that me, Kath and Jess had the same father, and he wasn't Buddy's. And of course Don was Andy's father.

'So . . .' I faltered. 'He's my father?'

Mother laughed out loud. 'If it says so on your birth certificate it must be true, mustn't it?' she said gaily.

She must have seen the look on my face, as she said, 'Look, one day I'll tell you all about it.'

Just then the old man shuffled into the kitchen. I could smell him from where I was standing.

'Morning, Grace,' he mumbled.

'Morning,' answered Mother.

He was staring at me. 'Who's this?' he asked.

'Tess,' said Mother. 'I thought it was about time she met you.'

I was gazing back at him, trying to keep the shock and disgust from my face.

'Go on, Tess,' Mother was urging me. 'Take your old dad into the front room and keep him company while I get his breakfast and a nice cup of tea.'

With legs like lead I walked out of the kitchen, past this old man, and up the hall to the front room. I stood with my back to the window. I felt nervous, and wasn't sure why. Was it because I was so disappointed that this broken-down old man was my father? Or was Mother having a laugh? It was true I didn't always understand her sense of humour.

I heard Filth shuffling up the hall. What do I call him? I asked myself in a panic. I can't call him Filth to his face, surely? Mr Stevens? But that would be mad if he really was my father. I so hoped he wasn't.

In any case, when he came into the room I was tongue-tied. He grinned at me, showing horrible teeth, all broken and yellow.

'Well, now,' he said in a rasping voice, 'this is nice, ain't it?'

Silence.

He sat down in one of the armchairs. Part of my mind registered the fact that the seat was covered with newspaper. Mother was obviously not going to have him dirty her furniture.

'Why don't we get acquainted?' he said. 'Come and sit on my lap.'

Sit on his lap? My whole self recoiled. What, get close to that stinking bundle of rags? Why?

When I hesitated, he called out in a surprisingly strong voice, 'Grace!' And I heard my mother tap-tapping up the hall in her high-heeled shoes.

'What's the matter?' she asked.

'Little Tess here doesn't want to be friendly,' he said. Then he cackled. 'She ain't so little, though, is she!'

Mother came over to me and put her face close to mine. 'When I tell you to keep your old dad company, I mean you to do what he says,' she hissed.

'Too right,' came Filth's voice behind her. 'Starts the day off well, don't it!'

Mother dug her nails into my arm and spat out the words. 'Sit. On. His. Lap.' Then she let me go and headed to the door, saying, 'Bacon and eggs in ten minutes!'

The old man grinned again and rubbed his hands together. He beckoned me over, curling one of his dirty fingers with its broken black nail.

I felt sick, but the thought of Mother's anger made me move one foot after the other and stand before the old man. He took my hand and pulled me on to his lap. I sat rigidly, trying not to breathe. He reeked of old sweat, stale beer and tobacco, and other things I couldn't even identify. Why did he want me to sit on his lap? I could just as easily sit in the other armchair and talk to him if it was company he wanted.

I realised he was shifting slightly under my bum. Was he uncomfortable? Was I too heavy? Well, he'd only have to say and I'd be out of there like a shot.

The minutes dragged on, me sitting there with my fists clenched, trying to keep down the sick I felt rising in my throat. At last Mother called from the kitchen, 'Breakfast!'

I jumped up, turning round to say, 'Did you hear Mum call?' And that's when I saw it. His grubby, stained trousers were gaping open, and something was poking out, an ugly, swollen thing like a big slug. I realised immediately what it must be. I'd seen my brothers, after all, and knew they had a willy between their legs. It never bothered me in the slightest, it was just what boys had and girls didn't. Now for the first time I saw a man's willy, and it was disgusting. I ran out of the room across the hall to the bedroom. I climbed on to the bed, shaking. I felt like crying. For some reason I couldn't explain, I felt dirty. I heard him shuffling back down the hall.

Then Mother called, 'Tess! Get off your arse and give me a hand, you lazy cow!'

I dragged myself back to the kitchen, where Filth was sitting down stuffing food into his mouth, and slurping from a cup of tea.

Mother nodded towards the scullery. 'Get on with the washing-up,' she said. 'We'll be going out soon, so make sure you finish everything off before I get back.'

She looked at Filth. 'Special day, today, isn't it?' she said to him, and he nodded. Mother added, 'Makes it all worth while, today, Tess.' Seeing that I didn't know what she was talking about, she grinned and went on, 'Pension day.'

'We've got an arrangement.'

Later that morning Mother was back, while I was in the kitchen cutting bread for sandwiches. I didn't look up, just kept slicing the bread and putting it on a plate.

'Look,' she said sharply. 'It's not much to ask, is it?'

Now I did look up, and stopping slicing. I looked at my mother in some surprise. If I didn't know better I'd have thought she was a bit embarrassed.

'It's just that every month he gets his pension, and gives me my cut for bed and board.'

Bed and board? In a shed?

Mother continued. 'The thing is, we don't want him to rock the boat, do we? As it is, it's a nice little earner, so what's wrong with keeping him sweet on pension day, eh?'

Sweet? I'd never seen anybody so absolutely not sweet in my whole life. But Mother's voice was soft, reasonable, and I found myself nodding.

'Good,' she said crisply. 'That's that.' She started to leave the room, and turned round at the door. 'Do you know, Tess, I really do rely on you to help me. You're the only one of all the kids I can trust.'

Now that made me smile. I was always a sucker for kind words, especially from Mother. My heart glowed with pride.

Mother went on, 'In fact, now you're so helpful, and growing up so fast, there's another way you can help me. And I think you'll like it.'

I looked at her eagerly. It was true, I was growing up, nearly ten and a half by now.

'You know I have parties here sometimes,' she said, and I nodded. 'Well, this Saturday I'm having a special party. A lot of important people are coming, and I want it all to go smoothly. That's where you come in.'

A party! When us kids were locked up we'd sometimes hear music coming from the front room, people chatting and laughing, and the smell of cigar smoke would waft down the hall. I liked the sound of this. All that day and the next, I felt myself lifted up, and couldn't wait for the evening.

'You've got to look really nice,' Mother said. 'I'll curl your hair for you.'

My hair usually looked a fright, a straight ginger mop, but Mother had a knack of twisting strands of my hair in strips of rag so that it all went wavy and looked much better. She usually didn't have time to do it, but tonight was obviously important. So she washed my hair and towelled it, then curled it up. While it was drying, I cleaned the big living room where the party was going to be held, sweeping the flower-patterned carpet, dusting the furniture and the lampshades, plumping up the cushions, polishing the mirrors till they sparkled, cleaning the ashtrays. By now, the pretend crepe curtains were a thing of the past, and the windows had real red velvet curtains. In fact Mother had brought in quite a lot of new furniture, including a three-piece suite that matched the curtains. Then I washed all the glasses in the sink in the scullery and dried them carefully.

I busied myself preparing the party food, undoing packets of crisps and crackers and making sandwiches, both salmon and cucumber and shrimp paste, cutting them diagonally as they looked fancier like that. Mother showed me how to make dainty little snacks with small chunks of cheese and tinned pineapple, sticking them on what she called cocktail sticks. That was a new one on me. Very sophisticated. I arranged everything prettily in bowls and on plates to put out in the living room. Meanwhile Mother was stocking the glass shelves of the new cocktail cabinet with lots of different bottles. This cabinet looked like a sort of cupboard till you pulled the door down flat and it turned into a little table to put the glasses on and pour out the drinks. As soon as you pulled down the door, a light went on inside, illuminating all the bottles.

Mother surveyed the living room, and my efforts. 'Lovely,' she said. 'That'll do nicely.'

I glowed. Only Mother could make you want to work for her and then feel grateful for the privilege.

'Now,' she said, 'you'll need something to wear.' She thought for a moment, then nodded. 'Your pencil skirt, that looks nice. Oh, and Lucy's left a blouse behind – it should fit you.'

Lucy was one of Mother's lady friends who stayed in the house from time to time, but she'd left suddenly, so Mother said. She fetched the blouse, which was a lovely cream colour, with lace insets and ruffles down the front. She nodded. 'That'll do. Now I'll just take out those rags and you can go and stay in the bedroom till I call you.'

She unwound the strips of rag, smoothing them out, and when she combed my hair I must say it looked lovely. Not for the first time, I wished I had natural curls. Then I went to the bedroom, carrying the blouse. The other kids had gone to bed hours earlier and seemed dead to the world. Mother let me keep the door open so I could see by the hall light as I tiptoed round, looking for my skirt on a hanger behind the door, and getting changed. The blouse was a bit wide at the shoulders, but otherwise I thought it would look good. A pair of clean ankle socks and my flat-heeled ballerina pumps completed my party outfit. It was unusual for me to dress up, and I must say I liked it! When Mother closed and locked the door, I sat down on the edge of the bed to wait, smoothing my skirt under me, careful not to disturb the kids. If they woke up and made a noise, Mum would be angry, and, apart from anything else, I didn't want to miss my treat.

At last there came the sound of the key turning in the lock, and Mother stood in the doorway. 'Tess,' she whispered, beckoning me.

I moved quietly into the hall – and wasn't Mother all glammed up! She was wearing one of her ballroom dancing gowns, a gorgeous turquoise colour, with a satin bodice and full skirt covered with net. She had her dainty high-heeled shoes on, and really looked a million dollars. I hoped I might look like a couple of quid, anyway.

Mother put a tray of nibbles in my hand and said, 'Take this round,' and I walked up to the living room doorway, feeling nervous. The ceiling light was off, but the table lamps were glowing and it all looked very glamorous. The guests did too, the men dressed in sharp suits, the girls dolled up in wasp-waisted evening gowns, their hair sleek and shiny, jewellery sparkling round their necks and wrists and fingers. I recognised Mother's friend Maureen, as well as a younger woman called Barbara, who always seemed to be at the house. The air was already thick with smoke and perfume. As I stood uncertainly on the threshold, a man spoke.

'This can't be Tess!' he cried. 'How she's grown! Well, well, little Tess – not so little now! You're growing up nicely.'

I didn't recognise him, just tried to smile. Other people laughed, but they seemed friendly.

'Go on,' said Mother, giving me a push. 'Off you go.'

I edged round the room, clutching the tray. Everybody smiled at me, thanked me, and I began to relax. This was fun. While Mother and Don kept the drinks topped up, I circulated with plates of nibbles. I even managed a tray or two of drinks without spilling anything. Someone started up the radiogram and dance music filled the room. A couple started slow-jiving. Other people were chatting, laughing, drinking and smoking. I've always loved the smell of cigars, more sophisticated than cigarettes. It was like a scene from a film, a nightclub maybe.

One or two of the men brushed against me as I went round, but I didn't think it was deliberate. One man pinched my bum, but in a friendly, jokey way.

Finally Mother had me washing glasses in the scullery, then I had to go to bed. It was hard to go to sleep. Doesn't get much better than this, I thought.

6

Mother's Little Earner

'Your mum's a prozzie, a dirty old prozzie! Your mum's a prozzie, a dirty old prozzie!'

I was rooted to the spot in the playground, staring in shock at the two girls in front of me. They were pointing at me as they chanted, 'Your mum's a prozzie, a dirty old prozzie!'

What? What was I hearing? One minute I'd decided to spend the rest of the dinnertime break playing hopscotch, the next minute these girls were in front of me, taunting me, jeering at me.

My mind raced. This was crazy. What were they talking about? As if my mother could be a prozzie! Everybody knew prozzies were dirty women, who went with men to do dirty things for money. As the enormity of what they were saying sank in, I felt my blood rise.

'You shut your mouths!' I yelled. I balled up my fists and stomped towards them. If they wanted a fight, by God they were gonna get one!

They skipped out of my way, giggling and nudging each other. I had half a mind to follow them and give them a bashing, but they were soon out of my reach, heading indoors. I had to be content with just glaring at them.

It really shook me. What a terrible thing to say about my mother. Why should they say that? When the bell rang and it was time for lessons, I took my time walking back to the classroom. I hardly heard the next lesson, and when the teacher said, 'Now, children, take out your books for silent reading,' I was relieved. I could sit and think and it would look like I was reading.

As I gazed at my story book, the words just swam in front of my eyes. I could still hear those girls chanting those awful words: 'Your mum's a prozzie, a dirty old prozzie!'

I was shocked to my core. Where had they got that idea? What lies were they spreading about my mother? As if she could be a prozzie! She was so clean, always so clean. My mind wandered back to something Don had said a while ago. He'd been in a good mood for once, and was talking about the time he'd met Mother. As I recalled, it had a lot to do with her being clean.

Don had a lovely speaking voice, rich and melodious, like James Mason I thought, with a hint of a Liverpool accent. He'd been living with a relative there for a long time before coming south.

'I'd come to Croydon for a job,' he told us kids, 'and I was looking for a room. A bloke told me that Grace Stevens let out rooms, so off I went to the address he gave me. When I walked up the front path I saw a woman scrubbing the front step as if her life depended on it, and I called out hello. She stood up and looked at me – and that was it. She had the most beautiful skin, the most beautiful complexion, she was all fresh and clean, and her cheeks were glowing. I knew I was going to fall in love with this woman.'

At the time I thought it was just a lovely story. Now I thought, Doesn't that prove Mum isn't dirty? And as for going with men, well, as far as I could tell she was only ever with Don. They might fight like cat and dog and terrify us kids with their almighty rows, but they always made up eventually.

As the afternoon wore on, I worried away at what the girls had said. I remembered other times when I'd seen girls huddled together, pointing at me and giggling, but nobody had ever said anything out loud. Was everybody going around saying my mother was a prozzie?

By the time the final bell rang and we were off, I'd decided to say nothing about it. I knew if I made a fuss the girls would know they'd got to me. That's what bullies like. The best thing was to ignore them, pretend it hadn't happened. If they tried it again, I'd have to push down my quick temper and walk away. Look down my nose at them. And I certainly wouldn't say anything to my sisters. In fact I wasn't sure if they even knew what prozzie meant. I just hoped nobody would tease them about it. As for what prozzies actually did – well, I had a sort of idea. I'd giggled about it with other girls at school. One of them had declared, 'Men do a wee inside you,' but I thought that was ridiculous, as well as disgusting. I knew it was something to do with willies, and what us girls had between our legs, but, quite honestly, the whole idea was as puzzling as it was disturbing, so I didn't waste much time thinking about it.

As for saying anything to Mother – forget it. She always said, 'Fight your own battles,' so that was what I had to do. Anyway, the thought of even mentioning prozzies to Mother made me cringe with embarrassment. She might be so insulted, and she was bound to take it out on me.

When I got home, I tried to act normally. Mother was on the phone. We were proud of that phone. We were one of the first families in the area to have one. I still remember the number: Croydon 4209. I never used it myself, and nor did the other kids. Mother had said, 'Don't you dare touch this or I'll have the hide off you.' And I heard her saying to Don, 'This is gonna be so good for business. We'll wonder how we managed without it!' I was glad she had something to help her in her business.

Mother was talking quickly. 'Betty, make sure Ruby's here by eight o'clock sharp. Don't let the dozy mare drop off again. Mickey's gonna come round and we're on a good thing there.'

She saw me looking at her and said into the phone, 'Hold on, Betty.' To me she said, 'I need you to help tonight – get the kids their tea and off to bed, then get ready yourself.'

I nodded and headed for the kitchen. I recognised the names Betty and Ruby. The two women had been round here several times recently. I'd been very struck by Ruby, thought she was gorgeous, not at all dozy. She looked like a gypsy, with fine dark eyes and beautiful long curly black hair. She was always very well dressed, with a pencil skirt and low-cut blouse showing off her good figure. She wore stockings with seams and stilettos with killer heels. She couldn't have looked more different from Betty. She was a strange one, Betty, very intense. She was short and on the stout side, with a Tony Curtis haircut – though it was usually men who copied his DA, the duck's arse as everyone called it. She dressed like a man too, always in slacks, shirt and jacket. By way of contrast she wore thick make-up, which Mother called Panstik, and bright red lipstick. She was very fond of glitter – on her hair, on her clothes. She was a caution. She and Ruby seemed to be very close friends. Whenever I saw them, Betty hardly took her eyes off her.

So they would be here this evening. I supposed Barbara would, too. She'd become a bit of a fixture. In fact she seemed to be living with us full-time, taking up the third bedroom. She was a funny little thing. She was about eighteen but looked much younger, could easily pass for thirteen. She wasn't what you'd call good-looking, in fact I thought she was downright plain, with her sharp nose, piggy eyes, short greasy dark hair and, what's more, a noticeable moustache. I once heard Don say something rude about the way she looked, something like, 'Who'd fancy that little rat?' and Mother said, 'Who looks at the mantelpiece when they're poking the fire?' They laughed, though I didn't get the joke at the time.

As I was busy making sandwiches for the kids' tea and then getting them to bed, I pushed what had happened at school to the back of my mind. I'd think about it later. When I had the kitchen to myself again, preparing nibbles for the party, a thought suddenly occurred to me. I slowly put down the knife I was cutting bread with.

Prozzies. How could I have been so stupid? Women who go with men . . . surely that's what Ruby was doing. And Barbara. It all made sense. Or – no, it didn't. Prozzies were dirty women, and Ruby was lovely, she had a lovely smell. Barbara might not be much to look at, but she wasn't dirty, her clothes were always clean and as far as I could tell so was she. In fact I thought of Mother's women friends as the painted ladies, they were always so prettily made up. And prozzies worked in dirty places, doing things for dirty men. Our home was squeaky clean, and as for the men who visited – well, if they were anything like the men at Mother's parties, then they'd be well dressed and smooth, very smooth. Some of them were really good-looking. One of them in particular, Teddy, always made my heart beat faster just to look at him.

So what was going on? There was no question of Mother being a prozzie herself, that was absolutely ridiculous. Maybe she was doing a favour for Barbara and Ruby and the other girls who would drop by or stay for a while. That's it. She was helping out her friends, letting them use her nice clean house so they wouldn't have to go anywhere nasty. Those stupid girls at school had got hold of the wrong end of the stick. Then I had a brainwave. Maybe this was Mother's 'business' she was always going on about. Such and such was bad for business, or good for business. Maybe it was like her deal with old Filth (I still couldn't bring myself to think he was really my father). If he paid her for board and lodging, maybe the girls did too. Everybody needed something for their trouble, I knew that.

Once a bit of light dawned, other odd things began to click into place. Mother and Don seemed to have a kind of running joke about the bus stop outside our house. 'Buses are slow tonight – look at the queue!' And they'd laugh.

I never paid much attention, till I was up and around more than usual, rather than being locked in with my brothers and sisters. One afternoon a few weeks back Mother had sent me to the local shop to buy some cigarettes, and I was dawdling back, on the opposite side of the road. As I came up, I saw the bus at the stop outside our house, and noticed something odd. There was a queue, mostly men, but only one or two of them actually got on the bus, along with a couple of women. The rest of the men, half a dozen or so, stayed in the queue. Now this was strange, as I knew only one bus stopped here. If the men weren't waiting for the bus, what were they doing there?

I was intrigued – or nosy. I leaned against the fence of the slaughterhouse opposite and watched. Sure enough, the men weren't looking up the road for the first sight of a big red double-decker, they were checking out our front door. It opened, and a man came out quickly, pulling the door to behind him and walking down our front path, not looking at anybody. Just as quickly, the first man in the queue walked up the path and went straight in.

Well, well. Now I knew. As I mechanically buttered bread and spread it with shrimp paste, I could see it in my mind's eye. They were queuing up to go into our house. I remembered Mother had a couple of lady friends round that day. I'd made them cups of tea. So the men were queuing up to see them. This was making the pieces fit, all right.

Then there were the times I'd been in Surrey Street market with Mother. All the barrow boys seemed to know her. Walking down the street, every other minute it was 'Hey, Grace, how're you doing?' Mother never bought much, but she'd stop to chat. Sometimes the men would hand her little parcels and, I noticed, Mother didn't pay them. She just said, 'I'll see you right,' and everyone smiled. Now I thought about it, more than once I'd heard a barrow boy say, 'All right if I bring Beryl round?' Or some other girl's name. Mother always smiled and said something like, ''Course you can, love. Ten bob to you – cheap at the price!' Like a kind of joke. Maybe this was the same kind of thing, only the men would bring their own girls round. They probably didn't have anywhere as nice to go to. After all, these were the days when most young people didn't have flats of their own. They'd just live at home with their family till they got married.

So Mother's a sort of landlady, I thought. Just as we pay rent to the council for our house, other people give money to Mother to have the use of it now and then. The barrow boys would bring their girls round, or other men queued up at the bus stop. There wouldn't be much room for them to wait indoors. They'd be the ones meeting Mother's friends and staying a while with them.

Just then, Mother joined me in the kitchen. 'Get a move on,' she said. 'People'll be here soon.'

I speeded up, arranging the crackers on a plate and reaching for another packet. Mother was looking at me. 'I meant to say,' she said, 'I've got another nice blouse for you. Hang on a sec and I'll get it.'

She came back with a pretty lacy blouse, a light green that suited my colouring.

'Try it on,' said Mother.

It was comfortable, but I thought it was a bit low for me. It gaped round the chest.

But Mother said, 'You'll grow into it. By the look of you, that won't take long.'

I felt myself blushing, but Mother reassured me. 'Don't be embarrassed about your boobs, they're lovely. You're very lucky to have big boobs. Men love them, they think they're really beautiful.'

That was something going for me at last, then.

That night, as I handed round the nibbles and drinks, I couldn't bring myself to think that the girls were prozzies. They were so well dressed, so pretty – even scrawny little Barbara looked quite good in the soft light from the table lamps. Nothing would make Betty look glamorous, but she didn't really seem to belong at the party. She sat hunched in her chair in a corner, not talking or laughing or dancing like everyone else, just staring at Ruby as she smiled and waved her cigarette and asked for a drink. 'Gin and It, please!'

There were about a dozen people all told, and I recognised most of them by now. I liked it when they called me by name: 'Thanks, Tess, you're a love.' I was more confident now, moving round the room with my tray, proud to be helping Mother.

As I took plates and glasses back to the scullery, I thought, Well, I give up. I can't work it out. I just won't worry about it. Who cares what the stupid cows at school say anyway? They don't know anything.

One thing I did know, and was absolutely sure about, was that Mother could never do anything wrong. She was always right, and that was a great comfort to me. What's more, I realised at last why us kids had to be locked in for so long at a time. It was to keep us out of the way. Maybe there were things Mother thought we were too young to see. I always felt Mother would defend us if push came to shove.

Later, of course, I knew that when a bloke is getting his end away with a working girl, the last thing he wants to hear is kids mucking about, running around and yelling and laughing. Put him right off his stroke. And as I was to find out, this is one game where the customer always comes first.

7

Mother's Little Helper Goes Out

I didn't mention anything about Mother's business to my brothers and sisters. They were too young to understand, I told myself. But deep down, I knew the real reason, and it wasn't anything to do with their age. It was that I just loved knowing something about Mother that they didn't. It made me feel special, singled out. This way, Mother and I could get closer.

I made sure I was as helpful as possible. On pension day, when old Filth came into the house, I tried to hide the disgust I felt. If being nice meant sitting on his lap, then that's what I did. I made sure to turn my head so I never caught sight of his willy. I didn't like to feel it against me, though.

And recently Mother had asked me to do something else on a party night. One of her lady friends, Lisa, was coming but her babysitter had let her down. 'Could you look after the kid, Tess?' Mother asked me. 'He could go in your room.'

Could I? Of course I could. I was used to looking after my little brothers, especially Andy, so this kid would be no problem.

''Course I will,' I said, and when Mother smiled at me and said, 'I knew I could rely on you,' my own face broke out into a grin. I felt warm inside. Mother and I were getting along so well.

It meant I couldn't help out at the party, and I missed that. Still, there was a baby to look after, and he wasn't much trouble. Lisa brought him in his pram and I put it by our bed. She left a bottle for him, and a clean nappy.

'I know what to do,' I said to her. 'I did it enough times for my brothers when they were babies.'

Lisa smiled. She was a new girl, one of those who popped up now and again in our house, and like most of them she was pretty and friendly.

'Thanks, Tess,' she whispered, so as not to wake the sleeping kids. 'You're a good girl for your mother.'

A good girl for my mother. I glowed with pride.

'You did a good job last night, Tess. Pity you missed Teddy, though. He was here, with Renee.'

Teddy? I felt myself blushing, and Mother added, 'You fancy him, don't you?'

We were sitting at the kitchen table next morning. Mother was smiling at me, in the friendly way I was getting more used to. I knew she was teasing, and that was a new one on me, but I didn't mind and it was lovely to see her smile. Usually Mother just came straight out with what she wanted to say. It must be a sign that we were getting closer.

And she was right. I'd always liked Teddy. From the very first time I caught sight of him I was smitten. He was so good-looking, a classic case of tall, dark and handsome, his thick black hair swept back into a quiff. He wore the sharpest suits, immaculate white shirts and fancy ties, while his shoes were always top-quality ox-blood leather. You'd never catch him in the teddy-boy style that was all the rage at the time, with draped jackets, drainpipe trousers and bootlace tie, along with thick crepe-soled shoes that I thought were really ugly. When the weather was cold Teddy would wear a very stylish topcoat with a velvet collar. I'd never seen anyone so classy, so glamorous.

That evening, I was supposed to be handing round the drinks and nibbles as usual, but one look at him and my heart started pounding and my mouth went dry. I didn't dare look him in the eye, just pushed the tray at him, tongue-tied. I was so embarrassed, and sure I must have been blushing like mad.

He was polite to Mother, smiling and charming. He even had a kind word for me. What a dreamboat! Renee was another one of Mother's girls, as fair as he was dark and as plump as he was lean. Just as good-looking in her way, though. It was common knowledge that she was mad about him. More than once I'd heard Mother say, 'You're a fool to yourself, Renee. You're in it for the business. When all's said and done, Teddy's a punter like everyone else.'

Punter – odd word, that. I'd heard it before, and realised it meant one of the men who visited. Teddy seemed more than just a punter, though. He was a gentleman, like a romantic hero in a film.

Now, as Mother looked at me, I shifted in my seat, mumbling, 'Yeah,' and not knowing where to look. I couldn't figure out why I felt the way I did when I saw Teddy, or one of the other good-looking boys who came round our house. I told myself I didn't like it, but then I knew part of me did. It was kind of thrilling.

Mother was smiling some more. 'You're growing up, all

right,' she said. 'I can tell. When you fancy boys, that means you're growing up, you're not a little kid any more.'

She inched her chair closer to mine. We'd just finished breakfast and the other kids had scattered. As it was a Saturday we weren't in a rush.

'And you know what?' Mother was saying. 'You fancy boys, and they fancy you. And as it happens I know someone who fancies you.'

My heart leaped. Teddy? Oh, no chance. I knew he was too grown-up for me. Who, then?

Mother was looking very pleased. 'You haven't met him,' she said, 'but he's a friend of Teddy's. They were out and about down Surrey Street when they saw me and you shopping. "Who's that girl?" this bloke – his name's Kenny – asked Teddy. Teddy said, "That's Tess, she's a lovely girl."'

I blushed with pleasure.

'This Kenny said he'd like to meet you, and Teddy said he'd have a word with me. Which he has.' Mother sat back with an even bigger smile on her face. 'It's all arranged,' she said. 'We're going round his place today, so doll yourself up. The taxi'll be here at eleven o'clock sharp.'

Taxi? My brain whirled. We never got taxis. All I could think to say was, 'What about the washing?' Saturday was the day the laundry usually went to the bagwash.

Mother waved her hand. 'Oh, don't worry about that. It'll keep. This is more important, Tess.'

She leaned towards me. 'We're on to a good thing here. This Kenny's a nice boy, and Teddy says he's loaded.'

'Loaded?'

'Money, girl, dosh, readies. You never know, if he likes you he might get you a present.'

I wasn't sure I understood that. I found it strange that anybody could like the look of me and want to meet me. I knew that the men fancied the girls in the house because they were beautiful, or at least most of them were, but I knew I wasn't beautiful, so why would anyone fancy me?

Mother was standing up. 'Right,' she said, 'when you've done the washing-up and cleaned the kitchen, get ready.'

An hour later the taxi called, and off we went in style. It was the first time I'd ever been in one of those black cabs, and I felt like a film star. I nearly waved at people on the street!

The taxi went right across town and pulled up outside a smart detached house. The garden was very neat, if a bit bare this late in the year. Mother rang the bell and a man answered the door. This couldn't be Kenny. Teddy had said he was a nice boy, and this was a man, a middle-aged man, quite stout, and going bald. He was wearing a shirt and tie and beige trousers with a sharp crease.

'You must be Kenny,' my mother was saying.

'Yes indeed, come in, come in,' said the man, smiling back and holding the door open. 'I'm very glad to meet you, Mrs Stevens, and – ah – Tess. Delightful. Would you like a cup of tea? I'll just put the kettle on.' He disappeared off to the kitchen.

While he was out of the room, Mother drew me towards her and whispered in my ear. 'I want you and Kenny to be friends. He's a very nice man. Teddy says so. You do what he says and you'll be a good girl.'

Do what he says? I felt uneasy, but then thought, Well, if Mum says so, it must be all right.

Then in a loud voice Mother said, 'Oh, would you believe it – I'll be forgetting my own head next.' As Kenny came back in she laughed and said, 'I'm just popping out for some cigarettes – won't be long.' As she went towards the door her smile disappeared and she hissed at me, 'Remember what I said.'

I flinched. That was more like the old Mother, looking so fierce. Then the door banged and she was gone.

'Let me take your coat,' said Kenny. I took it off and he hung it on a hook in the hall. Then he said, 'Sit down, Tess, make yourself at home.'

He gestured towards a plush settee and I sat down, hands in my lap, feet pressed close together. I felt nervous. What did he want? He sat next to me, a bit close, I thought, and started chatting, asking the same questions grown-ups always fire at children they don't know well.

'How's school?'

'What do you want to do when you grow up?'

So far so ordinary, with the usual answers.

'All right.'

'Dunno.'

I began to relax, didn't feel so shy. Then he said, 'You'll be going to big school next year, won't you?'

I nodded.

'Well, you're getting to be a big girl, aren't you?' He smiled. 'Yes, a big girl, especially here.'

And he brushed his hand over my chest. Uh-oh. I sat rigid, not saying a word, not looking at him. I stared at the window as he undid the top buttons of my blouse and pushed his hand inside my vest. He was touching my bare skin.

I sat frozen. What was I supposed to do? Was this being nice to him, just sitting there? Where was Mother? Why was she taking so long?

I kept looking at the window. There were clouds in the sky – was rain on the way? He was running his hand over my boobs, squeezing them, rubbing the tips with his thumb. Mother had said men like boobs, they think they're lovely, and mine were lovely. So this was how men showed they liked them? I realised he was moving his other hand. Out of the corner of my eye I saw it was inside his trousers. He was rubbing himself at the same time, only harder, and faster.

He was breathing hard by now, muttering words I couldn't understand. Suddenly he jerked upright, and shuddered. For a moment he was as still as I was, then he was taking one hand out of my vest and the other out of his trousers. That hand seemed a bit wet, and I couldn't help noticing a stain on the front of his trousers. Had he wet himself?

With his hand gone, I came back to life and quickly did up my blouse buttons. I desperately wished Mother would come back. I wasn't sure what had happened but I knew I didn't like it. Did I do right? Would Mother be pleased?

'Ah, there's your mother,' Kenny said, going towards the door. I hadn't heard her ring the bell and I was flooded with relief. As she came in I stood up.

She looked me in the face and said, 'All right?'

'Yeah,' I said automatically.

'Good. Well, get your coat and we'll be off.'

'Well, we have had a nice time, haven't we, Tess,' said Kenny. 'You must pay me another visit some time.'

Again, 'Yeah.'

He waved us off and Mother and I went out of the door and into the street.

For something to say, I said, 'Are we going to get another taxi?'

'No,' said Mother. 'Only works one way. We'll get the bus.'

We walked towards the stop. My head was still reeling, filled with pictures of what had gone on. I had to know. Gathering the courage from somewhere, I stopped and took Mother's arm.

'Mum?'

'What? What is it?'

'I'm ever so sorry, but I don't like him. I don't think Kenny is a nice man.'

She said nothing, just looked at me.

'We don't have to go there again, do we?' I asked, feeling tears begin to prick my eyes.

She was still looking at me. Then she shrugged and said, 'No, we don't. Not if you don't want to.'

I breathed easier. What a relief. I was so grateful to hear her words.

Mother didn't ask me what went on in Kenny's room, and I didn't tell her. I just thought, Well, she doesn't know him very well. Teddy can't know him very well either. They don't know he does rude things.

The next time Mother said she'd need my help for one of her parties in the evening, I did feel apprehensive. What if Kenny was there? She must have read my mind, as she said, 'Don't worry, Kenny's not the type to come here.' So I could go about my waitress duties quite happily. In any case, Christmas was coming, and like all kids we were looking forward to it. I tried not to think of Kenny and what he did.

Christmas was the only time Mother pushed the boat out for us kids. Well, as boats go it would have been a tiddly little thing as far as other people were concerned, probably not much more than a model boat on a pond in the park. But it was enough for us.

Mother had been using the promise of presents for weeks now.

'The one who's quietest will get the best present,' she said, and we bust our guts trying to be quiet as mice, competing with each other to be well behaved.

For a few days before Christmas we were making paper chains for the living room, licking those little coloured strips and linking them together. We had a tree stuck in a bucket, supplied by one of Mother's contacts in Surrey Street market. We decorated it with tinsel, silvery tinsel so sharp you could cut your hands on it. What with the balloons we blew up, the room looked very festive.

And Christmas Eve was really special. Mother actually lit the fire in the room where we slept, the only day in the whole year. We loved lying there, the dark lit up by the rosy glow of the flickering flames. And when we woke up in the morning – well, the magic continued. We couldn't see too well in the dim light, as the fire had burned out hours ago, but we could see five socks had somehow appeared on our bed. Each one had a tangerine stuffed in the toe, and there were a couple of cracked walnuts too, as well as dates individually wrapped in paper. A feast! We sat up in bed stuffing ourselves, looking forward to the rest of the day and our presents – or rather present. We got one each. Mother didn't bother to wrap them in Christmas paper, just left them in the brown paper bag, but that was fine by us. Though I must admit to a slight disappointment. All the time she'd said the quietest of us would get the best present, but as it happened there was no difference in what we got. Us girls each had a little doll, one of those I'd seen on a Surrey

Street market stall, and the boys each had a push-along toy car, which I'd also seen in the market. Oh well, Mother didn't have much money to spare, and of course it's the thought that counts.

Dinner was special, though, like a bigger version of our Sunday roasts, only with a large chicken and all the trimmings. This year we even had crackers, red and green with silver and gold stars. Beautiful to look at, even if most of them didn't go off with a crack when we pulled them.

All told, we had a lovely Christmas, and I could push Kenny and what he did right to the back of my mind. If I pushed hard enough, maybe I'd forget about him altogether.

In the New Year, life went on much the same as usual. At school those stupid girls who'd called Mother a prozzie didn't try their tricks again. At least, they did once, and I whacked them both so they went flying. Good job there was no teacher around in the playground, or I would have copped it – and there was no way I could have told anyone why I hit them. They still nudged each other and pointed and whispered, but they didn't dare take me on again directly. At home I was busy when Mother needed me. When she wanted us all out of the way, we were locked in our room, or sent out to the pictures. I'd just about forgotten Kenny.

One evening I was clearing up the kitchen after tea when Mother said, 'I need you to do a good turn for someone, Tess.'

Always happy to help, I thought.

Mother went on. 'It's my old friend Peter,' she said. 'He's taken up photography – you know, as a hobby. He's looking for a model, and I said you'd help him out.'

A model? Me? This sounded odd. I knew about models, of course, I'd seen them in the paper. They were beautiful, they wore gorgeous clothes and walked about so everyone could see them and take pictures of them. Didn't sound like me at all. And come to think of it, I'd never heard Mother mention Peter before.

'So I said I'd take you round to his place in the morning,' Mother added.

My heart sank. Next day was a Tuesday, so that meant she'd be taking me out of school. Still, modelling didn't sound too hard, and, as ever, if I could do anything to please Mother, then I would.

'You'll need your swimsuit,' Mother said. 'Don't forget it.'

'My swimsuit? What for?'

'Don't ask questions.' My mother was getting irritable, always a danger sign, so I shut up.

Next morning, after the kerfuffle of getting the kids out to school and nursery, I dug out my swimsuit. It was ruched elastic and navy blue – I'd got it for swimming lessons at school. I was just stuffing it in a bag when the taxi called.

This time the cab drew up outside a new block of flats. There were a lot of them being built in Croydon at the time. Everything looked spick and span, and I could see it was a swish part of town. As we waited inside for the lift, Mother said something that chilled my blood.

'Peter is a special friend of mine, so I want you to be nice to him. Do whatever he says.'

I thought my heart would stop. Immediately my thoughts flew back to the last time she'd said those words. Kenny, and what he did.

Mother took my arm and swung me round to face her. 'I hope you're not going to be difficult,' she said sharply, her eyes narrowed.

I could only gasp, 'No.' But I was filled with dread.

Mother gazed at me, frowning. Then she seemed to make up her mind about something. 'You needn't worry. This time he won't touch you.'

If I hadn't been in such a panic, those words might have registered more at the time.

'Oh, for God's sake, he only wants to take your bloody photo, so behave!'

The lift whirred smoothly upwards and we got out on the tenth floor. It really was posh here, fitted carpets everywhere, and very quiet. Mother rang the bell, and I wondered what was waiting for me on the other side of the door.

'Grace!'

'Peter!'

And we went in.

Peter was a little bloke, middle-aged, with thick grey hair and round glasses. He was quite dapper, wearing a crisp blue shirt and black trousers. He even had a cravat – that was classy. And his flat was classy. Carpet everywhere, and polished furniture. There was a distinct smell of lavender furniture polish in the air.

He patted me on the head. 'I'm very pleased to meet you at last, Tess. Ah, is that your swimsuit in the bag? Good. Just go and get changed in the bedroom will you, please?'

As I moved to where he pointed, my mother spoke. 'I'll just pop out for some cigarettes,' she said, and those words were like a dungeon door slamming.

I was shaking so much it was hard to get my clothes off and my swimsuit on. He won't touch you, he won't touch you, I kept saying to myself. Mum says he won't touch you. When I came out, to my surprise Peter had changed too. He was wearing black swimming trunks, quite short and close-fitting.

'Thought I'd join you,' he said with a laugh. 'Get in the swim, ha-ha!'

I thought he looked quite funny, with his spindly little legs, but I was careful not to show it.

I stood awkwardly in the middle of the room while he fussed about with his camera.

Then he said, 'I'd like you to look as if you're about to jump off a diving board, Tess. On tippy-toes and your hands together above your head. That's it.'

He was darting about the room, taking photos of me at all angles as I struck various poses he asked for. I felt very silly, but he seemed harmless enough. Until he said, 'That's lovely, Tess. Now, we'll just have you with swimsuit off, shall we?'

I froze. What? Oh, no. I couldn't do that. I couldn't stand there in front of him with nothing on. I knew that was wrong, absolutely wrong. Surely Mother didn't mean I should do that?

I shook my head. I couldn't speak.

'Now then, Tess, I'm sure you don't want me telling your mother that you haven't been helping me. She said you were such a good girl, eager to please.'

I stared at the floor, trying to catch my breath. My heart was hammering and I felt like crying. I couldn't let my mother down, I couldn't. I couldn't bear the guilt. But I couldn't take my swimsuit off, I just couldn't.

'Tess?'

I looked up, and saw a horrible sight. Peter had pulled down his trunks and was holding his willy in his hand. It was shiny and pink and looked swollen. Part of my mind registered the fact that the camera was nowhere to be seen.

'Look at this,' he said. 'Would you like to hold it?'

'No!' The word was out my mouth before I'd even thought of it.

'Well,' he said, 'it's that or taking off your swimsuit.'

'I won't!'

'Hmm . . . your mother is not going to be pleased if she finds out you've let her down.' He must have been reading my mind. 'Tell you what,' he went on, 'pull down your top a little way. Just slip off the straps.'

If I could have put it into words, I'd have said, 'Lesser of two evils.'

Reluctantly, I pulled down the straps, and tugged my swimsuit down an inch or two.

'Just a bit more . . . a bit more . . . yes, you might as well pull it down to your waist. It's more comfortable like that, isn't it?'

So I stood there with my boobs exposed, staring fixedly at the ceiling. I studied the lampshade of the ceiling light, which was patterned with red flowers and had a pink fringe all the way round. Peter was muttering and breathing heavily. I didn't look at him once.

'Right, that's it, go and get dressed.'

Keeping my eyes averted from him, I walked mechanically into the bedroom, took off my swimsuit and dressed in my everyday clothes. By the time I came out, Mother was back, chatting with Peter, who was also dressed again.

Could that really have happened? Everything in the room seemed so normal. Peter seemed normal, saying goodbye to us.

'I'll send you some prints!' was the last thing he said, as Mother and I got in the lift and the doors closed.

'All right?' she said to me.

And this time, my throat closing up and tears pricking my eyes, I couldn't say, 'Yeah.' I could only shake my head. True, that man hadn't actually touched me, he hadn't even got close, but he'd made me feel awful. I couldn't have put it into words, but he was worse than rude. It was like being rolled in mud, dirty sticky mud, and being laughed at. It was what being used felt like, and I was shocked to my core.

8

Mother Talks to Me

'What's the matter with you, Tess? Why aren't you eating your tea?'

I kept my eyes fixed on my plate, staring at my banana sandwich. Usually I'd wolf it down, but I didn't feel hungry. My whole throat seemed to be closed up, and I didn't trust myself to speak. I felt that if I opened my mouth I'd start crying, and wouldn't be able to stop.

That afternoon was burned into my mind. I kept getting an image of Peter with his swimming trunks down, holding his willy and telling me to touch it. I felt sickness rise in me, and pushed my chair away from the table.

'Gotta go,' I mumbled, and dashed to the toilet down the hall.

My mother's voice floated after me. 'Tess, are you all right, love?'

I shut and bolted the door, and knelt in front of the toilet bowl. I felt sure I was going to sick up all my guts, but all that came up was some liquid that burned my throat. Then I did start crying, great choking sobs. I tried to keep the noise down. I didn't want to make Mother angry.

We hadn't spoken at all on the way back from Peter's. We walked to the bus stop, and waited in silence. We sat next to each other on the bus. She shot me the odd glance, but I still couldn't trust myself to speak. When we got home, she surprised me by saying, 'I'll get the tea.' Usually it was me. I helped her anyway, slicing up the bananas while she cut the bread and buttered it. Everybody was quiet at the table.

Now I stared into the toilet bowl through my tears as my body shook. I tried to take deep breaths, and gradually I could breathe more normally.

I knew I had to go back in. I couldn't stay in the toilet for the rest of my life! I'd better try to be normal.

I opened the door – and there was Mother standing in front of me. Was it my imagination, or did she seem worried?

'You don't look well,' she said. 'Go and have a lie-down on the settee. I'll get the kids off to bed, then I'll bring you a nice hot cup of tea.'

The sympathy in her voice made me want to cry all over again. Instead, I just nodded and stumbled up the hall to the living room.

Lying on the red velvet settee, with my shoes off, I stared out of the window. The days were getting longer now it was spring, but it still got dark quite early.

As I sat there, I felt a weight in my chest, which seemed to grow bigger and bigger. I was so upset. Peter had frightened me. Wanted me to do something I knew in my heart was wrong. Mother would never have wanted me to do something so wrong, surely? Peter was just saying that, while Mother's back was turned. I buried my face in a cushion, trying to hold in the misery. I didn't want to be in pieces when Mother came in. At least she didn't seem angry.

I heard her telling the kids to get ready for bed. We were in the back bedroom tonight. Mother must have plans for the big front bedroom. It was going to be a bigger squash than usual, then, as the bed was only an ordinary double, not the huge one we usually shared. On the plus side, there were no shutters at the window, just a piece of old curtain Mother had tacked up. The window only looked out on to the back garden, so there'd be nobody there to care what sort of curtains it had. If you didn't count Filth, of course, living in his shed. I didn't think Mother would care what he thought about anything.

After a while I heard the door open, and Mother come in. I rolled round to face her as she put a cup and saucer on the coffee table.

'Here you are, love,' said Mother. 'Nice cup of tea. Do you a world of good.'

I sat up and swung my legs round. She was sitting in the armchair opposite, her hands on her knees, her eyes on my face.

'Thanks,' I managed to say.

We sat in silence for a while, till Mother said, 'I'm sorry you feel rotten, Tess. I didn't think you'd have a hard time. He didn't touch you, did he?' she asked, suddenly urgent.

I shook my head. 'No,' I muttered. 'I just had to . . . had to . . . do things.'

'Hmm. He'd better not have laid a finger on you,' said Mother, 'or I'll give him something he won't forget in a hurry.'

I looked up in surprise. Mother sounded really concerned for me. At least I was right in thinking she'd always look out for me.

I picked up my cup and took a sip. The tea was good and hot.

Just then, Mother stood up and came and sat beside me on the settee. As I clutched my cup, she looked into my eyes.

'I've got to tell you straight, Tess,' she said. 'You've just about saved my life today. I can't thank you enough.'

What? I put the cup down. My puzzlement must have shown on my face, as Mother added, 'The thing is, I needed the money. Kenny and Peter promised me money if you would keep them company. They like the company of young girls, they said. I didn't know you'd be so upset, Tess. Cross my heart, if there was another way of coming up with the dosh, I never would have let you go to them.'

I looked back at Mother. Her blue eyes were soft, her forehead creased – that'd be concern for me.

I still couldn't speak, but took a deep breath. I felt wobbly.

Mother went on. 'I wish I could hide it from you, Tess. You're just a kid, you shouldn't be worried with all this grown-up stuff. But the thing is, if it wasn't for you, we'd be right up the creek without a paddle in sight. You've saved us all.'

I've saved them all? Me? I felt myself blushing.

Mother explained some more. 'As soon as money comes in the door, it's out the window. Always stuff to buy, food and clothes and shoes – and the rent. What we pay that bloody council, we should own this place by now. And the rates! And the gas and electricity, not to mention the phone. I tell you, Tess, it's a struggle to make ends meet. Sometimes I can't sleep at night.'

Well! I shook my head. This took a little while to sink in. I knew we were hard up, as Mother was always saying we were, but I'd had no idea it was this bad. What a worry for Mother.

'You see, Tess, with what you've brought in, we can all go another month. You've saved our bacon!'

The weight inside me began to feel a bit less heavy. I could breathe normally now.

Mother was looking round the room. 'See all this, Tess? Nice now, isn't it? But do you remember how it used to be – those poxy paper curtains!'

I smiled.

'That's right, love. That's how poor we were. And do you remember how I got some of the stuff? The rugs?' She jerked her head to the nice thick patterned rugs lying on the lino.

Now that did make me smile. I remembered all right.

It was one particular tallyman who called on us, trying to sell some rugs. I knew we were broke, and from what Mother said to Don, I gathered there was some kind of list of people who couldn't pay what they owed. 'We'll be at the top of that!' said Mother. Apparently this salesman was new, or he hadn't checked us out, so he offered Mother the rugs, laying them down on the floor of the front room.

'Yes, they're lovely,' Mother said. 'There's just one thing – my husband doesn't believe in credit. If you leave them here, I'll check with him. Come back on Monday and I'll let you know.'

On Monday, the hopeful tallyman came back. Standing on the doorstep, the man said, 'If you want the rugs, I've got the credit forms here. Otherwise, I'll just take them back.'

Mother's face was a picture of surprise. 'Rugs?' she said. 'What rugs?'

'The rugs I left here the other day, of course.'

'What do you mean? You never left any rugs here – I've never seen you before in my life.'

'What!' The man was looking flustered. 'You know bloody well that I left two rugs here on approval.'

'I know no such thing,' said Mother. 'And I'll thank you not to swear.'

The man was sweating by now. 'I can tell you exactly where they were,' he cried. 'They were in your front room. One was in front of a settee, the other in front of an armchair. I put them there myself.'

Mother shook her head. 'I'm afraid you're confusing this house with another one,' she said.

'No, I'm not!'

'Well,' said Mother in a patient tone, 'why don't you look for yourself?'

'I will!'

The man pushed through into the hall, opened the door of the front room, and saw – a bedroom. Complete with bed, wardrobe and dressing table, with tatty old rugs laid over the floor. Mother had juggled the furniture!

The tallyman goggled. 'But . . .'

Mother sighed and tapped her foot. 'Are you satisfied now, young man?'

He knew when he was beaten. He crept away, muttering under his breath.

We all had a good laugh over that one.

Don often said she could talk herself out of a hanging. Or, more politely, she could sell ice to Eskimos and sand to Arabs.

Now Mother was sitting back on the settee, laughing at the memory of the poor tallyman. I laughed a bit too.

'That's better,' said Mother. 'Nice to see a smile on your face.'

Then she looked serious. 'I know it's hard, Tess, the things you have to do. Life doesn't seem fair, does it? Well, let me tell you, I know what I'm talking about. I've told you about my mum and dad, haven't I?'

I nodded. Us kids had heard about Mother's life with her family. She was a Croydon girl through and through. They all lived not so far from where we lived now. It was only a small house, but there were lots of children, seventeen in all.

'Think of that!' Mother would say. 'You might think it's crowded here, but think of all of us in that little house, just three bedrooms. And that whole house would have fitted in our two front rooms here.'

We were seriously impressed. We couldn't begin to imagine how they managed.

What Mother always went on about, though, was how strict her mum and dad were.

'What are you complaining about?' she used to say to us kids when we were crying after she'd given us a good hiding. 'This is nothing. My dad used to take a belt to me, and that was a thrashing. You lot don't know you're born.'

Now she said to me, 'Did I ever tell you the story about my sister Doreen?'

I shook my head.

'Well, she was older than me, and engaged to be married. The day before her wedding she was going out with her fiancé, and Father had told her, "You be back before ten o'clock or it'll be the worse for you. Ten, do you hear?"' Mother's voice took on a deeper note.

'Well, something happened, some hold-up, and Doreen's young man got her home a few minutes after ten. Before she could even knock on the door it opened, and Father dragged her in. He yelled at her fiancé, "She's not yours till tomorrow. She still belongs to me!" And he slammed the door shut and beat seven bells out of Doreen with his belt. He gave her hell – and she was getting married next day!'

I shut my eyes at the horrible image of the beating. Mother never used a belt on us. Then something occurred to me.

'What happened?' I asked. I felt quite caught up in the story. 'Did she get married?'

Mother grinned. 'Yeah, managed to drag herself round to the church. Couldn't wait to leave home. Mother and Father didn't go, though. She was forbidden to set foot in the house again. In those days, children did what their parents said, or it was the worse for them.'

'Poor Doreen,' I said.

'Yeah, she never had much luck. She fell pregnant, but something went wrong. I think it was the same thing that happened to me, when I had to go to hospital and you kids went into care.'

I shuddered at the memory. In my mind Beulah Heights was like an ogre in a fairytale.

'What happened to her?' I asked.

'Oh, she died of it,' said Mother, 'Great shame, she was a lovely girl. I named you after her, you know.'

Of course. I was Sandra Doreen Rebecca Joy – quite a mouthful. I liked the idea of having my aunt's name, even if she'd had such a sad end.

As I was taking this in, Mother added, 'Did I ever tell you about the worst thrashing I ever got?'

'No, I don't think so.'

'Well, us kids used to have to sleep squashed up in a couple of beds. Really squashed, not like you lot. One of my brothers had a dirty mind, and he tried to feel me up – do you know what I mean?'

I nodded. I had a horror of that, the most private part of your body being got at.

'I told Mother straight away, and do you know what she did? Slapped me round the face as hard as she could and called me a filthy girl! Me! Calling me filthy when it was my brother who was a wrong 'un.'

I was indignant. 'That's not fair,' I declared.

'Too right,' said Mother. 'Well, it got worse. She said she'd tell Father, and sure enough she did. "Evil thoughts!" he yelled at me. "Filthy slut!" And he thrashed me with his belt till I was screaming and bleeding. I couldn't move for days.'

This was horrifying. Poor Mother. And her brother got clean away with it!

'Yet I know he had his reasons. They were terrified about girls getting into trouble, so if there was the slightest suggestion of anything dirty, he had to beat it out of me. You had to be respectable. I know it's not fair, but life's like that. Hard. And for all they did, I never questioned them. I always loved them. I'd give my right arm to have them back with me for one day.'

Mother grew quiet, and seemed to be looking into space. I suddenly realised I wasn't feeling that heavy weight in my chest. It was as if Mother had driven it away.

She was looking directly at me again, and suddenly smiled. 'Think you could manage something to eat now, Tess?' she asked. 'You have to keep your strength up. If you don't fancy banana, what about some toast and dripping?'

'Yes, please!' My all-time favourite.

'Right, I won't be a minute. You just make yourself comfy.'

In the doorway Mother paused and looked thoughtful.

'You know what, Tess? I think it's about time you and me had a proper chat about your dad. Okay?' And she disappeared off to the kitchen.

I sat back against the cushions. Mother was talking to me more than she ever had. She was really taking me into her confidence. What a life she'd had! And she loved her mother just as I loved her. I started to feel more relaxed.

And she was going to talk about my father! I knew she meant the Irishman. That had just been one of her jokes about old Filth being my father – at least I hoped it was. If she'd wanted to cheer me up, she couldn't have come up with anybody or anything better. I never tired of hearing the slightest titbit about my father.

I knew Mother didn't meet him until she was quite old, about thirty. She'd been living with her family all the time. Well, I supposed some of the children would have left to look for work as well as get married, but I do know Mother was there all the time. Apart from the strictness and the beatings, Mother never said much else about her family. Their surname was Wood, that I did know, and my grandmother's name was Fanny. That meant she was called Fanny Wood: 'If anyone would do it, Fanny Wood!' I used to joke. Not in front of Mother, though. She wouldn't have taken kindly to me being cheeky about her beloved mother.

Mother didn't talk much about her schooldays, either. The only thing I remembered her mentioning in particular was a little boy she palled up with. He was nicknamed Bunny as he was the school wimp. A girlish boy, who all the other boys made fun of. As Mother described it, she would always stand up for Bunny, and protect him from the bullies. She had a strong right arm even in those days, and Bunny was eternally grateful.

'And we've been friends ever since,' Mother would say.

Back to Mother's young days, when the war broke out, and she was still living in the family house.

'The war drove a lot of people apart, but it brought a lot of people together,' Mother would tell us girls. 'And it brought me and your dad together.'

He was a soldier, a sergeant-major, stationed in barracks near Croydon. Mother met him one day walking home from work. She had a job in a local factory making bits for aeroplanes.

'Our eyes met,' said Mother. 'And that was it. He was the one for me.'

Mind you, the way she described him didn't make him sound exactly like a dreamboat. She said he was sixty, which seemed very old to me, but Mother should know. He was Irish, from the south, and he used to run a pub at one time. His name was Mick, he was six foot tall and rugged, a real man's man, he had bright blue eyes and he was ginger like me, or rather of course I was like him. We had to take Mother's word for it, as we never saw as much as a single photo. Mother said she'd had various boyfriends before she met Mick. 'Nothing happened with them,' she said. 'Mother and Father had drilled that into me.'

Anyway, Mick asked her out right then and there. They met next evening in a pub. She told her parents she was doing overtime in the factory. Then they were off.

'It wasn't long before I was knocked up with you,' Mother told me. She was fond of saying, 'You were conceived in the bushes in Wandle Park, near the ponds. Must be why you're such a water baby.'

That always made me smile – I did like being clean.

'Then came the bombshell,' said Mother. 'Mick was married, he and his wife had children, and he couldn't leave her. Catholic, you know. They don't hold with divorce. But he loved me passionately and I loved him just as much. I managed to get the place here, and he saw me when he could get leave from the barracks. Kath came along next, then Jess, and then the war ended. He had to go home, to Ireland.'

Her face would fall, and she would look very sad. Us girls would be sad too.

And now Mother was going to talk some more about him. I settled back on the cushions. This really was something to look forward to.

Mother bustled in with a plate of toast and dripping. It smelled wonderful, and as soon as she gave it to me, I realised I was really hungry. I started chewing while she took up the story again, sitting back in the armchair.

'Your dad would be very proud of you,' she said, and though I was stuffing my face, my heart leaped. 'What a good girl you've turned into. He knew the minute he saw you how special you were. I was waiting outside the barracks with you in the old pram and he had a right look at you. "She's a proper ginger nut, that one!" He laughed. "She'll go far." And he put a threepenny bit into your little hand as you looked up at him. It was his idea to call you Sandra.'

She sighed. 'You know, I've often said you remind me of him. The hair and the eyes. And he was a charmer, a silver-tongued charmer. He could entertain people, hold court for hours. You've got a touch of that, young as you are.'

Had I? This was good news. I did try to be good company for people, and I was glad she'd noticed.

We sat in silence for a while. Mother must have been casting her mind back into the past. She looked serious now. 'Of course when I fell pregnant with you, I was out of my mind with worry. Mick said he'd leave his wife, but that would have ruined him. He would've lost his children. I couldn't do that to him. We just managed as best we could.'

I'd swallowed the last of the toast and dripping, and now asked, 'Did you tell your mum and dad?'

Mother made a face. 'I had to. But first there were some things to take care of.' She looked at me. 'This is what I haven't told you.'

I was all ears.

'It was a terrible thing to be an unmarried mother in those days, just as bad as it is now. Even though things are different in wartime, and a lot of it went on, believe you me. There was only one thing for it. I'd have to get married – but who to?'

She paused. I loved the way Mother told a story. She'd act it out, all the different parts. It was like watching a film!

'Well, there was an old bloke I'd known for years. Harry. He'd been in the last war and something happened to him. Shellshock or something. Whatever it was, he was never the same again. A bit simple. Couldn't look after himself. I knew he liked me, so I took him out a couple of times to the pub, and we got talking. I gave him a bit of encouragement, and to cut a long story short – he asked me to marry him!'

Mother laughed. 'I looked at him, all broken down and dirty, rotten teeth, and thought of my Mick. Fine upstanding man, all his own teeth – why couldn't he be the one asking me to marry him? Still, needs must, beggars can't be choosers, so I said yes. That made Harry's day all right.'

She looked directly at me. 'And you know what his surname was?'

I shook my head.

'Stevens.'

This shook me. 'Stevens?' I thought quickly. 'You said Filth's name is Stevens . . .'

'You got it.' Mother grinned. 'Filth is Harry Stevens. He gave his name to you – I told you, it's on your birth certificate. Same for Kath and Jess too.'

I knew it! I knew that horrible old man couldn't be my real father.

'Oh, Mum . . .' I struggled to say something. I was so happy I knew the truth for definite now. And just as happy that Mother was telling me her story. I wanted to hear the rest of it.

'What did your mum and dad do when you told them?'

Mother shrugged. 'My mother had already guessed, and hit the roof. Good job that was all she could hit by now. She and Father were getting on a bit, no question of thrashing me now. Father cut himself off from me, but Mother didn't. Mind you, she told me what she thought of me. "You bring shame on this family," she said, "carrying a bastard."

'I'd told her about marrying Harry. With a wedding ring on my finger I'd be a respectable married woman, but that cut no ice. I tried telling her, "It's not a bastard. It'll have a name." Mother just snapped back, "The wrong name." And she never softened. She held it against you even before you were born.'

Well, that made sense. Pieces were beginning to fit.

'So that's why she didn't like me!' I said. 'I remember sitting under her kitchen table, and every time I tried to get out she'd kick me. All I could see was a little black boot, one of those old-fashioned ones with buttons.'

Mother nodded. 'That's right. I used to go there to do her housework, and I had to take you with me. But she wouldn't look at you.'

The memory was clearing in my mind now, and I added, 'There were lots of boxes, blue and white cardboard boxes, under the table . . .'

'Ah, that'd be the old Energen Crisp Rolls. We both had them, me and Mother, because of the diabetes.'

'Oh, did she have it too?' I knew Mother had suffered with it for years.

'Yeah. Must run in the family.'

We were both quiet for a moment, thinking back. Only once had I peeped out from under the table and got a good look at my grandmother.

'She looked a bit like Queen Victoria, didn't she?' I said. The minute I'd first seen a picture of the old queen, all dressed in black, with a long dress and her hair in a bun, I'd thought, Grandmother!

Mother smiled. 'She was very severe, all right. But I miss her every day.'

We were quiet again. Mother's story was running through my head, and I wanted the ends tidied up.

'So you and Filth – I mean Harry – moved here when you got married?'

'Yeah, we got the place from the council. A lot of people needed new homes during the war, and I was a priority, with a baby on the way. So we moved in and set up house. Not that I could stand Harry in the house, the filthy bastard. Wasn't long before he moved to the shed! Still, I kept to the deal – remember I told you we had a deal? I'd look after him, and he'd pay over his pension. Just keep a bit for his baccy and beer.' Mother grinned, her eyes sparkling. 'Bet the old bastard has got a stash somewhere. I'll find it!'

She really did seem to be in a good mood. I thought I'd ask for some more.

'And my dad was in the army place all the time?'

'The barracks, yeah. We just met when we could. When he had leave he'd pop over here. Couldn't be too often for me.'

'But he had to go away?'

Her face changed expression, her mouth turning down and the light going out of her eyes.

'After the war ended, there wasn't much use for an old soldier, was there? He had his marching orders, and he had to go home, back to Ireland. And to his wife and kids. I went to the barracks one last time, the day before he left. I walked all the way as usual, pushing the pram with Kath and Jess in it. You walked beside me, holding on to the handle. You were a good little walker, didn't complain.'

Mother sighed heavily. 'We had one last talk. He kissed each one of you girls, and said goodbye. He took the boat to Ireland, and took my heart with him. He was the love of my life.'

I was spellbound. I could see the scene in my mind's eye – the tall soldier in uniform, the young woman with three little children. A heartbreaking farewell. I so wished I had a memory of his face. Did he ever think of me, his little Sandra, and what became of me?

Mother was looking into space again. Grieving for her lost love. It was like a romantic film. Though I couldn't help wondering, if my father was the love of her life, what did that make Don?

He'd come along when Buddy was just a baby. Mother had never told us who Buddy's father was, only that he was a bookie. I wondered for a moment if I could ask her now, but thought better of it. She looked so wrapped up in her thoughts. Poor Buddy, the only one of us not even to know his father's name.

I was about five when Don came into our lives. He might have fallen for Mother on the spot, but he wasn't so keen on us kids. My earliest memory of him was when we were all sitting at the table in the kitchen, having tea, and he suddenly burst out at me. 'You eat like a pig and you look like a pig!'

What? I was shocked, and started to cry till Mother told me to shut up. That did stick with me, though – pig. I was fat. That set a pattern with Don.

Us kids called him Don when he moved in. We didn't pretend he was our dad or our stepdad. He looked quite foreign, with deep brown eyes and dark hair, not very big but fit and active. I remembered Mother once telling us where Don had come from before he landed in Liverpool, something like Puerto Rico. Anyway, he had the look of a Latin lover in a film.

Mother always said that when Don came to her, he was an alcoholic and she cured him. Well, Mother didn't like booze, though she happily served it at her parties, so an alkie could be someone who just had a couple of pints a night. Anyway, Don did come in one night, genuinely pissed, falling about all over the place, and Mother went ape. The story goes that she got a funnel from somewhere, forced it into his mouth and poured salt water down him. He never touched a drop after that. On the other hand, she'd talk about how she had him sent to an asylum, as the drink had made him go crackers. He begged her to get him out, and promised he'd never drink again if she did.

Ever since I could remember, they'd always fought a lot. If Mother so much as looked at a man, Don was like a cat on hot bricks. Once they got into a row on a bus, and he kicked her off the platform. To get her own back, she threw hot chip fat at him, complete with chips. Us kids were terrified of their rows; they seemed to shake the house when they were at it hammer and tongs. Then they'd make it up.

When Andy was born, Don was over the moon. He always doted on him. As Andy was a blue baby, he had extra special attention, and everybody walked on eggshells round him. Till, of course, that day he held his breath one time too many and Mother blew up at him. That put him in his place.

One day Mother laid down the law to Don. He must have clumped one of us, not Andy, and Mother was there in a flash. She was blazing.

'They're my kids, they're not your kids. If you hit them, you don't hit them with love. I hit them with love. You keep your hands off them.'

So I always thought Mother would protect me. That's why I was so worried when she left me with first Kenny and then Peter. I'd be safe as long as Mother was there.

Sitting back on the settee, I looked at her, and such a feeling of love rose up in me. Mother glanced over and smiled at me. Just for once in my life I felt everything was perfect.

Then Mother was looking serious again.

'There's one more thing I have to say, Tess,' she said. 'You know what happened today with Peter, well, it mustn't go beyond these four walls. Other people won't understand, and we could all get into trouble.'

'What do you mean?'

'Well, people might blame me. I might have to go to prison, and you'd have to go back to that awful Beulah Heights place. I couldn't bear that.'

'Neither could I!' Just the thought of it made me sick, and I felt again the hand of Mrs Danvers across my face.

'So it'll be our little secret, okay?'

I nodded. I was feeling really grown-up now, so proud that Mother needed me and trusted me.

'I'm already skating on thin ice,' Mother went on. 'The law says I shouldn't have working girls in my house, but I say it's my house and what goes on here is my business and nobody else's. Everybody's happy and nobody gets hurt.'

That made sense.

'If it gets out, though, if the police find out, they'll get me for it. They'll put me away for sure.'

That sent a chill down my spine.

'So we'll keep it to ourselves, shall we?'

I nodded again. Of course I wouldn't say or do anything that could get Mother into trouble. I wouldn't say anything about what went on in the house, or about me with those men.

She could always rely on me.

9

Bad Boys

For the next few days I felt I was walking on air. I looked at Mother with new eyes, knowing what she'd been through. Growing up in that family, with so many kids crammed into a small house and her mother and father so violent. I knew she loved them, but they seemed terrible to me. They thrashed their kids even if they'd done nothing wrong.

Most of all, though, I dreamed of her romance with my father. Grace and Mick – it was like something out of the films. My heart ached for her, losing her true love like that. She was so brave, letting him go back because it was the best thing for him. And marrying Filth, or rather Harry. Fancy doing that! It was for us girls, of course, to give us a name. There wasn't anything Mother wouldn't do for us.

When I took my brothers and sisters to school, or made their tea, I looked at them and thought, Little do you know. Little do you know how hard our mother works for us. She might lose her rag now and then, and dish out the odd good hiding, but that was nothing compared to what she had to put up with when she was young. And she loved our father so much – at least, the father of us girls. When he had to go away her heart broke into a million pieces. Yet she carried on, made a home for us, worked her fingers to the bone for us. And she still does.

If I thought of those times with Kenny and Peter at all, it was like from a distance. As Mother herself often said, 'Needs must when the devil drives.'

I really felt a new closeness with Mother. As if I'd grown up all of a sudden. That's not to say I didn't still get the rough edge of her tongue along with the others.

One evening a couple of weeks later Mother was having a party, so I was getting ready as usual. The other kids were fed and tucked up in bed, when there was a knock on the door. Bit early, I thought, but I opened it, to see a man standing on the step. He looked vaguely familiar, tall and chunky, wearing a smart camel coat. Before I had a chance to say anything, he'd barged in past me, saying, 'Where's yer mother?'

'In the kitchen,' I called after him as he stomped up the hall. Fine manners he's got, I thought.

I followed from a distance, curious to know who he was, and whether Mother would tell me off for letting him in.

'Gracie!' I heard him say.

'Charlie?' said Mother. 'You're early – can't you wait?'

They both laughed, then Charlie said, 'I didn't wanna hang around with the stuff. Here, get rid of it.'

'Okay,' said Mother. 'Same cut as usual?'

'Yeah, that'll do.'

'You staying?'

'Nah,' said Charlie. 'Got business tonight. Be seein' ya.'

Ah, he's coming out. I whizzed down the hall and into the front room. As Charlie's heavy tread passed the door, I was busy dusting the cocktail cabinet.

The door slammed behind him, and I wondered, What's all that about? What stuff? Oh well, Mother's bound to say it's none of my business.

It didn't take me long to finish in the front room, and I headed back to the kitchen. When I got in, I saw Mother standing in front of the mirror over the fireplace, turning her head from side to side. She was obviously admiring a necklace she was wearing, and from what I could see it was gorgeous. A rich, glowing green, sparkling in the light.

'That's a lovely necklace,' I said. 'Did Charlie give—'

Before I could finish, Mother whirled round, a look of fury on her face. 'You little cunt!' she snapped. 'What do you mean sneaking up on me like that?'

I was shocked rigid. It'd been quite a while since Mother had been so sharp with me, and I felt sudden tears pricking my eyes.

'I didn't mean to,' I stammered. 'I was just coming in to make the sandwiches.'

Mother glared at me for a moment, then she seemed to soften.

'All right,' she said. 'I'll let you off this time. But listen, Tess. I have to tell you something. Sit down.'

We both sat at the table. I was nervous, dreading what was coming.

Mother took off the necklace and put it on the table. 'Yeah, it is lovely. But you haven't seen it, right?'

I was too surprised to say anything. What did she mean?

'I'll say it again, Tess. You have not seen this necklace. I was not trying it on. Got that?'

I nodded. If she said so.

Mother made a tutting sound. 'Do I have to spell it out?' She looked straight at me. My face must have looked blank as she went on, 'Look, it's bent, okay?'

I blinked. 'Bent?' It looked fine to me.

'Oh, for Christ's sake. It's hot, it's nicked, it's stolen. Now do you understand?'

Stolen! I was shocked. Mother was still speaking.

'Yeah, Charlie gave it to me, but not to wear. I was only trying it on to see what it looked like. He'd spit feathers if he knew I'd not put it away. And you' – Mother's voice rose – 'will never mention it. Right?'

'Right, sure.' But I couldn't help asking, 'If you can't wear it, what are you going to do with it?'

Mother raised her eyebrows to heaven and sighed. 'Where have you been?' she said. She sounded weary. 'I'm gonna pass it on to someone who'll want it. Who'll give me money for it. I keep a little bit for me and give the rest to Charlie. It's the way it works, business for him and business for me. We get our bit, and the insurance coughs up to the owner. Nobody gets hurt, nobody loses out. See?'

Ah, so this was another string to Mother's bow.

'And,' she went on, 'I need hardly add that it is not something the law will know about. So you keep your lips sealed good and proper. It'll be another little secret between us.'

I nodded.

Mother looked straight at me again and said, 'Look, Tess. I'll level with you. I'd rather you didn't know about this, for your own good. You don't want to tangle with the likes of Charlie. He's a real hard nut, a proper villain. One of the really bad boys. He's not like the small fry who go hoisting, nicking from shops. He's the genuine article, and we don't cross him, not if we know what's good for us.'

Her face was serious now. 'And we do know what's good for us, good for us all, don't we?'

I was serious too. 'Yes, we do.'

'Good girl.' Mother stood up and added, 'You get cracking with the grub while I put this little beauty somewhere the sun don't shine.'

That made me smile, and I set to cutting bread with a lighter heart.

As I worked, I thought, Well! What a turn-up. Mother was involved in stealing. But she didn't actually steal anything herself, so that wasn't so bad. She sold stuff on to people who wanted it, so they were happy. She and Charlie were happy with their cut, and the owner of the stuff didn't lose out either. Of course, as Mother said, the law wouldn't see it that way, but as she had pointed out many a time, the law can be a total prick when it comes to real life. When honest people are hard up and have to bend the law a bit just to survive.

I had a sudden memory of our trips to Surrey Street market. Those little packages the boys had passed to Mother, and she hadn't given any money back. Was that bent stuff too? The boys didn't seem like villains, though. Maybe they were the small fry Mother mentioned.

My mind running on this, another memory popped into my head.

'I know them!' I said to Mother. 'Haven't they been round here?'

I pointed to the photographs on the front page of the daily paper. Two lads, one dark and the other fairer.

'Yes,' said Mother shortly. She seemed very quiet, not her usual self.

I searched my memory and dragged up their names. 'They're Chris and Derek, aren't they?' I'd noticed them now and then about the house. They were always polite to Mother, and I thought they were nice boys, and quite handsome too. The teddy-boy look suited them. It was usually Chris who did the talking. Derek was much quieter.

Mother was nodding. 'Yes, that's them all right,' she said grimly.

'Why are they in the paper?' I asked.

'Read it yourself,' and Mother shoved the paper over to me.

God, it was a shock. This was serious stuff. They'd tried to break into a warehouse, Barlow and Parker's in Tamworth Street – that was just a few streets away from us. Someone had spotted them and called the police. The boys hid on the roof, and when a policeman climbed up and grabbed hold of Derek, Chris had fired a gun at him. A gun! I could hardly believe my eyes. Those two nice boys – what was Chris doing with a gun?

The cop was hurt, but not too badly. He managed to put Derek under arrest, while Chris got out of the way.

It got worse, much worse. The police sent more men, and the first cop to reach the roof, a PC Miles, got shot by Chris. In the head. He died.

Oh, my God. Murder.

I looked at Mother. She was staring straight ahead.

'This is awful,' I whispered.

She nodded again. 'And it'll get worse. The cops won't rest when it's one of their own. Someone's gotta swing for this.'

I'd never seen Mother so serious. And of course she was right. It was November 1952, and the young men were Craig and Bentley. Young Derek was going to go down in history as the victim of one of the worst miscarriages of justice in the country, ever.

They were in all the papers, and when I read what was going to happen to Derek, I said to Mother, 'But he didn't shoot the cop! Chris did it.'

Mother's voice was hard. 'Chris is too young to hang,' she said. 'He's only sixteen. But Derek's over eighteen, so he's the one to get it. I told you, someone has to swing, and if it can't be Chris then it'll be Derek.'

There was quite a commotion all over the country, with petitions to Parliament and everything. Mother herself campaigned for Derek when he was in Wandsworth Prison. She took to the streets of Croydon with a petition. She was out in all weathers, and gathered thousands of signatures. Of course it was a terrible thing that a man had died, but there was great sympathy for Derek. No way was he responsible for what Chris did.

'Let him have it, Chris' – that's what the police said Derek had said to his pal. That made him responsible for the killing. I couldn't understand this, it seemed so unfair. How did the police know Derek wasn't telling Chris to hand over the gun? That's if he said it at all.

All the protests were to no avail, though. As everyone knows, Derek Bentley was hanged. It was in January the next year, less than three months after the copper was killed. Like a lot of people, Mother always reckoned that the whole thing stank. 'He was stitched up all right,' she'd say. And sure enough she and all the others were proved right years later when Derek was pardoned. Fat lot of good it could have done him, though. Or his sister Iris, who campaigned for him and died before the pardon. At the time, it was like a dark cloud over our house. Now, as I buttered slices of bread and opened some jars of Shippam's paste, I thought about those boys. They'd been passing bent stuff to Mother, that was obvious. Were they some of the small fry? If they were, then they got a hell of a sight bigger. I wondered if that horrible Charlie had a gun. How did he get hold of the necklace? Did he grab it from a shop, or break into someone's house? I shivered. From what Mother said, Charlie by himself was bad enough. Just think what he'd be like with a gun!

As it happened, I'd find out.

'Open the door, Grace, for Christ's sake! Quick!'

The letterbox clanged shut, and the door knocker beat out again. With my ear glued to the bedroom door, I could hear my mother shuffling along the hall, saying, 'All right, all right, hold your bloody horses. I'm coming.'

She undid the bolt, opened the door and cried out, 'Charlie! Where the bloody hell have you been? What's going on?'

'Never mind that now,' the man said in a hoarse whisper. 'Let's get in.'

I could hear his footsteps going quickly down the hall, while Mother closed the door and shot the bolt. Then she followed Charlie. They must have gone to the kitchen, as everything went quiet again.

I made my way back to bed in the dark. God knows what time it was, but the only light coming through the cracks in the window shutters was the faint yellow of the streetlamp. It must be the small hours.

It was a wonder all the kids weren't woken up by the loud knocking. It had made me jump out of my skin. What was going on? Mother didn't usually get visitors this late – in fact most of them would have gone home by now.

As I lay there trying to get back to sleep, I couldn't help wondering about Charlie. Since that last time he was in our house, some weeks ago now, he seemed to have disappeared. I heard Don saying that he hadn't seen Charlie for a while, and Mother had said, 'Nobody's seen him. He's gone to ground. Can't say I'm sorry.'

Next morning it was the usual rush to get everyone ready. Then I was busy at school, and I almost forgot the drama in the night. It was Mother herself who reminded me, when I got home.

'I want to talk to you,' she said, looking straight at me.

My scalp crawled. What had I done? What did she have in mind? Even though we'd been getting on pretty well on the whole, when Mother said something like that I immediately jumped to a conclusion. Was she sending me out again?

With knees knocking, I followed her into the front room. The other kids were noisy in the kitchen, having their tea.

As we sat down in the armchairs, Mother said, 'We've got a bit of a problem.'

We! She said 'we'! I sat up straight, trying to look serious and grown-up. Well, it wasn't long now to my birthday. I'd be eleven.

'Well,' she went on, 'we had an unexpected visitor last night.'

'I know,' I blurted out. 'Charlie.'

Her eyes narrowed. 'How do you know that?' Her voice was sharp.

'I just heard you say his name, Mum. I wasn't listening or anything, but the knock woke me up and I heard you say his name.'

She looked doubtful, then shrugged. 'Yes, well, it was
Charlie. He's been out of town for a while, nobody knew
where he'd gone. Now he blows in out of nowhere and lands
on our doorstep. "I'm in shtook, Grace, and that's the truth,"
he says to me. "I've cocked it up big-time, and now they're
after me."'

My eyes must have been as big as saucers.

'Charlie told me he'd done a job with some of the local lads,
jewellery it was. Heavy job.' She lowered her voice. 'They had
shooters. You know what they are, don't you?'

'Guns,' I breathed.

'That's right. Well, the job went off fine, and Charlie took
the stuff to a bloke in Manchester.'

Ah, like he brings stuff to you, I thought. Only I didn't say
anything.

'Well, this bloke only went and did a runner, and bang
goes everyone's cut. Charlie's fuming, chewing the carpet.
"Honest to God, Grace," he says to me, "he's not gonna get
away with that." So he goes looking for him, and he's still
got his shooter. He clocks him in a pub, and when he goes
to the gents', Charlie follows him. Bang! Got him in the
kneecap – slow him down a bit. Now he's had a taste, he
knows what's coming if he doesn't come across with the
goods. Next time—' Mother sliced her finger across her
throat.

'Right, job done, Charlie scarpers out the window and lies
low. Next day, he has a sight of the local paper, sees a headline
– "I got the wrong geezer!" he tells me. "I'd only gone and got
the wrong geezer!" Well, now Charlie's really in it. Police'll be
looking for him, and the local boys are none too pleased
either.'

She shook her head. 'He says to me, "I need your help, Grace. Can you put me up for a bit?"'

She looked at me. 'What could I say, Tess? Every man is some woman's son, isn't he? Honest mistake, as far as I could tell. So the deal is this. He'll lie low here for as long as it takes. Now the law must never know he's here, so we all have to keep shtum. You get me?'

I nodded.

'Even the kids might notice him as he'll be here all the time,' she said, 'so we'll make up a tale. Say he's a friend of Don's paying a visit, or some such. We'll never mention his real name. Don't want one of the kids coming out with it at school – you never know who's listening. I can trust you to keep them in order, can't I, Tess? It'll be another one of our little secrets.'

Again I nodded. I was still so thrilled to be in her confidence, to help her. I felt ten feet tall. What did I care about robberies and shootings and people getting hurt? Here was another sign that my mother trusted me.

As it happened, Charlie stayed with us for over a month. I don't think he set foot outside all that time. He kept out of our way and we kept out of his. Often the only sign of him was the smell of his cigar. Well, we wouldn't see him anyway during the week, being at school, and then going to bed soon after. At the weekends, now the weather was getting warmer, I usually took the kids out to the park for hours, although I hoped Mother would give me the money to take them to the pictures, always a treat for me.

Charlie might not have left the house, but some other men came round to see him, 'local boys', I heard Mother call them. And I couldn't help hearing raised voices.

'You bloody fool, Charlie, you've landed us right in it.'

'You should have stuck with the geezer, not let him go off with the gear.'

'Now the fucking cops'll be sitting up and taking notice. Last thing we want.'

'A man deserves a shooting, well and good – but an innocent man, that ain't right.'

And there was a lot along the lines of 'All this aggro and we don't even have the fucking tom now!'

That puzzled me for a bit, till I found out it was rhyming slang, short for 'tomfoolery' – jewellery.

Anyway, eventually the fuss died down and I didn't hear any more about it. One day Charlie was gone, and that was the end of it.

Blame it on Barbara

'It's Barbara's fault,' said Mother. 'The little cunt. Gone off in a huff and left me right in it.'

We were sitting in the kitchen, me and Mother. She'd kept me off school again, to clear up after one of her parties, and we'd sat down for a break. Mother made the tea and I broke out a packet of custard creams. Of course I didn't dream of saying no to Mother, and as ever I enjoyed being with her, but I didn't like to miss school. Especially today. I was going to change my library book. I'd just finished *Good Wives*. It wasn't bad, but not a patch on *Little Women*, I thought. Still, I liked following the fortunes of the March sisters, and at least it was a happy ending for most of them, even though Beth died and that made me cry . . .

'Did you hear what I said?' she snapped.

I jerked my head, all attention now.

'Yeah,' I said. 'Barbara's gone and left you in it.'

'And do you know what I mean by that?'

'Er, she's gone away?'

'Yes, she bloody well has gone away, without so much as a by your leave. Little cow. After all I've done for her too.'

Inside my head I smiled. After all Mother had done for her? By now I knew just how hard Barbara worked in Mother's business. She didn't always stay in her bedroom. Quite often she went out, and I gathered it was somewhere special. 'Off to school?' Mother would say with a grin. I knew Barbara had a couple of school uniforms, and I couldn't work out why she'd want them. It was at least three years since she was at school. Anyway, she must have got the money rolling in. More than once I heard Mother say, 'She's our fucking meal ticket.'

Barbara had been with us for two or three years, and I'd learned something about her story, how she happened to come to us.

'Fucking ran away, didn't I?' she'd said on one of the rare occasions we bumped into each other in the kitchen and had a chat. 'I wasn't gonna stay in that fucking hell-hole.'

The hell-hole was a care home. I wondered if it was anything like Beulah Heights. If it was, I didn't blame her for getting out of there.

'What about your mum and dad?' I asked her.

'They chucked me out,' said Barbara. 'Told me to get out and stay out.'

I was horrified at that. Being turned out by your mum and dad. I'd always been scared of being parted from Mother, and the thought that she would actually get rid of us haunted us for years. Poor Barbara. She told me she'd lived rough for a while.

'How do you do that?' I asked her.

She shrugged. 'Doss down where you can. Shop doorways. Lot of shops in Croydon.'

'Did people give you money?' I asked, thinking of the beggars I'd read about in stories.

She grinned, showing her small pointed teeth. 'If I played my cards right.'

It turned out that someone on the street told her that Grace Stevens would see her right. And Barbara had been here ever since, off and on. I wondered what had set her off this time. She was always a prickly girl, one minute all over Mother like a rash, the next minute shouting at her and flouncing out of the house. Just recently, she'd been acting really oddly.

She started wearing boyish clothes like checked shirts and blue jeans. She even got some shoes that looked like work boots, and a black donkey jacket that was too big for her. Mother cut her hair for her, and Barbara slicked it back with Brylcreem. She stopped wearing make-up, and was walking in a different way, too, with a bit of a swagger. It was like she was turning herself into a barrow boy. She wouldn't look out of place behind one of the stalls in Surrey Street market.

I found this all very puzzling. Why wear boys' clothes when you could choose from all the pretty dresses I knew she had? What made everything even stranger was the way she was acting towards Mother. If you didn't know better, you'd think Barbara was in love with her, sitting gazing at her all moony-eyed or following her like a lovesick puppy, calling her 'love' and 'darling' and sounding as if she meant it. I could see Mother was a bit annoyed at this, but as she said to Don, 'I've got to put up with the mad little cow. Don't want her running off.'

Barbara actually brought Mother bunches of flowers from the market, and asked her to go to the pictures with her – like a date! When they set off down the street, Barbara took Mother's arm, as if she was helping her. Don thought it was funny. I was with him at the front room window, watching them go, and he said, 'Will you just look at them. Fucking Laurel and Hardy.'

Though Mother was only average height, she always held herself straight. 'Hold yourself straight and look the world in the eye,' she'd say. Next to tiny Barbara, she did look huge. I suppose it was a bit comical.

Anyway, it wasn't long before Don stopped finding it funny. In fact he got really annoyed. 'That bloody girl's taking you over,' he complained.

But again Mother said she had to put up with it. 'Just a phase,' she said. 'She'll get over it.'

But she didn't, and one evening things came to a head. With the kids in bed, I was washing some underclothes in the scullery, when an almighty row broke out in Mother's bedroom. I could hear all three of them, Mother, Don and Barbara.

What was going on? I crept across the hall to hear better.

'You can't tell me I can't sleep in my own bed with my own wife!' That was Don, yelling his head off.

'She's not your wife!' Barbara shot back. 'You're not married.'

'Don't give me that, you little freak. I'm telling you to get out and get out now. I've had enough of you creeping about—'

Mother broke in. 'Don, Don, don't make so much of it.'

'Much of it? I'm entitled to make what I like of it, and I don't bloody well like it. She can't come in here and take my place, what's the matter with you?'

''Course not,' said Mother soothingly. 'We can sort this out.'

'But he doesn't love you like I do.' Barbara's voice rose to a shriek. 'I love you, you belong to me.'

'No, she does not!' roared Don.

'I don't belong to you either!' cut in Mother sharply. 'I don't belong to anybody. Now let's sit down and sort this out.'

'Nothing to sort out,' snapped Don. 'She goes or I do.'

'He goes or I do.'

'Oh, for God's sake, the pair of you,' said Mother. 'I've had enough of this.'

Barbara flared up. 'And I've had enough of you. You don't love me. If you loved me you wouldn't have this filthy man in your bed. I hate you. I'm going and you can't stop me.'

I quickly stepped back into the kitchen, and heard her wrench open the door. She stormed into her room, and sounds of banging and crashing filled the air. Next moment the front door slammed.

Mother was telling Don off. 'What did you have to go and do that for? You know how touchy she is. I would have got round her. Now she's buggered off – we'll be in the shit if she doesn't come back.'

'She'll come back, she always does.'

Well, obviously not.

Mother's voice broke in on my thoughts. She was still complaining.

'Roof over her head, food on the table, clothes on her back – who pays for it? Me, that's who.'

Again, I could have smiled, but didn't dare to. Barbara was always grateful for Mother's presents – the clothes, a man's watch – but it must have been her money paying for them. Don had always had a job, as a sheet metal worker, but as Mother often told him during one of their rows, 'You don't earn enough to keep a pig in shit.' It suddenly occurred to me that this money business was just the same for Betty and

Ruby. Ruby would work all week, 'a right goer' in Mother's words. I knew Betty was in charge of the money, and she must have been raking it in, even allowing for Mother's cut. On Saturday Betty would take Ruby shopping, usually to one of the cheap clothes shops in town, and Ruby would come back gushing about how generous Betty was.

'Look, Bet's bought me this lovely skirt and a nice pair of stockings. Oh, she's so good to me, she really is.'

But she was earning the money! I just didn't get it. Later of course I'd know it was love, of a sort. I'd heard about lesbians – lezzies – but when I was a kid I didn't realise what that meant. I just thought they were girls who wanted to be men, like tomboys – maybe George in the Famous Five books – only more grown-up.

Now I became aware that Mother was gazing at me, leaning with her elbows on the kitchen table and holding her teacup in both hands.

'So what am I going to do?' she said.

She was looking at me intently now, right into my eyes, frowning.

I was stumped. It wasn't like Mother to be at a loss over anything. I just shook my head.

'Well, we're in a jam and no mistake,' she said. 'I've got a couple of very important customers who are going to be very disappointed if Barbara doesn't come back. I wouldn't be surprised if they buggered off and went somewhere else, and then where would we be without the money coming in?'

Money worries again. I knew just how hard it was for Mother to make ends meet. I was becoming anxious now. If we didn't have any money, what would we do? Where would we go? Again, I couldn't think of anything to say. Mother shifted her gaze away from me and looked up at the ceiling.

'Hmm, there might just be a way out . . .'

'Yeah?' I was immediately relieved. How could I have doubted my resourceful mother? Of course she'd have a plan.

She looked at me again. 'You're the only one I can turn to now, Tess. If you can just help me out again and pay a little visit or two . . .'

And I felt two different emotions then, almost at the same time. First a swelling of the heart that Mother still needed me, relied on me, and that I was so important to her. Immediately followed by a rush of panic, a sick dread washing over me. If she meant what I thought she meant . . .

Mother must have seen the look on my face, as she quickly said, 'Oh, don't worry, love. You know I'd never do anything to hurt you, don't you?'

I nodded, my heart thumping.

'It's just that I've got these commitments, and it'd be so bad for business to lose them. I really don't know anybody who could do what Barbara does as well as you could.'

But what does Barbara do? I drew a deep breath and asked Mother that question. 'What does Barbara do? I mean, she's grown-up—'

Mother cut in. 'I don't mean you'd do exactly what Barbara does,' she said soothingly. 'Of course you're still a kid, that wouldn't be right. What do you take me for?'

She sounded indignant. I blushed to think I could doubt my own mother. Of course she'd look after me, have my best interests at heart. By now I had a clearer idea of what went on between men and women, and the thought of doing anything like that made me feel sick.

'But I can't expect you to understand if I don't explain,' she went on. 'These particular customers are very special. What we call privileged. They're rolling in dosh – gold-plated. They live in lovely houses – you'd love their gaffs, Tess, you really would. The last word in luxury. And what's more . . .' She leaned towards me. 'They're famous.'

'Famous?' I was immediately interested. I couldn't help wondering if they were film stars. One of my favourites? Dirk Bogarde or James Mason? As if, God help me, being famous would make it better.

Mother spoke the customers' names in a solemn voice – and they didn't mean a thing. I'd never heard of them.

'One's an actor, a proper actor in a theatre. Shakespeare,' she added impressively. 'He's a very distinguished man. And the other one is a dress designer, who works with society ladies, all very classy. His clothes get pictured in all the best magazines.'

By now I was wondering. If these men were so special, so rich and so posh, it was a puzzle what they saw in little Barbara, who was no pin-up.

Mother must have guessed what I was thinking, as she said, 'Now why these men, these gentlemen, like Barbara is because she's so small and looks so young for her age. This sort of gentleman is interested in young girls, and he wouldn't dream of hurting them.'

Mother leaned forward.

'And if they like young girls, what's even better than Barbara is a real young girl – fresh and pretty and interesting, like you, Tess! You can cheer up the old gentlemen.'

Well, if you put it like that . . .

'I'll take you there like before,' she said. 'You like the taxi, don't you? We'll make it a day out, just you and me. And I shouldn't be surprised if there's a present for you.'

Mother's words were some comfort, but I still felt dread in the pit of my stomach. I could see Kenny and Peter again – no, my mind flinched away from them. Don't think about it, I told myself.

As it happened, I did enjoy some of it, that first day. There was the journey, of course, and I loved being with Mother, just us two together. This was quality time all right. On the way to the dress designer, we took the train from Croydon to a big London station, Victoria, I think, then joined the taxi queue. It was a typical April day of sunshine and showers, but we were standing under cover. There was a whole string of taxis, and though there was a long line of people, we didn't have to wait long. We were going to a place called Earl's Court, which I thought sounded like something out of a story book.

The dress designer's house looked like it had come out of a story book too: it was tiny, with old-fashioned windows with lots of little panes joined together. The door was a smart navy blue, and the knocker was polished brass. 'Smells of money,' Mother said as we walked up the little lane off the main road where the taxi had dropped us. This lane didn't have a smooth surface like the road, but was paved with little round stones, which I later learned were called cobbles.

The dress designer answered Mother's knock, smiling and waving us inside. He seemed very nice and friendly, not so very old, though his thick hair was pure grey. The first thing I noticed was that the carpet in the hall was so soft my feet seemed to sink into it. Then we were in a room, which much to my surprise seemed to be full of dresses. Dresses all over the place, draped over armchairs, hung round the walls from picture rails. They were gorgeous, frothy with lace and netting and ruffles, or smooth and silky. And such lovely colours – glowing gold and silver, deep red and emerald green. They spelled glamour, what I'd seen film stars wearing at the pictures.

The man must have seen me gazing at these dresses with longing, as he said, 'Would you like to try one on?'

Would I! He walked over to one wall and selected a dress, in a shimmering green material. Was it real silk?

'Here,' he said. 'This is the colour for you. It'll go perfectly with your hair.'

He turned to Mother. 'You help her on with it while I'm busy in the kitchen.' Walking out of the room, he called, 'Let me know when you're decent!'

I took off my old cardigan and my blue and white gingham dress and pulled this one over my head. It must have been silk, it was so smooth and cool, with a rounded neck, nipped-in waist and long flowing skirt. There was a full-length mirror in the room, tilted back on a wooden stand, and I gazed at myself. I was a princess! Well, sort of. But the dress was so beautiful it would have made anybody look good.

Mother was smiling. 'It suits you,' she said. 'Maybe you'll have one like it some day.'

I hoped so.

The designer called from the kitchen. 'Can I come in now?'

Without waiting for an answer he came back in and stopped dead at the sight of me.

'Well,' he said, looking me up and down. 'Don't you look like a million dollars! A proper little film star if ever I saw one.'

I was really relaxing now. This wasn't so bad, in fact it was fun. I was wondering if I'd have a chance to try on any more dresses, when the designer said to Mother, 'You did bring the other gear?'

Other? Mother nodded and reached into the shopping bag she was carrying. She brought out a neatly folded white blouse, a navy blue skirt and a striped tie. It was a school uniform. Was it one of Barbara's?

'While I see your mother out, dear, just slip the dress off and put on this on, will you?'

See my mother out? 'Mum—' I started to say, before Mother cut in with, 'I'm just popping out for some cigarettes. Won't be long.'

She was gone in an instant. I stood frozen. Popping out for cigarettes. That's what she said last time, and the time before that . . . Did it mean he was going to touch me? I was vaguely aware of voices coming from the front door, and from nowhere came the thought that I didn't want him to see me in my vest and knickers. I quickly pulled off the green dress and put on the blouse and skirt. I had some trouble with the tie as I'd never worn one. At my junior school we wore our own clothes. So I just draped it round my neck and hoped that would do. Just why he wanted me to wear a school uniform I couldn't begin to guess.

I heard the door bang, and the designer was in the room again. 'All change today, hey?' he said, smiling. 'The uniform suits you too – not as fancy as this dress, of course.' And he picked it up, smoothing it with his hands, and put it back on its hanger.

Then he turned and faced me, his head on one side. 'Well, now. You and I should get acquainted. Come and sit beside me on the sofa.' He swept aside a pile of dresses and patted the cushion beside him.

My feet felt like lead but I moved towards him. I forced myself to remember what Mum said: he doesn't hurt little girls, he doesn't hurt little girls. I sat down beside him, holding myself stiffly, and found myself saying in a rush, 'I'm sorry about the tie, I couldn't work it out.'

He laughed. 'Oh, don't bother about that.' And he pulled it from round my neck and dropped it on the floor. Then he started stroking my hair, looking at me all the while. His hand moved to my chest and I thought, This is it. Sure enough, he started to undo the buttons, but slowly. Soon they were all undone, and he was slipping his hand inside my vest, feeling my boobs. Oh well, just like before. As Mother had said so often, men like boobs, they're beautiful. The one part of me that was.

While he was busy, I kept my eyes fixed on the wall opposite, trying to count how many different dresses I could see. If I could just keep my mind on that, I didn't have to take much notice of what this man was doing.

Soon he was breathing more loudly, and suddenly he was pulling up my skirt and sticking his hand up my knickers, touching the most private part of my body. Now this I could not, would not, take.

'No!' I cried out, pushing his hand away. 'You mustn't! I'll tell my mum!'

No good. He pushed me off the sofa on to the floor and his knees were either side of me. He fumbled with his trousers and pulled out his willy. It was all stiff, and now I was hysterical with fear. I struggled and struggled, hitting him with my fists on his head and shoulders, but he just held me down with his other arm. He was so heavy. Now he was breathing harder than ever and his face was red. He suddenly jerked, and all this white stuff came out from his willy, splattering over my face and my vest. I was crying so hard I thought I would never stop. It was like being trapped in a nightmare.

He rolled off me and sat with his back against the sofa. He was speaking to me. 'Stop, please stop crying. I didn't mean to frighten you. Tess, please stop. I'm so sorry, so sorry.'

I heard his words, but what did they mean? Sorry? Did he mean it? Did it mean that I could go home now? I clung to that hope, taking deep breaths, sobbing now rather than crying my eyes out. I managed to pull myself together, and stood up, wiping my face and straightening my clothes. He came towards me again, and I opened my mouth to scream. Before I could make a sound he was stuffing notes down my vest, crackly paper banknotes, going, 'Sorry, sorry, sorry. Take this, I'm so sorry.' He seemed really nervous.

I was too astonished to say or do anything. I just stood there while he stuffed notes down my vest. Then there was a loud knock on the front door. Thank God! That must be Mother.

'Wait here, will you?' said the designer. 'I want a word with your mother.' He smoothed down his thick grey hair and went out of the room. I didn't know what to do with the money. But I did know I didn't want to wear that uniform. I quickly took off the blouse and skirt and dropped them by the tie. Then I slipped my old dress over my head, and buttoned up my cardie. I pulled my hankie from the pocket and scrubbed my face to get rid of that horrible gunge. I was beginning to feel more normal, calmer. The shock waves were getting less. And now Mother was here, everything would be all right.

By the time she came into the room, I was breathing normally and had dried my eyes. The banknotes were itchy against my chest. I'd tucked my vest firmly into my knickers. Something told me that I shouldn't lose the money.

'All right?' she said. She spotted the uniform on the floor and picked it up, putting it back in her bag.

I didn't reply.

'Let's go,' she said.

The designer held the door open as we went out. He didn't speak, just nodded.

Me and Mother walked back along the little lane. She was holding my arm. As we turned the corner, and I knew we were out of sight if the designer was still at his door, I stopped and said, 'Mum, there's something I have to say to you.' I felt like crying again, and started breathing jerkily.

'Can't it wait?' she said.

'No, please, Mum.'

'Oh, all right then – spit it out.'

And in a rush I started to tell her what had happened . . . 'And then he got me on the floor and I was so frightened, I thought—'

Mother's voice cracked like a whip. 'That's enough of that!'

I leaned against the wall of a building and felt like it was swallowing me up. I couldn't bear it.

Then Mother spoke again, her voice softer. 'Listen, wait till we get home and you can tell me all about it. We'll have a nice cup of tea. And you know what? As a treat we'll get a taxi back too, shall we?'

I nodded, unable to speak but clinging to the lifeline she offered. I was so grateful for it.

Then in a normal voice she said, 'Where's the dosh he gave you?'

Dumbly I started pulling the notes out of my vest.

'Don't flash it around! You want anyone to see? Quick, give it here.'

I watched her as she gathered the notes neatly together. 'Hmm, fivers too,' she murmured, folding the big white notes, the ones that haven't been around for many years. 'Thought it'd just be one-ers.'

True to her word, Mother did sit down with me when we got home. The house was quiet, as it was early afternoon and the other kids were still at school or nursery. As soon as we got in I dashed to the scullery and filled the sink with cold water – I didn't wait to heat any up. I scrubbed my hands and face as clean as clean. The thought of that stuff splashing on me made me want to vomit. I'd put my stained vest in the bagwash later, but at least for now I'd got rid of the worst of it. Coming home in the train, I was in an agony of embarrassment, convinced people could smell the stuff on me.

Now Mother heard me out, right to the end, by which time I was crying and hiccupping. When I mentioned he'd touched me 'down below', she frowned. 'He wasn't supposed to do that,' she said. 'The thing is, your boobs are so beautiful he must have got carried away.'

Was it my fault then?

'If you're really unhappy about this, we could do something,' she went on. 'But as I've said before, if anyone else finds out, we could all get into trouble.'

I remembered what she'd told me, how she might get the blame and be taken away from us. That would be the worst thing of all, and the thought made me cry harder than ever.

'Oh, no, Mum, no! I'd never say anything, I won't ever tell a soul! Honest I won't!'

She patted my hand. 'You're a good girl, Tess. I knew I could rely on you. It'll just be one of our secrets, won't it?'

I was still crying, but her words really touched me, and after a while the tears stopped. I wiped my eyes, and clung to what she'd said. I hated what the man did, but I loved Mother. My love for her was bigger than my hate for him, I had to remember that. Nothing was more important than Mother, and she'd shown that I really meant something to her. We had a special bond. Now I looked at her, and managed a smile.

As Mother pushed her chair back from the table, she said, off-hand, 'Next time, just above the waist then, yeah?'

I tried to forget about the dress designer, though there was still the other important customer to think about, the actor. The familiar dread rose up a few days later when Mother said we were going to visit him.

'It'll be a trip to the country,' she said. 'A day out.'

As usual, we took a taxi, but this time from our local station, and whizzed through Croydon till we were out on open, empty roads, with green fields either side.

The house was lovely, like in a picture book, very old and higgledy-piggledy, surrounded by gardens full of daffodils. The actor was much older than the dress designer, with a wrinkled face and big teeth, and thin silver hair. He took us to what he called his study. The walls were covered, just like the designer's, but this time with black and white photos. 'Me in my prime,' he declared, waving his hand at them. Anything to do with films and performing always interested me and I had a good look. Most of them showed a younger man wearing old-fashioned costumes, like Errol Flynn wore in *Robin Hood*. Some of the photos were of other actors, with their autographs, and he was obviously proud of them, showing them off to me and Mother.

After a chat, Mother said, 'Just popping out for some cigarettes.' And now I knew that it was going to start.

As it happened, it wasn't as bad as I feared. I had to wear the school uniform again, and he told me I'd been naughty and had to be punished. Which meant he sat down, put me across his knee, pulled my skirt up and smacked my bottom. At least I keep my knickers on, I thought. All the time he was huffing and puffing. After a few minutes, he pulled my skirt down and told me to stand up.

I felt silly, and a bit embarrassed, being treated like a little child, but it was nothing like the dress designer. And he didn't smack me hard. It was all a puzzle, though. I told myself that what he wanted me to do was maybe a bit like acting.

When me and Mother were going back in the taxi, along empty roads and not a building to be seen, no shops or anything, something suddenly occurred to me.

'Where did you get your cigarettes?' I asked Mother.

She just looked out of the window.

11

Watching and Waiting

Barbara was away for months, the longest time ever. I realised that must put Mother in a jam, what with Barbara being her main meal ticket. I dreaded the thought of being sent out again to those special customers, but knew I had to do everything I could to help Mother. I tried not to think of it, to push it to the back of my mind. That worked during the day. I was usually busy then, what with looking after the kids, and school. I started at secondary school, and just like in junior school, I was a good girl, not one of the troublemakers, and I enjoyed my lessons. After school, it was a case of getting the kids their tea, and putting them to bed. It was at night that the worry washed over me.

If we'd all been locked in early – and it still happened, as Mother didn't always want me around – I didn't much feel like joining in our games of I Spy. Even my favourite way of passing the time, talking about the future when I would live the life I wanted, didn't fire my imagination like it used to. When my brothers and sisters were all fast asleep, I lay awake for hours, feeling a weight in my chest that made it difficult to breathe. I'd think, I'm not like you any more. I'm not a kid. I'm more like a grown-up.

'I wish there was someone I could talk to,' I'd say to myself – then immediately felt guilty. As if I needed anybody more than Mother! The kids were out of the question, of course. It was a grown-up I needed. Someone kind and sympathetic, who could help me deal with everything. Make it feel better.

I thought of the grown-ups I knew now, and those I had known. Outside the family there were my teachers, and they were mostly good to me. In fact sometimes I thought I caught them looking at me in a way that seemed to say, 'Poor you.' But I might have imagined it. They certainly didn't know anything about my home life, and what I had to do. They never would know, either. Teachers were official, like policemen. Mother would get into terrible trouble. She might be taken away from me, and I couldn't bear that. No way could I confide in them. I wished I was still friendly with Mrs Hodge, but I would never go behind Mother's back and visit her upstairs again. In any case, there was bad blood between her and Mother. Us and the Hodges didn't actually bump into each other very often, which was odd considering there were nine of them and at least seven of us, and only one front door. The Hodges kept themselves to themselves, right enough.

Inside the family – well, there was only Mother's family, of course. My heart ached when I thought about my father. If he was here, I wouldn't have to do what I did, I was sure of that. For a start, Mother wouldn't be so hard up. Maybe she wouldn't even have to have any girls working in the house. Then there'd be no need for me to go and see those men. Though I was more than glad to help Mother, I couldn't persuade myself it was easy.

If only I'd had a kind grandmother or grandfather. I'd read about them in stories, and seen pictures of white-haired, roly-poly old people in rocking chairs. Grandma was usually wearing a shawl, and Grandpa often had a moustache. My grandparents were nothing like that. I hardly ever saw my grandfather, and my grandmother never liked me.

I had uncles and aunts, too. I'd got to know a couple of Mother's sisters: Phyllis, who married a Polish airman during the war, and especially Cathy, always called Bubby for some reason. I could remember a time when Bubby invited me to her house, one of the few times I ever went anywhere. She was married, but didn't have any children of her own. Maybe that's why she took an interest in me. For my part, I found her kind and friendly, and thought her very glamorous. She looked like Ruth Roman, with her short curly dark hair, wide smile and good figure. But for some time now she hadn't been round, and when I heard Mother and Don having a blazing row, I realised why.

'You fucking cunt!' Mother yelled. And that was just for starters. She really let rip. She accused him of having it off with Bubby, said she knew all about it and wasn't as stupid as he thought.

Don couldn't get a word in. Eventually he shouted, 'I'm not standing for this. I wouldn't touch your fucking sister with a bargepole. You're out of your fucking mind, you crazy cow!'

I'd crept out of the kitchen to hear the row, but it sounded as if things were going to turn really nasty, so I whizzed back in. That explained why Bubby had stopped calling, anyway. It wasn't the first time Mother had accused Don of playing away, as she called it. 'You and your wandering hands! Mine'll wander round your fucking throat!'

As I got back to preparing the tea, I thought this over. Of course I didn't know what Don got up to, but it wouldn't have surprised me if he had been chasing girls. He liked talking dirty, making rude comments about people, even people he didn't know, just saw on the telly. Maybe it was having girls in the house. He'd been known to chance his arm with them too, and Mother had flown off the handle.

So, none of the grown-ups in my life could help me. I'd think again about happy families in books, especially my favourite, the Marches in *Little Women*. When I read about them, I'd get a kind of glow in my heart. I thought, I bet Marmee wouldn't have sent her daughters out to strange men! But of course Mother had her reasons, very good reasons. I was her right-hand girl, helping all the family.

And recently I'd had a sign that I was really growing up. I'd started my periods. I'd had a bit of a belly ache for a while, and my boobs seemed to be getting more swollen. Mother had never told me the details, but somehow I'd picked up some info on the school grapevine. So when I went to the loo and passed some blood, I knew what was what, after a fashion. When I got home I told Mother, and she simply said, 'Oh, okay then.' She tore up a bit of old sheet and folded it. 'Use that for now. Then nip off to the chemist. You'll want a sanitary belt and a pack of towels. The girl in there'll sort you out.' I soon got the hang of the towels, and learned to burn the old ones in the open fire in the scullery.

'Easy for you girls nowadays,' Mother said. 'When me and my sisters were at home we didn't have proper towels like these. We had to use old rags, and wash them out each time – no getting rid of them on the fire. That'd be a waste. And Mother had an eagle eye. She kept tabs on us girls, kept a calendar. Every month we had to show her our bloody rags to prove we weren't pregnant, and God help you if you were late. You'd get a beating just in case.'

Meanwhile, knowing how much Mother was missing Barbara's money, I walked on eggshells, expecting her to send me out again any minute.

A couple of weeks after I'd gone to the old actor's place, one Saturday morning, I was checking through the bags of washing in the scullery, making sure the whites and the coloureds hadn't been mixed up. Mother went mad if any colours ran. I was wondering if I'd be the one to take the bags to the wash today. If I was, I hoped Mother would give me the money for the bus fare. Carting those bags about was heavy work, and it was a long walk to the laundry place in town. Maybe Kath would come with me. Just then, Mother came in.

'Tess, I want you to do someone a favour today.'

I froze in the act of pulling some towels out of a bag. My heart thudded, and it was hard to breathe. The day I'd dreaded had come. Mother was sending me out again.

She spoke sharply. 'Don't stand there like a waxwork, you dozy cow. Get a move on!'

I turned slowly to face her.

'Nip off to Mr Chickens,' she said.

She must have seen I wasn't taking it in properly, as she shook my arm quite hard.

'What's the matter with you? Can't do a favour for a neighbour?'

Mother was very hot on us helping people. She always said, 'If you see an old woman with a heavy shopping bag, carry it for her. If someone needs a seat in the bus, don't wait to be asked.'

'What about the washing?' I whispered.

'Oh, bugger the washing,' she said. 'Just get down the road and do what he wants. I've been trying to get him here ever since his wife did a runner, so you be nice to him, understand?'

What could I do? I nodded mechanically, and made my way out of the scullery, my feet dragging. Even though I'd been expecting something, it didn't make it easier when it happened.

Mr Chickens wasn't his real name. It was what Mother called him (though not to his face) as he kept chickens in his yard. He sold the eggs and sometimes killed a hen or two. He lived just down the road, in the basement of a big old house like ours. Mother had pointed him out to me in the street. He wasn't very old, but he walked with a stoop. 'A long streak of misery', Mother called him. Now she wanted me to be nice to him.

I opened the rickety old wooden front gate and walked up the path. I had to go round the corner and down some steps to the flat. I could hear the chickens before I saw them, clucking away. They seemed happy, scratching in the dirt in the sunshine. They were in a kind of wire cage, nearly as tall as me, with a little wooden shed at the end. I lifted my hand to the door knocker, wondering desperately what would happen before I could go home again. Mother might be just up the road, but here I was alone.

The door opened and there was Mr Chickens. He stood there blinking at me through his glasses. I couldn't help noticing that his clothes were grubby, and his cardigan was missing a few buttons.

'Ah, it's Tess, isn't it?' he asked, and I nodded.

'Here you are,' he said, giving me a piece of paper. 'Ten bob should be enough.'

He was giving me money? What was going on?

I opened the paper and realised it was wrapped round a ten bob note. There was writing on the paper, and my head whirled. What did the words mean? Were they telling me what to do?

Mr Chickens was speaking. 'I hope it won't be too heavy,' he said. 'Wait a minute, you haven't got a bag. I'll go and get one.'

He disappeared indoors while I stood gazing at the words on the paper. Tea (Typhoo Tips). Sugar. Marge. Milk . . . A shopping list! Was that all it was? Was this the favour?

He came back and handed me an old string bag. 'Thanks a lot,' he said. 'I'm just not up to traipsing round the shops these days.'

'Okay,' I said, taking the bag. 'Won't be long.'

I walked quickly back down the path, thinking, Is this it? Is this really it? Just get his shopping? A flood of relief washed over me and I could have laughed out loud. I practically skipped along the pavement to the grocer's. Two bob change, and I was walking back to Mr Chickens.

This time when I knocked on his door I was feeling cheerful. He opened it, and I gave him the bag and his change.

'Thanks, Tess,' he said. 'Will you come in?'

Come in? Immediately my heart sank. He wanted me to come in – why? He called me from inside. 'Tess?' I shut the door behind me and walked into a little room. It was cluttered with all sorts of stuff, and smelled sour. Everything looked as shabby as Mr Chickens. I could see him in the tiny kitchen that led off this room, putting the shopping away in a cupboard next to the stove. The only other thing was a sink, which even from where I stood looked filthy.

I stood still, holding myself in. What was going to happen? What would he do?

He came back into the room and stretched out a hand to me. I had to stop myself flinching.

'This is for you,' he said. Then he smiled, though he didn't show his teeth. 'Don't spend it all at once.'

It was sixpence, a shiny little sixpenny piece. I took it and looked at him.

He must have seen a question on my face, as he added, 'Oh, I know this place is a bit of a mess, but don't worry. I can cope.'

Was that really it?

'Thank you,' I said, edging back to the door.

'Thank *you*,' Mr Chickens called after me as I shut the door.

I walked home. I was walking on air, clutching the coin. I knew what I'd spend it on. Next time Mother sent me out to get shopping, I'd call in at my favourite shop, just round the corner. We called it Audrey's, as Audrey was the woman who ran it. If it had a proper name, we didn't know it. It was where I got Mother's cigarettes, but more interesting to me were the sweets. I could see them in my head now: blackjacks, flying saucers, pink shrimps, Refreshers, sherbet dabs . . . Me and the kids would have a feast!

I put the sixpence carefully in my pocket. I didn't want to lose it.

After that, I fell into getting shopping for Mr Chickens twice a week, usually Wednesdays and Saturdays. He never wanted much, living alone as he did. Every time I saw him he seemed to be stooping more and more. His voice was growing quieter, so that when he spoke I could hardly hear him. He seemed to be fading away. I felt sorry for him, really. I thought he was nice, the only nice man I knew outside school. I started to look forward to seeing him, hoping I could cheer him up with a chat or a joke.

It made me smile to think how worried I'd been when Mother first told me to go and see him. Not all men were nasty.

The next time Mother sent me out, it was the other way round.

'Got a treat in store for you tomorrow,' Mother said. It was a Friday afternoon, when I was clearing up in the kitchen after tea.

A treat? Maybe it was the pictures. I hoped so.

'Trip to the Smoke,' she added.

'Smoke?'

'London,' she said impatiently. 'We're off to Earl's Court again in the morning. That little house where you tried on that lovely dress, remember?'

I stopped smiling. I remembered. 'You mean . . . that dress designer bloke?'

'That's the one!' Mother seemed quite cheerful, but I felt as if I'd been punched in the gut. It had been weeks since the last visit, and by now the memory usually stayed in the back of my mind. Now I felt just as I had when Mother told me to go and see Mr Chickens.

'But, Mum . . .' My voice faltered. What could I say to her? The image of him kneeling on top of me flashed into my mind, and I cringed. 'What he did . . .'

'Oh, don't worry about that,' said Mother, waving a hand. 'It's sorted. I put the fear of God in him. If he tries that again,

I'll have his guts for garters. He can go so far and no further, know what I mean?'

I nodded slowly. Just above the waist then. I could manage that. It was dawning on me that things weren't so bad if I knew what to expect.

And as it happened, the dress designer kept himself in order. Just like last time, Mother popped out for her cigarettes, and he sat close to me on the settee. He didn't push me to the floor, and he didn't let his hand wander downwards. Just undid my school blouse, lifted up my vest and felt all round my boobs. When he got his willy out, I knew to look away quickly. I studied the dresses again, wishing I could try on another one. They really were lovely. Keep looking at them, wait till he's finished.

There were no tears from me this time. On the way back, Mother said, 'That wasn't so bad, was it, love?'

I shook my head. I was relieved it was over, and that Mother seemed pleased. As she said, it wasn't the worst thing in the world, but that didn't mean I liked it. I hoped and prayed Barbara would come back and I wouldn't have to go out again. Meanwhile, though, if Mother needed the money, how else could she get it?

In the event, it was like the US Cavalry in a western, galloping over the hill to save the cowboys.

Not that Jane looked anything like a soldier. The first time I saw her, she made a big impression on me. I'd heard Mother telling Don about some new girl on the scene, and unusually for Mother she was really excited.

'We're in fucking clover,' she said, laughing her head off.

I gathered this girl, Jane, was on the run, but what she was running away from I didn't know. She was different from other runaways Mother took in, though, in a different league. She was more than good-looking, she was beautiful, with gleaming blonde hair, lovely blue eyes, high cheekbones and a gorgeous figure. She looked like a film star. Not quite Marilyn Monroe or Diana Dors, she was quieter somehow. Of all the film stars I admired, she was more like Belinda Lee than anyone, very high class.

Mother was beside herself, fussing round Jane in the kitchen, asking if she wanted anything. Jane just sat there with a slight smile on her face. Mother got me to give Barbara's room a good going-over. 'Nothing too good for Jane,' she said. So Jane came to live with us, just as Barbara had.

I learned bits and pieces about Jane's story. I couldn't ask directly, or Mother would tell me to mind my own business. But I kept my ears open, and often heard Mother going on about her.

'Beauty queen,' she said. 'Well, you wouldn't be surprised, would you? Just look at her!'

Another time she said, 'Modelling, real modelling, all professional. Pictures in the papers and everything.'

It all sounded very glamorous. I wondered what on earth could have made Jane run away from that kind of life. I had learned that awful things went on in some homes, but Jane looked so perfect, as if nothing had ever touched her.

She was in great demand, I soon realised that. Mother was often on the phone, talking her up as she usually did with her girls, but this time she didn't have to exaggerate. Sometimes Jane would go out to a punter, accompanied by Mother,

sometimes she'd stay in. I looked forward to seeing her at one
of Mother's parties, and I wasn't disappointed.

She was the star of the show, absolutely gorgeous. Her
shiny hair cascaded in waves over her shoulders. Her dress
was a deep blue, matching her eyes. It had a low neckline, and
clung to her figure all the way down before flaring out round
her ankles. She wore a necklace that sparkled in the light –
could it be real diamonds? When she smiled she showed off
perfect teeth. I'd never seen anyone with such white teeth. All
the men were hanging around her. 'Bees round a fucking
honey pot,' Mother said gleefully in the kitchen when we were
fetching more food.

I wondered how the other girls felt, left talking to each
other. If they minded, they didn't show it, and thanked me
when I took round snacks and drinks.

Mother was in a good mood for weeks. Money must be
rolling in, I thought. I thanked my lucky stars that Jane had
arrived – no need for me to earn any more!

I found out there was another string to Mother's bow
where Jane was concerned. I heard her on the phone, speaking
in what I called her posh voice. Not that Mother spoke
roughly. Even when she was swearing her head off she still
sounded her aitches. She didn't sound like other people round
about who spoke in what she called a Cockney accent. But this
time she sounded like one of the announcers on the wireless.

'Oh, good afternoon. You don't know me, but I'm acquainted with a certain young lady. I believe you've had the
pleasure of knowing her yourself. Such a charming young
lady. She's told me all about you—'

Here Mother broke off. Obviously the person on the other
end was getting their oar in.

'Certainly not,' said Mother. 'I assure you I have no such intention. What do you mean, threats? As the young lady is unavailable at present, I'm simply wondering if I may be of assistance. I could offer a replacement, should you be interested.'

Another pause, and then, 'Well, if you don't want a replacement, the newspapers could be on to this. I could earn a lot of money . . .'

Ah, money. That was where it was leading. Mother always said, 'Knowledge is power,' and she knew something all right. In which case, knowledge must mean money too.

At the time, I couldn't quite get my head round this. It was before I ever even heard of blackmail. In any case, I didn't learn much more.

One day I came back from school to find Mother in a very bad mood. She was stamping round the kitchen, spitting feathers as Don sat drinking a cup of tea at the table.

'Fucking press,' said Mother, scowling. 'Sniffing round here – who tipped them off? If I knew who it was I'd smash their faces in. Like a bat out of hell, she was. Grabbed her gear and legged it. God knows where she's gone.'

I'd been standing in the doorway.

'What do you want?' Mother snapped.

'Is it Jane?' I asked.

'Yes, it bloody well is, for your information. Not that it's any business of yours, what goes on here.' Then she looked directly at me and changed her tone. She sighed. 'Well, we'll just have to get by, won't we?'

I had a horrible feeling I knew what she meant. I couldn't see the US Cavalry coming for me.

* * *

At least next time it was only the old actor. Like before, Mother and I had a taxi out into the country, and she left me alone with him. I noticed she didn't say anything about cigarettes this time. She just went off somewhere.

The old man started talking about naughty girls and punishment, then I was over his knees again. This time he was smacking me a bit harder. What was worse, he suddenly pulled down my knickers and smacked me on my bare skin. That hurt quite a lot and I couldn't help saying, 'Ow!'

He breathed faster. 'That's what little girls get when they're naughty,' he said, between huffing and puffing.

This was really embarrassing and I felt very silly. I couldn't for the life of me figure out why he wanted to hurt me, but it was over quickly. When he pulled up my knickers I pushed myself off him.

He stayed slumped in his chair, in front of all the old black and white photos from the films. He waved his hand.

'Off you go. You'll find your mother in the hall.'

I couldn't get out of there fast enough. Again I tried to wipe the memory. Just concentrate on the trees, I thought, as the taxi took me and Mother back along the country roads to Croydon. Looking back, I realise I was finding a way of dealing with these men. It was a case of having to.

12

Growing Up

I might have had troubles of my own, but some months later I found out just how bad things could be for other people.

It was a Sunday afternoon. I'd taken all the kids to the park, and we'd had a good time on the swings. We were walking up our road, chatting and laughing, when I saw a small crowd on the pavement a few doors from us. People were on the opposite pavement too, staring at the house where Mr Chickens lived. An ambulance was parked right outside, and people in uniform were walking up and down the path.

As we got closer, I realised Mother was there, by the front gate. She saw us, and came hurrying up.

'Get indoors, kids,' she said. Our door was open and we all trooped in. I was last, and turned to Mother.

'What's going on?' I asked.

Mother shook her head. 'It's Mr Chickens,' she said. 'Poor bastard.'

Mr Chickens? Last Wednesday he'd asked me not to call again for a while. I had a sudden memory of his sad smile as he gave me the sixpence. He gave me sixpence every time.

'Why?' I asked. 'What's he done?'

'Only gone and gassed himself.'

Gassed himself! What a shock. Poor Mr Chickens. I felt really sorry for him. A terrible thing to do, put your head in a gas oven. He must have been desperate, hopeless. I wished there was something I could have done. It made my worries seem like nothing. After all, I wasn't lonely. I tried to imagine living all by myself, with no one to talk to, no one to eat with – and no one to love me. I had Mother, and my brothers and sisters. I was lucky, I shouldn't complain.

Mother just said he'd lost the will to live, and that was that. And she'd find out if any chickens were going cheap.

Not long after, a new tenant moved in. I saw him carrying bags along the path and round the side. I wondered if he knew someone had died in his new home. I didn't fancy the thought myself. He was a young man and looked fit, so he wouldn't need anybody getting his shopping. That was a pity. To tell the truth, I was missing my shilling a week. Maybe there was another neighbour around who'd need help. By now I wasn't so stuck in the house, and Mother might let me run errands for other people again.

'You're really growing up now, Tess,' Mother kept saying. 'I can really talk to you.' It was true, I'd be a teenager in just a couple of months. I wasn't getting packed off to bed early like the other kids. In the evenings I helped Mother round the house, or got everything ready for one of her parties. What I liked most was taking the kids out for an evening at the pictures, when Mother wanted us all out of the way. When we got back home, there was another treat. I'd knock on the door, but not loudly, and Mother would open it with a finger to her lips. 'Sshh!' We'd tiptoe into our room, and there on our bed would be our late-night supper – plates of sandwiches and cakes. It was like one of those midnight feasts I'd read about in school stories.

There was another change around this time that I liked best of all: I wasn't locked in at night. Mother turned the key on the other kids when they went to bed, hours before me. But she unlocked the door when I'd finished helping, and she didn't lock it again. I was overjoyed. There was something about being locked in that made me feel buried, suffocated. It didn't matter that the door looked exactly the same from the inside whether it was locked or not. It was just knowing that I could open it if I wanted to. I could breathe more easily. Mother trusted me to be quiet if I had to nip out to the loo – I was so thrilled I never had to use that disgusting chamber pot again. The other kids still had to use it, though.

'Don't tell them or they'll be running all over the place,' Mother had said.

I smiled to myself. Another of our little secrets, even if it was only about an old pot! The other advantage about not being locked in was that we didn't have to wait for somebody to let us out in the morning. Mother often slept late, and Don usually didn't think, so it had been pretty hit and miss what time we got out. And on school days that could be a bit hairy. But now I could wake everybody up and see to them while Mother was still asleep.

And there was no question of me having a Saturday-night bath like the others, when we'd get punished as well as scrubbed by Mother. I had a bath to myself now.

My only worry was that Barbara was still away; nobody had heard anything from her. That meant a couple more trips to London and the country. I told myself to be strong, remember I wasn't like poor Mr Chickens. There were people who loved me, depended on me. As long as I had Mother, I'd be all right in the end. I found it easier each time to take my mind off what the men were doing. Concentrate on the designer's collection of dresses, imagining myself all glammed up like a princess. I couldn't look at much while I was over the old actor's knees, just a plain brown carpet, so I thought of scenes from films I'd seen, putting myself in the leading lady's place. At the same time I'd tell myself, 'Nearly over, nearly over, not long now.' I shut my mind away from pain and shame. No point dwelling.

I knew Mother was feeling the pinch. She told me so. 'I wouldn't send you out if I wasn't desperate,' she said to me. 'I'd give my right arm to keep you at home, but what can I do? It's that bloody Barbara's fault.' There were other girls in the house, and as far as I could see there was usually a queue of men at the bus stop outside, so some business was going on. 'But it's not enough,' said Mother.

One Saturday morning, she said to me, 'You and me are going on a little trip today.'

My heart sank. Who'd it be this time?

Mother looked at me and laughed. 'A nice walk in the sunshine, that's all. What could be nicer than mother and daughter taking a little walk together?'

What did she mean? Mother wasn't one for going for walks for fun. When she walked it was to get somewhere. I must have looked as puzzled as I felt, as she spelled it out.

'I'm going to Streatham, to the common, to see who's around. Who's who and what's what. Where there's girls there's punters, and where there's punters there's girls. Spread the word, let them know there's a good gaff here. See what I mean?'

Light was dawning. She was looking for new girls to work in the house, and new customers. It was news to me that girls worked outside. I just hoped I was there to keep Mother company and not for anything else.

We took a couple of buses and made our way to the common. It was a lovely sunny day, and the grass and trees were all green. We walked quite a way in, Mother looking around as we went. We were walking on a narrow path when Mother said, 'Hang on, that looks promising.'

A young woman was leaning against a tree. As we came nearer, she cocked an eyebrow.

'Hello, darling, all right?' said Mother.

'Who wants to know?' said the young woman. She had a very white face, with dark eye make-up and bright red lipstick. She was swinging a shoulder bag from one hand.

'I do,' said Mother. 'I might be able to do you a favour. I'm Grace, from Croydon. Ring any bells?'

The woman straightened up. 'Yeah, it does, as it happens.' She looked interested.

Mother smiled warmly, and handed her a piece of paper. 'That's my number. Ring any time. I'm looking for good girls and I can see you've got what I'm looking for. I'll see you right, don't you worry.'

The woman glanced at the paper. 'Right,' she said. 'I'll bear it in mind.'

'You do that, darling,' said Mother. 'Be seeing you.'

She took my arm and we walked on. 'That's got the cunt,' she muttered.

We wandered all over the place through the afternoon. Mother spoke to about half a dozen young women, and she seemed satisfied with the result. She also went up to three or four men, who were hanging about here and there among the trees and bushes. 'I can spot a punter at a hundred yards,' she told me.

They made me feel uncomfortable, so I kept my distance when Mother went up to them. I could still hear her, though.

'Hello, darling, looking for something special? You want to ring this number' – and she passed over a piece of paper. 'Lovely girls, all fresh and all up for it. Worth every penny. Guaranteed.'

The men looked a bit shifty, glancing around, but they all kept the piece of paper. I saw one of them look at me, and jerk his head. Mother looked round, and she shook her head.

After a couple of hours, I was feeling tired, and so was Mother. 'Let's go and have a cup of tea,' she said. 'There's a nice caff near here, and you never know, I might drum up a bit more trade. Good pick-up place.'

I was glad to sit down. The café was quite full, the air thick with cigarette smoke. The table was clean, though, and the tea was good and hot. Mother bought me a cream puff as a treat, and I must say that went down well.

As I tucked in, my eyes wandered round the room. Were all the women working girls? Were all the men punters? They just looked ordinary, drinking their tea and eating their cakes and sandwiches.

Mother leaned towards me, and murmured, 'Show you what I mean. There's a woman sitting behind me by the window – don't look! I reckon I can reel her in.'

I waited a moment before glancing over at this woman. She was sitting hunched up in her chair, stirring a spoon round and round in a cup of tea, keeping her eyes down. I could see one side of her face, which seemed to be bruised.

Again Mother murmured, 'Her old man's been duffing her up, I'll stake my life on it. Bet she's done a runner, now she's stuck. Watch this.'

Mother stood up and walked over to the woman's table. There was an empty chair and Mother pulled it close to the table. She sat down, put an arm over the woman's shoulder and her head close to the woman's head. She was talking in a low voice. Suddenly the woman stopped stirring her tea and put both hands to her face. Her shoulders shook. She must have been crying, but she didn't make any sound I could hear. Mother stroked her hair. She glanced over at me and winked.

When the woman stopped crying, Mother spoke to her for a few minutes, and gave her a piece of paper. Then she patted the woman on her shoulder, and came back to our table.

She grinned at me. 'Just as I thought,' she whispered. 'Easy meat.'

So Mother was right. She could reel her in. At the time, I remember feeling admiration for Mother's confidence, her skill. I felt a bit sorry for the woman, being in such a state, but to be honest I didn't spend much time thinking about her. I didn't know her. Though when I look back at that scene now, my blood runs cold. Those were the days before Erin Pizzey and her refuges for battered women. If a woman was beaten up by her husband, she couldn't expect help from the police. To them, it was just a domestic, they wouldn't want to get involved. That poor woman in the café must have been at the end of her tether, in fear of her life, to run away. And God help her if she had kids. She'd be easy prey, all right. Just like the younger girls who'd come to our door, running away from something they couldn't bear.

I've tried to sort it out in my mind, the way Mother acted, see it from her point of view. She was offering a safe place, of sorts. There'd be a price to pay, of course, no such thing as a free lunch. Mother didn't run a charity. What was worse for the woman? Living on the streets?

It took me a long time to realise that the way I thought about this was because I'd grown up in a brothel. Nobody ever used that word – for Mother it was always 'the business', and Don would make jokes about a knocking shop. For working girls to have sex with men for money was just a fact of life. Money was at the bottom of everything. Mother would never have sent me out if she hadn't been desperate for cash.

I suppose every kid takes life for granted. What they're used to is just the way things are. If I'd grown up in a rich family with ponies and ballet lessons like heroines in stories, then I would have thought that was normal. I knew not many families lived the way we did, but it was normal for me.

I was learning quite a lot about Mother's business. Now I knew how she found new girls. And once she found them, she had a favourite place to show them off. .

'Can't beat Surrey Street,' she told me. 'Down I go, this new girl on my arm, make sure the boys get a good eyeful. Fresh meat, their tongues are hanging out. We go and sit in a pub, word gets round – and Bob's your uncle.'

Mother obviously had to work hard to keep her business going. Then I saw another side to her work that really surprised me. Sometimes she deliberately shut up shop. No girls in the house, no punters at the door.

'It's like this,' she said, sitting at the kitchen table, cup of tea in one hand, cigarette in the other. The kids were in bed and we had the house to ourselves. Don must have been down the pub, though Mother always tried to put him off. She didn't want him turning back into an alcoholic. Anyway, I loved these times together, just her and me. We were having quite a lot of these cosy little chats, and I was proud Mother could confide in me.

'In this game you need friends on the inside. Bit of a sweetener here, bit of a sweetener there, know what I mean? The cops have to show they're doing something, so every so often they'll raid a place. But first they put a watch on.'

A watch on? Mother saw my confusion and laughed. 'I don't mean they put a watch on their wrist! I mean they watch the place, in secret. They see how many men are going in, how long they stay, that sort of thing. Then when they've got their evidence, well, it's a raid.'

She sipped her tea. 'Thing is, if they've got no evidence, they've got no case. They're up shit creek without a paddle. So when my boys in the station get wind of a watch, they let me know. Means we have to lie low for a while, but in this game you take the rough with the smooth. And the girls can always work harder when the coast is clear.'

She grinned. 'When I know they're out there, I might take a fit in my head. Go out in the front garden, by the bushes, take some air. "Any slugs out tonight?" I could say. Poke around with a stick, and I just might find a very big slug. Dressed in uniform. "Oh, sorry," I'd say. "Were you looking for something, Officer? May I be of assistance?"'

That made me laugh too.

'And that puts the kibosh on their obs all right.'

'Obs?'

'Observations. That's what they call it. They're observing me. But once they've been rumbled, that's it, they have to scarper.'

Mother took a drag on her cigarette. 'You just have to show them who's boss,' she said.

I remember gazing at her with something like awe. Was there anything that Mother couldn't do?

Not long after that, we had a visit from the police, but in broad daylight. It was early on a Saturday afternoon, and I was cleaning the kitchen. I was just thinking about Mr Chickens, and wishing I was earning another sixpence, when there was a loud knock on the door. The kids were all holed up in our room, and Mother and Don had gone back to bed, so I answered. Two cops in uniform were standing there, a man and a woman. My mind immediately flashed back to what Mother had told me about obs, then I realised with relief there was nothing secret about this visit.

'Hello,' said the woman, in a kind voice. 'Is this where Mrs Grace Stevens lives?'

I nodded.

'Is she in?'

I nodded again.

'Well, could we speak to her, please? I'm afraid we have some bad news to tell her.'

Oh dear, I thought. I'd better disturb them, then.

'Just a sec,' I said. 'She's in bed – I'll tell her you're here.'

I tapped on the bedroom door and called, 'Mum! Some police are here. They say they have some bad news for you.'

There was what sounded like a snort from inside the room.

'Tell them to come in,' called Mother.

So the police stood in her bedroom doorway. I was behind them, and Mother seemed to be alone in the bed.

'Mrs Stevens,' said the woman, 'I'm very sorry to tell you that your husband has been found dead.'

Mother burst out laughing, and said, 'As far as I'm concerned, this is my husband,' and she lifted the covers to reveal Don, grinning his head off. 'Bet this is the healthiest corpse you've ever seen!'

The cops looked at each other, then back at Mother.

Mother caught sight of me as I was hovering in the background, and said, 'Tess, take the officers to the kitchen and make them some tea. I'll be along in a minute.'

The cops sat at the table while I put the kettle on and got the cups. I could see they didn't know what to make of this.

It turned out that it was Filth who'd died. Of course, he was Mother's official husband. He'd been found stone dead in a local street and someone had dialled 999.

'Where's his body now?' Mother asked. She had a gleam in her eye.

'In the morgue,' said the woman cop. 'Would you like to see him?'

'Yes, please. I'd like to pay my respects.'

The cops looked at each other again.

'Of course,' said the man. 'Our car's just outside. We'll wait for you there.'

When the cops had gone, Mother chuckled. 'I wondered where the old bastard had gone,' she said.

I knew that recently he'd taken to wandering off, going AWOL, dossing down somewhere. If he wasn't around on pension day, the only way Mother could be sure to find him was to wait outside the post office till he came along.

Now Don had joined us in the kitchen.

'Why are you going to the morgue?' he asked Mother. 'What's the point?'

Mother buttoned her coat. 'He might still have his boots on, and his old cap. He always kept money in his boots and cap, thought I didn't know. Silly old sod. See you later.'

As she left and Don went back to their room, I sat at the table thinking about old Filth. Or Harry, to give him his real name. I knew he was only my official father, his name the one on my birth certificate – though come to think of it I'd never actually seen it. And I was very glad he wasn't my real father. He was dirty and disgusting and I hated having to sit on his lap on pension day because Mother said it kept him sweet. But still, he was dead. I'd never thought about it before, but he must have been lonely. He didn't have a proper family. Just like Mr Chickens.

'You count your blessings,' I said to myself, and went back to cleaning the kitchen.

When Mother came back, Don said, 'Any luck?'

She grinned. 'No sign of his cap, but he still had his boots on. Good job they left me alone, the poor grieving widow! I got them off and you'll never guess – half a dozen one-ers, the crafty old git!'

And she held up some creased one-pound notes.

'No wonder you're in a good mood,' said Don.

'Yeah, why not? If I'm a widow I'll be a merry one!'

To celebrate, Mother said us kids could go to the pictures, and have money for ice cream too. I wondered if I should feel happy that Filth had died, then thought, No, I'm just happy to be going to the pictures. Though I was happy I wouldn't have to see him again.

While the kids were getting ready, Mother told me a tale.

'You must hear this, Tess,' she said. 'Just shows what the poor old bastard was like.'

She lit a cigarette. 'One day Filth caught sight of one of the girls, and reckons he's fallen for her. Pretty little thing. He tells me this, and I think, Aha! I'll put one over on you. So I say to him, all innocent, "Funny you should say that, 'cos she says she likes you too. How about that?"

'I tell you, the way his old eyes lit up, it'd kill you. So I start the wind-up. "Why don't you buy her a little present? Give me ten bob and I'll go down the market, get her some nice perfume, tell her it's a present from you." So he hands over the dosh and I'm thinking, Like taking money from a baby!

'Of course the ten bob goes right into my pocket, but I play him along. "Oh, she really liked the perfume, she really thinks you're nice. What about some stockings?" Then I think he'll start getting suspicious, so I cut to the chase. "She wants to marry you," I told him. Then I think, Will he remember he's married to me? So I spin him another tale. "Don't worry about me." I said. "I won't stand in your way. I'll get a divorce so you'll be free." Christ knows if the old fool takes that in, but then I tap him again. "She'll need stuff for her bottom drawer, won't she? Pretty things, underclothes for the honeymoon, all smooth and silky." His tongue's practically hanging out, and he hands over another packet.'

Mother laughed and took another drag on her cigarette.

'Couldn't last, of course. Even he's bound to twig sooner or later.' She looked thoughtful. 'Come to think of it, maybe that's why he buggered off.' She nodded. 'Must be. But then he goes and dies. Oh well, serves him right.'

When she said that, I had a bit of a jolt. Mother was happy, and that could only be good, but all of a sudden I didn't like the sound of her laughing. It didn't seem right, with him only just dead and her taking the mickey out of him. Not to mention the money. But then I shook myself. Just be glad Mother's in a good mood, I thought.

Mother wasn't a widow for long. One Friday she said, 'We're off down town tomorrow.'

Every time Mother talked about a trip I got nervous. Just going shopping? Or was I going to see some man?

'I'm getting married.'

'Married?' I gasped. Before I could stop myself, I said, 'Who to?'

Mother laughed. 'Oh, for God's sake, who do you think? I'll give you a clue. He lives here.'

I felt silly then. Of course she meant Don. I just never thought of him that way.

'Not that I give a flying fart one way or the other,' Mother went on. 'As far as I'm concerned we could go on as we are, but Don wants it.'

In the event, we had a nice time. Mother looked as smart as usual, with a summery two-piece costume in green check and a little hat with a feather. Don wore his only suit and a clean shirt and a tie. I don't think I'd ever seen him wear a tie before. Mother had told me to get the kids ready and put on their glad rags, and we all looked a picture, I thought. The only other people there were a couple of girls I'd seen in the house, and a man who was a friend of Don's.

The ceremony in the registry office didn't take long, then we all went off to the Gun for a celebration. It was Mother's favourite pub in town. Though she hardly drank, I knew she often went there to see people, do business. It was a fine day so us kids sat in the beer garden while the grown-ups stayed in the bar. We had lemonade and crisps, a whole packet each. As we sat there drinking our lemonade and munching our crisps, everyone was happy. I wish things could always be like this, I thought.

I wondered if Mother and Don would row so much now they were married. Would it make any difference? Their rows had always frightened us to bits.

Now, as I looked round the peaceful pub garden, I could only hope things would get better.

Her good mood lasted for quite a while. Maybe being married made a difference. And soon, to my surprise, I had something in common with her, another thing that showed I was growing up. Just as she had a new husband, I had a new boyfriend.

Or maybe I should just say boyfriend, as he was my first. He appeared in the kitchen one morning as I was chivvying the other kids to get ready for school. He was sort of drifting about the place, a tall, thin young man with sticking-out cheekbones, not good-looking. In fact you could say he was ugly.

'Who are you?' I asked.

'Um, no one,' he said, or rather whispered. 'Your mother said I could stay here.'

Of course, Mother did take in waifs and strays, but they were always girls. This puzzled me. When I came back home, there was no sign of him. I said to Mother, 'There was a young man in the kitchen this morning.'

'Yeah,' she said. 'That'll be Victor. I ran into him last night, in the caff near the common.'

She must mean the one in Streatham, where we'd been before.

'He was just sitting there, looking lost,' Mother said. 'Didn't seem to know what day it was. So I got chatting to him, said, "Have you got somewhere to stay?" and he shook his head, poor little sod. So I offered him a place here.

'I felt sorry for him,' she went on. 'He's had a sad life. He was a baby during the war and one night a bomb hit his house. No trace of his parents, so he was adopted. He fell out with them and he's been living in a hostel. It was horrible, he said, so he jumped at the chance of coming here.'

Poor Victor, I thought. Another one with no real family, all alone. I felt sorry for him. Then a thought struck me. Anybody Mother took in had to work for her, I knew that. What could Victor do?

She must have read my mind. 'He's got a job,' she said. 'He's not thick. He's got some sort of job in an office in town. So he can afford to pay me for bed and board.'

Ah, that was it. Mother would be his landlady. Though as it happened, bed and board was pushing it a bit. He might have shared our meals, but there was hardly ever a bed for him as far as I could see. He'd just doss down in a handy corner. But he didn't complain. He was always polite. 'Well brought up,' said Mother. 'You can tell. Always says please and thank you, and never elbows on the table.' That was one of her bugbears, elbows on the table. That and not sitting up straight.

Anyway, Victor became part of the family, though he was so quiet you often didn't notice he was there. I was always happy to have a chat when he was around, and one day he said, 'Would you like to go to the pictures with me?'

He was asking me out! A boy was asking me out! Was this a proper date? I'd never had one, though I had met boys in the pictures. Once, when I was in the queue with my brothers and sisters, a boy I didn't know came up to me and put his head close to mine. 'Wanna sit in the back with me?' he murmured in my ear. Why not? It was the first time a boy had taken notice of me, and I was flattered. After I'd got the kids settled, I made my way to the back row, and sat down next to this boy. He grinned at me, and as the lights went down he put his arm round my shoulders. He kissed my cheek a few times, and then turned my head towards his. He pressed his lips on mine, did a bit of licking and sucking. I was delighted. This was like love scenes in the films, though I had a sneaking suspicion snogging wasn't all it was cracked up to be.

After a while he started stroking my chest, going, 'Mmm.' He seemed to like my boobs, so Mother was right when she told me all men and boys loved them. He slipped his hand inside my blouse and under my vest and started stroking my bare skin. This was nice too. Nothing like horrible old men having a grope. But then his hand moved downwards, and I stopped him, pushed his hand right away. He drew back. 'Fuck you,' he hissed, and got up out of his seat.

That was a bit of a shock, as I'd been enjoying myself, thought it was really romantic. Why couldn't he just have kept to my boobs? That was all right, didn't mean much, but not down below. I watched the rest of the film trying not to cry. Then I cheered myself up thinking, Well, at least he thought I was attractive in the first place.

After that, I'd met a few more boys in the same way. They'd feel my boobs, some would try to go further and some wouldn't. In any case, they'd leave before the film was over, and I'd wait outside for my brothers and sisters to come out. I realised word must have got around when one day a snotty girl at school said to me, 'You know what they call you?'

'Who?'

'The boys.'

'No – what?'

'Tit-up Tess.'

That wasn't very nice, but it was true, I supposed. I might sound really naïve, but it honestly never occurred to me at the time that they would have a low opinion of me, think I was a slag. As far as I was concerned, they were singling me out for my lovely boobs, and I felt flattered, even privileged. Mother's words had gone deep. I was just glad that though I was fat and ugly I did have something to offer. Then another girl told me of another name the boys called me, and this did hurt. Prick-teaser. I was leading them on, getting them worked up, then I put the shutters down. I thought this was unfair. Above the waist was all right, below wasn't. Couldn't they understand that? In any case, I'd seen men's willies and they were horrible. I didn't want anything to do with them.

I'd been wondering whether I should avoid boys in the queue if they came up to me again, and now here was a boy actually asking me out! Well, Victor. He might be in his twenties, but he seemed more like a boy to me.

'I'd love to,' I said, and he smiled. He was nice, I decided. Not handsome, but looks weren't everything.

Over the next few months we went out together regularly, usually to the pictures. I must say it was nice to go there with a real boyfriend. When we walked home the first time, I wondered if he was going to try anything. But no. We just chatted, friendly and nice. He was so gentle, a real gentleman.

Never laid a finger on me, just gave me a quick kiss on the cheek.

I got used to him, and he did seem to like me, in his quiet way. Then one evening as we were strolling back from the pictures, hand in hand, he suddenly turned to me and said, 'I love you. Can we get engaged?'

Engaged? To be married? I was staggered. Had I heard him right? Did he mean it?

'Do you mean it?' I asked.

'Of course I do,' he said. 'I've never been so happy. I know we can't get married till you're sixteen, but that's only a couple of years, isn't it? I can wait. So will you marry me?'

Well! This was a turn-up. In fact I wasn't even fourteen yet, only thirteen and a half, but that didn't bother me. I had a sudden picture in my head of me in a lovely white wedding dress, holding a big bunch of flowers, the centre of attention. As if I knew anything of marriage at that age! My head was as filled with romantic fantasy as any young girl's. I did know I didn't feel for Victor the way leading ladies felt for romantic heroes in the films, but I did like him, he was comfortable. He loved me! I was thrilled. Life couldn't get much better. Me and Mother were closer than ever, and now this!

'Yes,' I said.

13

Crashing Down

Victor was over the moon. He even kissed me on the lips. I was just so happy that someone loved me, actually wanted to marry me. When I told Mother, she cocked an eyebrow.

'Didn't think he'd go that far,' was all she said.

Well, I thought, he has, and I'm glad of it. I'd hoped Mother would be pleased for me, and it hurt a bit that she didn't seem to care one way or the other, but at least she hadn't said anything against it. I wondered whether to tell anyone else, but decided to keep quiet for the time being. I didn't have any special friends at school – in fact I didn't really have friends at all. I just didn't get in the groups that other girls did. And they could never have come round to see me. Anyway, I had a feeling that they might tease me about Victor as he wasn't good-looking, and I didn't want the boys to start calling me Tit-up Tess again. So no, I wouldn't spread it around. Just enjoy being engaged – not that I had a ring yet.

'We'll choose one together,' Victor said, and I was looking forward to that.

Meanwhile, there was another change in the air. The Hodges moved out.

*   *   *

The first thing we knew about it was one Saturday morning. We were in the kitchen, and there were all these thumps and bumps on the stairs.

'What the bloody hell is that racket?' snapped Mother.

She went out down the hall. We heard voices, then Mother was back.

'They're off!' she said, a big grin on her face. 'Good riddance to bad rubbish!'

'Who are?' I asked.

'Them upstairs,' said Mother. 'Lock, stock and barrel.'

I felt a sudden pang. I remembered how kind Mrs Hodge had been to me, how warm and safe I'd felt in her big kitchen. But Mother was cock-a-hoop.

'Why are they moving?' I asked. They'd been living here as long as I could remember. 'Where are they going?'

'Don't know, don't care,' said Mother shortly. She turned to Don. 'You know what this means, don't you?'

He looked blank. 'What?'

'Upstairs'll be empty. Empty, get me?'

Don frowned. 'Well, not for long. The council's bound to get in more tenants. There's always a waiting list.'

'Yeah, but I bet you it won't be straight away. Bound to be a gap. A gap I could fill. All those empty rooms . . .' She looked thoughtful, then smiled. 'I'm off to make a few calls.'

She bustled out of the kitchen. Me and Don looked at each other.

'There's no stopping your mammy,' he said.

We heard her voice from the hall. 'Don't call me Mammy!'

Mother was true to her word. As soon as the last of the Hodges had gone and the furniture lorry had roared off,

Mother was up those stairs in a flash, going, 'Come on, Tess.'

We whisked through all the rooms. I'd only ever seen the kitchen before, and was amazed at just how many rooms there were on the two floors. Seven, including a little boxroom. Mother was rubbing her hands. 'Get this place cleaned up, Tess,' she said. 'We don't want it to look like a poorhouse.'

I fetched a broom and a mop and bucket from downstairs, and some cloths and dusters. The rooms were bare, so it was mostly a case of sweeping the floors and wiping down the windows and mantelpieces. It felt odd to be in an empty room, seeing outlines on the floor where furniture had stood, and light patches on the walls where there'd been mirrors and pictures. It was sad, somehow.

Late that afternoon, a couple of men came round in a van.

'Here you go, Grace,' said one of them.

They'd brought a couple of beds, small doubles, in bits, along with old striped mattresses. They carried them upstairs and Mother told them which room to put them in. Then they put the pieces together again.

'I'll chuck a couple of sheets over, it'll do,' she told me.

And people arrived that self-same evening. Mother had already planned a party, so there were the usual visitors, like Teddy, but this time there were about half a dozen new faces. I was helping out as usual, and noticed that there was a regular toing and froing up the stairs.

Mother was in her element. Of course, I figured, more girls, more punters, more money. Maybe she'd been wishing the Hodges out for years, maybe that was why she'd taken against Mrs Hodge. That and me showing my liking for her.

The evening was obviously a great success. Mother was still

in a high old mood next day as we sat down to one of her roast dinners.

Don was a bit doubtful, though.

'There's gonna be tenants in there some time, though,' he said. 'What if they arrived when you were busy?'

Mother sniffed. 'They're not likely to move in at night, are they? We'll just keep the front door locked so we don't get unexpected visitors. And just in case, Tess can clean the rooms every morning, can't you, love? And put the sheets in the wash?'

I nodded. As it happened, there wasn't a lot of cleaning to do, just taking out bits of rubbish – cigarette packets, that sort of thing. Quite often I had to pick up what looked like little wrinkled balloons. They were cold and slimy and I dropped them in the bin with a shudder. I learned later they were called condoms.

After that first evening, Mother's business really took off. More beds arrived and there was a steady stream of punters. Not all the rooms upstairs were used, and Mother said Victor could use the boxroom. She found an old single mattress, and Victor was grateful. I didn't think he knew what Mother's business really was, but I was sure he was a bit afraid of her, and would never question anything she did.

With all this going on, Barbara reappeared. She was just there when I came home from school one day, sitting in the kitchen, smoking a cigarette. Mother and Don were out.

'They got hitched then,' she said, her mouth turning down.

'Er, yeah.'

She squashed the cigarette into a saucer. 'It don't change the way I feel.'

I stood there feeling awkward. 'Er . . . no.'

I was thinking, Thank God she's back. Mother was raking it in with the extra punters, but if the dress designer and the old actor wanted a girl, would she say no? Well, now Barbara was back on the scene. And looking at her, I could swear I was bigger than her. At least my bust was. She'd lost weight. She looked more of a child than I did. In fact, as she was still wearing men's clothes, she looked like a lad.

I expected all sorts of ructions when Mother and Don came back and saw Barbara, but to my surprise there weren't any. Don and Barbara were still a bit snippy with each other, but Mother welcomed her with open arms. 'Good timing!' she cried. 'Enough to go round for everyone!'

So Barbara settled back in. After a while, it really was as if she'd never been away. She was a familiar face to me again, like Ruby and the other girls.

Around this time other people started dropping in. Once I was out and about more in the house, afternoons and evenings, I realised that people were always coming round to visit Mother. She knew a lot of people, not only those in the business. Often they'd come round just for a chat and a cup of tea. Or Mother might find them a bit of work to do, an errand to run.

'Keep my finger on the pulse,' Mother would say to me, tapping the side of her nose. I knew she always liked to know what was going on.

Two of Mother's new visitors made a special impression on me. One was Lily, a little Irishwoman with a cloud of frizzy red hair and big green eyes. She was a laugh, and talked nineteen to the dozen.

'Ah now, Gracie,' she said one day, sitting back in her chair and blowing out a stream of smoke, 'you don't know what it means to me, to be comin' round here to you and gettin' away from himself. I swear to God he's gettin' worse. If he's not hittin' the bottle it's me he's hittin'.'

Himself was Liam, her husband. I had to walk past their house on the way to and from school, and one day Lily had waved at me from the gate. A big dark man was standing behind her. I didn't like the look of him.

'Hello there, Tessie,' said Lily. She turned back to her husband, and said, 'This is Tessie, Gracie's girl. I've told you about Gracie, haven't I, Liam?'

The man said nothing, just scowled at me. I gave a quick smile and a wave to Lily, and got on my way. When she talked about him round our place, I could just imagine him boozing, and beating her. I had a picture in my mind of a big bad old black cat and a little brightly coloured bird.

Mother's other new visitor was called Anna. She was a small woman, like Lily, but with short black hair and dark brown eyes. She was much quieter. I hadn't really noticed her until one day Mother called me into the front room where she and Anna were sitting.

'Come and hear this, Tess,' she said. She turned to Anna. 'Go on, Anna, tell her what you told me.' She turned to me again. 'You'll never believe it,' she said.

I sat down in an armchair, curious to know whatever it was. Mother seemed to be very lively today. Her eyes were gleaming.

'I do not know if I should tell the child . . .' Anna started. Her voice was low and deep, and she spoke with an accent. She sounded like the Germans in war films.

'Oh, go on,' said Mother. 'She ought to know what goes on.'

'If you think so,' said Anna. She turned to me and said, 'It was when I was in the camp—'

'That's a concentration camp,' Mother broke in. 'You know about those, don't you, Tess? Auschwitz and all that?'

I nodded. 'We've had it at school,' I said. I knew the Nazis put lots of Jews and other people they didn't like into camps, and treated them terribly. Nazis were evil.

'Show her your arm, Anna,' said Mother. 'Go on.'

Anna pushed up her sleeve. On the inside of her left arm a long number was stamped. It was blue. A number on an arm? That rang a bell.

'Isn't that what they did in the camps?' I asked. 'Stamped a number on people?'

Anna nodded. 'Well, it is a tattoo. It is permanent. I shall have this all my life.'

I gazed at her with astonishment. She must have had the most awful time you could possibly imagine, but she'd managed to come through. And here she was sitting calmly in our front room, drinking tea. She must be so brave. I wanted to know more about her story.

'How did you get here?' I asked.

'After the camp was liberated, I could not go home again. There was no place for Jews in Germany. So I came here, with other refugees. I had taught English in Germany, so I knew the language. I have worked as a translator, and now I have moved to this town to work for a charity.'

Mother looked at me. Her face seemed to be saying, 'What do you think of that?' Well, I was very impressed. What an amazing woman! I felt a great respect for her, and was glad Mother had introduced her to me. Now I said, 'Thank you,' to her and got up to go.

Mother interrupted. 'No, Tess, don't go. You haven't heard her story.'

There was more? I sat down and looked at Anna.

She still seemed reluctant about something. 'Are you sure?' she said to Mother, and Mother said, 'Of course. Go on, go on, Anna.'

Anna took a deep breath and said, 'All the guards in the camp were cruel. They hurt people deliberately. They took pleasure in it. But there was one who was cruel above all. He was twisted. When the women needed to go to the lavatory, he told them they could not pass water at the same time as . . . as—'

Mother broke in. 'He said they weren't allowed to wee at the same time as pooing. One or the other. If he saw them doing both at the same time, he'd shoot them!'

What! My mind whirled. I couldn't take this in. What a terrible thing to do. I could only shake my head. It was beyond belief. And mad, too. An evil, evil Nazi . . .

Anna was looking down at her hands. All I could think to say was, 'That's so awful, I'm so sorry . . .'

She shook her head. 'I was telling your mother, this was just one of the ways they used to break us down.'

'And he really did shoot women, right where they were, squatting on the floor,' said Mother.

I looked at her, thinking, Of course, she's shocked and sickened too. Her cheeks were flushed and her eyes were glittering. Unusual for Mother to be so emotional.

She was waving a book. 'I've been reading this book,' Mother said. 'It's about Auschwitz, but there's nothing like that in here.'

Anna said nothing, just picked up her cup.

I thought, Ah, that fits. Mother wasn't a great reader, but the books she did read were always about awful things:

torture, cruelty, crimes, horror. She'd get quite carried away. It was the same with films – she liked anything with blood and guts in it, hangings and beheadings. You wouldn't see her at a Doris Day musical.

I felt a bit uncomfortable now. I stood up and said to Anna, 'It was nice to meet you. I hope you enjoy living in Croydon.'

She smiled as I turned to leave the room. Mother was flicking through her book and didn't look up. Later on I heard her telling Anna's story to Don, and he said, 'For God's sake, Grace, that's disgusting. Shut up about it.'

And I wished I hadn't heard it. Horrible images would pop up in my head. The next time I went to the toilet I tried pooing without weeing, and it was impossible. What a terrible, cruel thing to do to someone. I've since wondered about Mother's fascination with the story. Did she just want to shock me? Or did she get a kick out of the whole thing? At the time I knew very little about what made people tick. I only knew that somehow Mother seemed too keen on something so twisted and revolting.

It was Mother's other friend, Lily, who set off my disaster with Mother. Just when we were getting along so well, and life seemed good.

I was walking home from school as usual, just coming up to Lily's house. I saw Liam leaning over the front gate, looking directly at me.

'Hello,' I said, trying to make it sound casual, though he did give me the creeps.

'It's Tessie, isn't it?' he said. His voice was deep, and like Lily he had a strong Irish accent.

I had to stop then, and say, yes, that's me.

'Will you be doin' me a wee favour, Tessie?'

What? Alarm bells rang in my head. I never liked the sound of favours. Then again, Mother was always saying I should be polite and helpful to neighbours, and though Lily and Liam were a couple of streets away, I supposed that counted as neighbours, and of course Lily was her friend.

'What is it?' I asked, trying not to sound nervous.

'Would you be comin' in and fryin' me an egg for me tea? I'm starvin', so I am, and there's no sign of Lily.'

Fry him an egg? What a funny thing to ask. I was no great shakes as a cook, as Mother usually said when I tried to help her get Sunday dinner, but still . . . I could probably manage a fried egg.

'I'll have a go,' I said.

'That's a good girl,' said Liam, opening the gate.

We walked down the path and into a small front room. There was a table and some chairs, not much else, and a low fire burned in the grate.

'Um, where's the kitchen?' I asked.

'Oh, you'll not be needin' that. There.' And he pointed to the fire. 'That's for the cookin'.'

Cooking on a fire? When I looked again I could see there was a kind of grill on legs over the flames. Maybe they didn't have a proper stove.

'And there's the egg and the pan,' Liam added.

The egg and the pan were on the table, next to a big chunk of white bread on a plate. The pan was black and thick with grease. Mother would have a fit if she saw such a dirty pan. But I went ahead and cracked the egg into the pan. Enough grease already, I thought. Then I placed the pan, which was surprisingly heavy, on the grill thing, and hoped the heat would be enough.

I could hear Liam pacing about the room behind me. He suddenly said, 'D'you see much o' me wife at your place?'

I looked round. 'Well, she's in and out,' I said, using one of Mother's expressions.

'Hmm. Well now, what does she do when she's there?'

'Do?'

'Yes, do. What does she do? Is there a party goin' on?'

'Not always. Sometimes.'

'Are there men there?'

I was taken aback. 'Well, sometimes.'

'Does she go off with them?' Liam asked, his voice suddenly deeper.

Off with them?

'What do you mean?'

'What d'you think I mean? Does she go around alone with the men?'

I didn't know what to say. I looked at the egg, which still looked raw. I said, 'I don't think so.'

'Hah!'

Then he was quiet for a while. The white of the egg started to cook. Then he burst out with, 'Does she talk o' me at all?'

'You?' All these questions, I thought. What's he getting at? As Lily was always complaining about him, I'd better be careful.

'Not really.'

'What d'you mean, not really?'

'Well . . . just now and then.'

'What does she say? Does she ever say I hit her, does she?'

I felt my head spinning. 'Oh, she might have said something, but I don't know.'

'I knew it, I knew it.'

He took me by the arm and looked straight at me. His eyes were a very deep blue, and a bit bloodshot.

'Look, Tessie,' he said in a quieter voice. 'I don't want you or your mother thinkin' I'd ever harm a hair of her head. She's always puttin' these stories around, and there's not a grain of truth in any of them. D'ye hear me?'

I nodded, thinking, Anything you say, just let me get out of here. I glanced back at the fire. 'The egg's burning,' I said.

'Fuck the egg.' And he let go my arm and slumped down at the table, his head in his hands.

I stood there for a moment, wondering what to do. I'd better move the pan off before it caught fire, anyway. I saw a tea cloth crumpled up on the table, and used that to hold the hot handle.

'There's the egg,' I said, as I put the pan on the table.

He didn't look up, just waved me away. I was glad to get through the front door and hurry down the path. Should I tell Mother about this strange man? Best not. She was always telling me not to talk to anybody about what went on in our house.

'How many times have I told you to keep your fucking mouth shut, you little cunt!'

Mother was slapping me hard across my face, this way, that way and this way again.

I staggered back against the front door, shocked to the core. It was the next evening. Me and Victor had come back from the pictures, and I was just lifting my hand to the door knocker when the door was hurled open, and Mother was standing there like an avenging angel.

'You never ever *ever* say anything to anybody about this place!' Now she was hitting me, punching me, on my head and shoulders. I shrank against a wall, trying to protect my head with my arms. As Mother ranted and raved, walloped seven bells out of me, there was one tiny thought at the back of my mind, behind the awful shock and the pain. Victor was seeing this. I felt so embarrassed he should see me like this.

Now Mother had stopped hitting me and was pointing at someone. It was Lily. I knew her from her bright red frizzy hair, not her face. Her face was a mess, with two black eyes, and purple bruises all over. There was dried blood under her nose.

'Look at her!' Mother yelled, gripping my arm so tight it hurt. 'Look at her! Look what your blabbing fucking mouth has done!'

I shook my head. Tears were pouring down my cheeks. I gasped, 'I didn't say—'

Mother gave me another clump round the head. 'You said enough!' she roared. 'When she got back he was waiting for her. Look what you've done! Now get to your room! I want you out of my sight. *Now!*'

And she shoved me into our bedroom and slammed the door. As I stumbled and fell on the floor, the key turned in the lock. For a long while I couldn't do anything but crouch there in the dark, my head and arms and shoulders hurting, throbbing, trying to keep my crying down so I didn't wake the kids. But I had a bigger pain in my heart. After all my efforts, I'd let Mother down. I shouldn't ever have said anything to that man, I shouldn't have gone into his house. I could have said I was in a hurry or something and just gone past. But I didn't. So Lily was beaten up and it was my fault.

And to cap it all, Victor had seen me. What must he think of me?

That night, when I'd managed to get my clothes off and slide into bed, I lay there in despair. Would Mother ever forgive me? And would Victor still want to marry me? Would he even want to see me again?

The next day I was stiff and sore. It hurt to get washed and dressed, but I had to go to school. I was so scared of seeing Mother again. What if she turned her back on me for ever? What if she sent me away? I knew people at school were looking at me, but I ignored them. I didn't care what they thought. I only cared about Mother and getting back into her good books.

When I got home, she was in the kitchen. She looked up. 'I'll never forget what you did,' she snapped. 'Get out of my sight and stay out.'

Later that day I bumped into Victor in the hall, when I was going to the toilet. He stood in front of me awkwardly, his face going red.

'I'm s-s-sorry, Tess,' he said. 'C-can I do anything for you?'

I shook my head. 'No. Nobody can.'

I kept out of Mother's way as much as I could. She didn't ask me to help at her parties, and she was locking me in again with the other kids in the evenings. I dragged myself through every day. I'd never felt so bad in my life. The only light was Victor. I could only see him during the day at weekends now, as I'd be locked in. But we did go for a walk in the park a couple of times, and I enjoyed that.

I plucked up courage and asked him, 'Do you still want to be engaged to me?'

'Of course I do!' He said it like a shot, so maybe he meant it. 'I'm sure you didn't do anything wrong. I think your mother was very hard on you.'

Oh, I thought, he's taking my part against Mother. I found that quite shocking, though it was nice to think that someone was on my side.

A couple of weeks after that awful evening, I got home from school and Mother was waiting for me.

'I've got something to tell you,' she said.

My heart sank. Had the worst thing happened? Was she sending me away?

'Victor's gone.'

14

On the Up Again

I stood there in the kitchen, just staring at Mother. What did she mean, Victor's gone? I'd been so keyed up for her to tell me I was the one to go that I just couldn't take this in.

Mother was obviously getting impatient. 'Did you hear what I said?' she snapped.

I nodded.

'Well then?'

Now I shook my head. 'W-what do you mean?'

Mother's voice was sharper. 'Don't you understand plain English? He's gone, skedaddled, vamoosed.'

Then I burst out, 'But he said he loved me!'

'Love!' Mother snorted. 'Well, that's as may be. He did tell me he thought he was too old for you, you should find someone your own age.'

'He could have told me himself!' I cried, the hurt sinking in.

Mother shrugged. 'Well, he's got a new life now.'

'A new life?'

'He's gone to Cardiff.'

'Cardiff?'

'What are you, a fucking parrot? Cardiff. It's in Wales.'

'But why would he go there?'

'To find his family.'

I sat down at the table. Victor didn't have a family. He was just making something up to get away from me. After that awful evening, he'd seemed to be kind, but he must have been so disappointed in me.

Mother sat down opposite me. 'Don't you want to hear what happened?'

I felt like saying, 'Would it make any difference?' But I just nodded.

'Well,' said Mother, 'I'd been thinking all this time how sad it was that Victor had no family of his own, how he never knew his real parents, and he's a nice boy. So I get to wondering whether anything can be found out, even after all this time, so off I go to the Salvation Army.'

I nearly repeated the name but caught myself in time. 'Why them?' I asked.

''Cos they look for missing persons, look up all sorts of records and files, put two and two together. Well, the long and the short of it is, they only go and turn up Victor's real parents! There was a right mix-up at the time. Always the way when a raid was on. There's no sign of a little baby so the parents think he's dead, killed in the blast. They left London and went to Wales. So there you have it!'

She sat back with a smile on her face. She did seem pleased with herself. Part of my mind realised that was the first time she'd smiled at me ever since I let her down. So while I was taking in her news – and it was wonderful for Victor, to be reunited with his parents – I felt a small hope grow in me that Mother and I would be reunited too.

I felt tears pricking my eyes, and I started sniffing, looking down at the table.

'Plenty more fish in the sea,' said Mother.

Was I mistaken, or was her voice not so sharp? I looked up at her and she was still smiling.

Then she said, 'I'll put the kettle on. You look like you could do with a cuppa.'

Just as my heart was sinking, Mother lifted it up! Trust her to do the right thing. It had been awful to be cut off from her. I might have lost Victor, and I was upset, but what really mattered was that I had Mother back.

It wasn't long after this that Mother showed how much she cared for me, by sticking up for me. It was at school, of all places. Mother had never set foot in my school, had never gone to meetings or seen the teachers or anything like that. She hadn't even come to prize-givings when I'd won a prize. She took no interest at all. I took home all my school reports, which were pretty good on the whole, but I don't think Mother even looked at them, let alone kept them. As for school photos: 'Waste of money. I know what you look like!'

Anyway, one day I got into trouble. This was unusual, as I was happy at school, worked hard and often came top of the class, especially in English. Mind you, this trouble was to do with sports, and I was never much cop at them. I liked swimming, and the long jump, but that was about it. This particular day, the sports teacher, Miss Judd, was having a go at me. I'd been hurdling, running round the track and jumping over those little fences, and I'd caught my foot. I came a cropper, sprawled all over the track. It was painful and embarrassing. But Miss Judd wasn't having any of it.

'Go back there and try again, Sandra,' she told me. 'Don't you know it's the best thing to do? If you fall off a horse, get up on it again straight away.'

Horse? I was having enough trouble with hurdles. I just stood there in my games kit feeling upset. These days I was uncomfortable anyway in my games kit. We wore navy blue knickers and I felt silly going about like that. We also had to wear a plain white vest, which was stretched across my boobs. I didn't have a bra, so that was another discomfort, jiggling up and down.

'I can't, Miss,' I wailed. 'I just can't.' I was sure that I'd catch my foot again and go flying.

Miss Judd was getting impatient. 'Oh, for goodness' sake,' she snapped, 'don't be such a baby.'

She grabbed my arm and shook it hard. I jerked away, going, 'No, I won't!' Then she suddenly cracked me one right across my face, slapped me really hard.

'You can and you will!' she shouted.

I was stunned. The slap hurt all right, and a stone in the ring she was wearing had scratched me, so that was stinging. On top of that, I was shocked that she'd hit me round the face. Teachers could hit you, but not round the face, I was sure of that.

It looked like Miss Judd had the same thought, as she made a noise like 'Tcha!' and strode off down the track. I didn't know what to do, so just crept back to the changing room.

When I got home that afternoon, Mother was in the kitchen. She glanced at me and did a double-take.

'What's that?' she said, coming over and pointing at my cheek. 'How did that get there?'

'Er, what?' I asked. I was playing for time. There was no way of knowing how Mother would react.

She pulled me over to the mirror above the fire. 'That,' she said.

And I saw the mark on my cheek was red and angry, the scratch showing up through it. Well, I had to tell her. 'Miss Judd hit me.'

'Who's Miss Judd when she's at home?'

'One of the teachers.'

'Right,' she said. 'We're going round that fucking school.'

She marched me back to school, with a face like thunder. We swept through the reception area and Mother snapped, 'Where's the one in charge here?'

I pointed at a door. 'That's the headmistress's office.'

'She'll do.'

Without delay Mother stepped up to the door. It always had a notice pinned to it, saying: 'STOP. THINK BEFORE YOU KNOCK. IS YOUR JOURNEY REALLY NECESSARY?' I was thinking, Well, no, my journey is not necessary. I was shaking with nerves. But after a quick look at the notice Mother growled, 'Knock? Fucked if I will.' And she barged straight in.

The shocked headmistress stood up behind her desk and tried to speak. 'Really! You can't just come in here—' and was stopped by Mother snapping, 'Miss Judd – where is she? Where is the fucking cow?'

The headmistress was opening and closing her mouth, but no sound was coming out. Her massive bosom was heaving, and her head was shaking, making the little kiss curl she always had on her forehead flop up and down.

Mother pulled me forward and said, 'Look – look at her face! What do you think of that, eh? Go and get that fucking teacher and tell her if she wants to hit anyone she can try having a go at me and see where that gets her!'

As Mother stood glaring at her, and I was wishing the ground would open and swallow me up, the headmistress pulled herself together.

'Miss Judd will have left the school by now, and I must ask you not to refer to a member of my staff—'

Mother interrupted. 'Are you gonna get her or not?'

'I've told you, she'll have gone home by now. She's not here. Whatever's happened, we can sort it out in the morning.'

'I'm not waiting that long,' said Mother. 'Tell you what, next time you see her, give her this from me, will you?'

And she whacked the headmistress right across the face. As the teacher fell back, Mother turned on her heel, grabbed my arm and marched me out.

She was hopping mad. Though I was embarrassed as hell, and dreaded what would happen the next day, part of me was thrilled that she'd stood up for me, protected me. That's what mothers do.

And much to my surprise there was no comeback at the school. Nobody said anything to me, not even Miss Judd. Obviously they were sweeping it under the carpet. I couldn't get over the fact that Mother had actually hit the headmistress. That must be a first. They'd all know not to cross her again!

After that, my life took a turn for the better. I'd never been so happy. Me and Mother were a team again, and I was her right-hand girl. Business was booming, and Mother was at the heart of it, organising everybody: the girls, the punters, the parties. More than once, Mother said to me, 'I really don't know what I'd do without you, Tess.' And that was the icing on the cake.

She was more open with me these days, talked to me as if I was a grown-up. One evening a young man might drop by with a small package for Mother, and later she'd tell me what it was, just as a matter of course. 'Nice bit of tom, Tess. I can get a good price for that.' She never had to tell me not to mention anything. I'd learned my lesson well, and it looked like Mother trusted me.

I was glad to help out at the parties again. I'd missed those evenings – the glamorous girls, the smart men, the cigar smoke, the music playing on the radiogram. I was opening the door to the guests now, taking the girls' fur wraps and the men's hats and putting them on the new hallstand. This was very smart, in a dark shiny wood, with pegs all round a big mirror and a seat with a lid that lifted up. I felt like one of those hat-check girls I'd seen in films.

All the old regulars were still around. I kept a special eye out for Teddy. I still had a bit of a thing for him, even if he had got Kenny on to me. I was sure Teddy wouldn't know anything about that. There were new faces to get used to, as well. One was called Big Joe, who frightened me at first as he was, well, so big. He had a large sticking-out chin, and reminded me of Desperate Dan in the *Dandy*. Much better dressed, though, like all the men who came to the house. And in the event, Big Joe was a gentleman, soft-spoken and polite, and very nice to me. 'Here you are, love,' he'd say, giving me a two-bob bit as I took his hat. Very generous.

There was another new face that reminded me of a cartoon, but definitely not so nice. This one was called Wally, and he looked like Bluto, Popeye's enemy. Big and rough and tough, with shaggy eyebrows, who always smelled of booze. When I took his hat he always stared at my chest, and made me feel awkward. Mother didn't like him, I could tell. She was very stiff towards him, not easy and relaxed like with the other guests. I heard her saying to Don, 'You want to steer clear of that Wally. He's a nasty piece of work. The girls don't like him. "He's too rough, Grace," they tell me. What can I say? I'm not getting on the wrong side of Wally. So I say to them, "I know, I know, it's tough, but what can you do? Just get it over with as soon as you can." '

'I'm not scared of him,' Don said. 'He'd better watch his step when I'm around.'

I thought that was a brave thing to say, considering Wally could have made two of Don.

'Who are you kidding?' Mother said. 'He'd make mince-meat out of you.'

Another new face was a man they called Coffee Jim. Coffee because his skin was dark brown, I suppose. He was tall and lean, with sharp cheekbones, a scar running down one side of his face. When I took his hat, he was perfectly pleasant, thanked me nicely, but I couldn't help feeling a shiver run down my spine. I'd heard about him, and it sounded like he was another bloke not to tangle with.

'Handy with a knife,' Mother said once.

I gathered he was involved with big-time villains in London. I started hearing a name, a funny name for a man, I thought. The Craze. Maybe he was a loony. I felt silly when I found out it was two blokes, called Kray. They were twins, Reggie and Ronnie, working out of the East End. 'The business', Teddy called them. From what I could tell, carrying round my trays of nibbles and drinks, the men all had a high opinion of these Krays. They lowered their voices when they said their names. Coffee Jim had something to do with them, or one of their outfits. They obviously had a lot of fingers in a lot of pies, and you didn't cross them if you knew what was good for you.

These were the early days of the Krays' criminal career, of course. They'd be making a big name for themselves later on.

While Coffee Jim did have a presence about him, something that made you notice him, that didn't go for another of the new faces. Claude wasn't much to look at, average height, average everything. Pale blue eyes, round face, fair hair slicked back. A whining voice, always complaining. The only interesting thing about Claude was that somehow he'd got an absolutely beautiful girlfriend. When I first saw Jean, at one of Mother's parties, I was reminded of Jane, the runaway Mother had taken in, the one who had been a model or something. Jean was tall and curvy, with lovely long blonde hair and deep blue eyes. Gorgeous. When she spoke, to my surprise she sounded posh, like someone playing a titled lady in a film.

'How come Jean talks so posh?' I asked Mother later.

Mother shrugged. 'Comes from good stock. I hear her sister's a nun, for God's sake.' She grinned. 'Must have come down in the world to be with that little turd Claude.'

'Yeah, what does she see in him?' I wanted to know.

Mother shrugged again. 'There's more than one way of skinning a cat.'

What did that mean? I must have looked puzzled as Mother added, 'He's got something she wants, and it's not his pretty face.'

But he didn't have a pretty face . . .

Mother laughed. 'You're such a little innocent, Tess.'

She seemed to mean it kindly, so I asked, 'What has he got, then?'

'It's drugs, isn't it?'

This still didn't mean a lot to me. I'd heard of drugs, of course. They were like extra strong booze, and they were against the law as they were dangerous. I was sorry that someone as lovely as Jean was doing something dangerous. She must want the drugs very much if she'd put up with Claude.

Mother was looking thoughtful. 'You never know,' she said. 'There might come a time . . .'

She was quiet for a moment, then her face lit up with a smile. 'I could do with Jean on the books,' she said. 'A girl like her – they'd be queuing round the block.'

Well, I thought, they're certainly not queuing at the bus stop any more. That had dawned on me early one evening when I was coming home with some shopping. The bus was just reaching the stop outside our house, and two men were waiting. They both got on. Not like in the old days. Now Mother had the whole house, there was obviously room for punters to wait indoors. That must have been good for business, too.

There was something else to cheer Mother up. An old friend paid a call.

It was me who answered the door, and standing there was a small man, with hair as ginger as mine, but short and parted on one side. He was wearing a brightly coloured flowery shirt and tight white trousers, and carrying a black shiny bag over one shoulder. He beamed at me, very friendly, and said, 'Hello, lovey. Don't tell me you're little Tessie, all grown up?' He had a high voice for a man.

Before I could say anything, he was stepping through the doorway. 'Is your mummy at home?' he asked.

'In the kitchen,' I said. 'Down the hall and on the right.'

'I know the way, sweetie,' he said, and off he went.

I looked at him, thinking, That's a funny way of walking. It was if his legs were joined at the top, making him wiggle his bum.

Then he paused outside the kitchen door, flung his arms wide and said, 'Gracie! It's little me!'

I heard Mother cry, 'Bunny!' Then he disappeared inside, while I shut the front door.

Bunny. I knew that name. He must be Mother's old school friend, the one she used to protect from bullies. He was a girlie boy then, now he was a girlie man, obviously. I didn't remember ever meeting him. Perhaps it was when I was little.

I could hear Bunny as I walked down the hall. 'Well, I stuck it as long as I could, Gracie, but you know what they say. Nobody wants a fairy when she's forty.'

That made me smile. Nobody wants a fairy when she's forty – that was one of Tessie O'Shea's songs Mother liked. I waited outside the kitchen while Bunny rattled on.

'So I said to them, you can keep your cabins and your cabin boys and your tropical uniforms and stick them where the sun don't shine, duckie. I'm off home. And not before time, Gracie. Now what's all this I've been hearing?'

Mother noticed me and said, 'Come in, Tess. Meet Bunny.'

He turned to me. 'So I was right, this is little Tessie,' he said, taking both my hands in his and gazing into my eyes. 'Well, she's a credit to you, Gracie, a credit.'

He was like a cheerful, chirpy, wind-up toy. I couldn't help liking him.

'Do you know, Tessie, if it wasn't for your darling mummy I wouldn't be here today? I'd still be up to my ears in shit, pardon my French, nasty boys shoving me down the khazi. Oh no, along comes Gracie and she hammers the whole bleeding lot of 'em, don't you, sweetie?'

Mother was smiling broadly. 'You bet I do,' she said. 'Anything for you, Bunny.'

'And anything for you!' he cried, letting go my hands and twirling round to face her directly. 'Here I am, yours to command. What can I do you for? Go on, Gracie, there must be something I can do. I can be a wossname – I know, a shop assistant, a knocking-shop assistant.'

Mother laughed out loud. 'Always a place for you, Bunny.'

He flung his arms right round her, hugging her tight. She didn't hug him back, Mother wasn't one for hugging, but she patted him on the shoulder.

'Right, let's me and you have a talk,' she said.

After that, Bunny kept popping up, and I was always pleased to see him. Mother had him running errands all over the place, and he helped me get things ready for the parties. He was easy to get on with, always one for a laugh and a chat – though it was usually him doing the chatting. In fact he and Mother only fell out when she'd had enough of the gab.

'Christ,' she'd say. 'No wonder you're called Bunny. Rabbit, rabbit, rabbit.'

Then Bunny would flounce off, looking hurt, only to reappear shortly afterwards as perky as ever.

Bunny wasn't the only one to do errands for Mother, of course. I was still popping to Audrey's for her cigarettes and anything else she wanted, as well as getting a big shop now and then. There was something new now, though.

'I'd like you to help out one of my friends,' said Mother one morning.

I went cold, my mind immediately leaping to the times I'd helped her friends before.

'It's Kitty, just round the corner,' she said.

Thank God for that. Not a man.

'Her kid's started school and she won't have time to take her in the morning. Could you pop in and take her?'

Of course I could. Happy to do anything to help. Kath and the others could just go on without me. It was only the little boys who needed help these days, anyway.

So a couple of days later I left home a bit earlier than usual, and went to Kitty's place. She had a flat in a big house with a lot of bells by the front door. I rang the bell for number 3, and after a while a woman answered the door. She looked quite old to have a young daughter, I thought. Her hair was streaked with grey, pulled back in a bun, and her face was pale and lined. She had a nice smile, though. 'You must be Tess,' she said. 'Come in, dear.'

I followed her in and up some stairs, and into a kitchen. A little girl with long fair plaits was sitting at a scrubbed wooden table, spooning out porridge from a bowl in front of her.

'That's right, Rosemary,' said Kitty. 'Make sure you finish your porridge, it's good for you. Now, here's Tess to take you to school.'

Blimey, I thought, fancy having a mother fussing round your breakfast, making sure you eat it all up. It was nice, though. And the kitchen was nice too, warm and homely, with sunshine-yellow curtains at the window above the sink. There was a rack suspended from the ceiling in front of the chimney breast, with neatly folded washing airing on it from the heat of the fire. Kitty was standing just under the rack, her back to the fire. With a shock I realised she'd pulled up her pinny at the back, a wraparound pinny with a cheerful pattern of roses, so that her bum was facing the fire. I couldn't help noticing she was wearing old-fashioned pink bloomers, before I quickly looked away and out of the window. It's her house, I thought. She can do what she likes. I nearly jumped out of my skin, though, when suddenly there was an explosion of noise from Kitty's direction, an almighty raspberry. It seemed to roll on for ever, till it finished with a 'pfft'.

She's farting up the chimney! I didn't know where to look. I fought down an urge to giggle and fixed my eyes on Rosemary, who was scraping out the last of her porridge like a right little Goldilocks.

'Now, dear, are you ready?' said Kitty to her daughter.

The next moment we were all trooping down the stairs, and Kitty was waving Rosemary goodbye. As I went out the door, Kitty touched my arm and said, 'I have terrible wind, you know. I'm a martyr to it.'

You don't say. I just smiled and nodded, and walked after Rosemary.

That was the only time she mentioned it, though the same thing happened every day. Rosemary finishing her breakfast, me gazing out of the window and Kitty letting rip up the chimney. I'll never get used to people's funny little ways, I thought.

Anyway, there was an unexpected bonus for me, having to go round to Kitty's. Kitty was letting me in one morning, just as a girl was coming out.

'Morning, Jenny,' said Kitty.

'Hi, Kitty,' said the girl. She looked at me and grinned. A friendly face, and she was very pretty, with blonde hair in a ponytail and a thick fringe flopping over her forehead. She was dressed very stylishly, in a tight-fitting ribbed polo-neck sweater and Capri pants that showed off her curvy figure.

'This is Jenny from number 4,' Kitty told me. 'Jenny, this is Tess. She takes Rosemary to school for me.'

Jenny smiled, showing regular white teeth. 'Hi, Tess' she said. 'So you live round here?'

'Yeah,' I said. 'Just round the corner.'

'We should meet up some time,' said Jenny over her shoulder, ponytail swinging, as she walked up the garden path.

'She seems nice,' I said to Kitty as we went upstairs.

'Oh, she is,' said Kitty. 'She's had a hard life. No family or anything. She lives here all by herself.'

'How old is she?' I asked. It amazed me that someone so young could live alone.

'She's only sixteen,' said Kitty. 'But she does all right, she's got a job. You don't hear her complaining.'

I bumped into Jenny a couple of times, then one morning she said, 'Fancy coming to the fair tonight?' There was a travelling funfair in the park at the time.

'Great!' I said. I'd always loved fairs, the bright lights, the loud music, and I had some money in my pocket from the tips I'd been getting at Mother's parties.

'I'm going with Terry,' Jenny went on. 'You can go with his mate Paul.'

A boy? Right.

I dolled myself up that evening and went round to Jenny's. She looked glam as usual, and all of a sudden I felt dowdy.

'Come on,' she said.

We met the boys at a hamburger stall outside the park. Terry put his arms round Jenny and kissed her. The lad next to him had to be Paul. He was on the plump side, with a shock of fair hair. 'Hi, I'm Tess,' I said.

He grunted something I couldn't catch. He didn't look very pleased.

We all went around together for the next half-hour, going on the dodgems and the waltzer, which I loved. It was thrilling to be whirled about like that.

Then Jenny and Terry were off. 'See you,' they said.

I looked at Paul.

'Gotta go,' he mumbled.

I made my way back home by myself. I wasn't surprised Paul hadn't wanted to stay with me. I'd seen him looking at Jenny, and I could tell he fancied her. Well, what boy wouldn't rather look at her than at me? No getting away from it, I was fat and plain. No boy would fancy me for my looks. They liked my boobs, I knew that, so that was something. But how I longed to be like Jenny! At least she seemed to like me, and it was good to have a friend at last.

Anyway, whatever happened outside, life was still good at home. I'd never known Mother to be in such a good mood for so long. At her parties she kept everyone entertained. 'You're a star, Gracie!' Bunny would say. I noticed new stuff round the place, like cushions and ornaments. 'Finishing touches,' said Mother. And she bought a lot of new shoes for herself, very dainty, with small heels and sparkly bits. 'Just right for dancing,' she said. Recently she'd been out more than usual in the early evening, going ballroom dancing, which she loved.

We hadn't heard anything from the council. Nobody had come round to look at the flat upstairs. It seemed that we could go on like this for ever. Then two months after the Hodges moved out, there was a bombshell.

15

Notice to Quit

'What? I don't believe it. I don't fucking believe it!'

Mother was speaking in a low voice, but very intense. She had a face like thunder, her teeth clenched. One hand held a cigarette that was burning down as she stared at the letter in front of her.

Don had just brought in the post. It came a bit later on Saturday morning. I was clearing the table after breakfast when Mother opened the long white envelope and started to read what was inside. Don was leaning back in his chair.

'What is it, love?' he asked.

Mother didn't look at him. Just went on staring at the piece of paper.

She started shaking her head, side to side, then suddenly crashed the hand holding the paper down on the table. Me and Don jumped.

'Look, Grace, tell me – what the hell is it?' Don was looking worried now.

Mother was breathing hard. 'Bastards. Fucking bastards.'

'Grace, if you don't tell me what's in that letter—'

'Read it yourself,' she snapped, and flung the crumpled piece of paper at him. She sank back in her chair, taking a deep drag on her cigarette.

Don smoothed the paper and read slowly from top to bottom, his lips moving slightly.

'Oh,' he said.

'Oh?' Mother's voice was rising. 'Oh? Is that all you can say? I'll give you fucking Oh. The bastard council are throwing us out and you just say Oh!'

'Well, what can I say?' Don protested. 'The council own the house, they can do whatever they like with it. I don't want to go any more than you do, I like it here. But if they're pulling the place down for redevelopment, we can't exactly stay put, can we?'

'Redevelopment my arse! They're taking my gaff away from me. Everything I've built up, can't you see it, you idiot?'

Don frowned. 'No point getting at me, Grace. I'm not the fucking council, am I? Anyway, you're a legal tenant, you got rights. They're not chucking us out on the street. It says here we'll be rehoused.'

'Rehoused!' Mother spat. 'I don't want to be fucking rehoused! I want to stay here.'

Don tried again. 'Well, you never know, this place they're offering might be all right. Might even be better.'

'Yeah?' Mother jeered. 'Yeah, there's bound to be a great big house just like this one. Plenty of room for the girls and the punters, nice big rooms for my parties.' She slammed her fist down on the table again. 'No chance. It'll be some poxy little rabbit hutch. No room to swing a cat or anything else. And fucking miles from anywhere. Who's gonna want to go all the way out there? What the hell is that gonna do to my business?'

Don shook his head. 'I don't know, Grace. But it can't be that small.' He grinned. 'There's gotta be room for us and six kids now.'

I pricked up my ears. I'd been keeping out of the way, but now I joined in. 'Six kids? What do you mean? Who's the other one?'

Mother scowled at Don. 'Trust you to blab,' she said.

That didn't stop Don grinning. 'Well,' he said. 'Why not? They're bound to know sooner or later.'

Mother turned to me. 'I'm six months gone,' she said. She didn't sound very excited, but I was.

'That's fantastic!' I said, looking down at her front. She really didn't show much. She wasn't fat, but she was what Bunny called well upholstered. She carried herself well, too, with a straight back. I wondered if I dared give her a hug. Then I caught myself. Of course not. But it was good news. I immediately hoped it would be a little boy, then we'd be three girls and three boys.

'Yeah, yeah,' said Mother, waving a hand. Then she said, 'I've got more important things to worry about now. Like what we're gonna do to keep body and soul together.'

Don was getting annoyed. 'You're overdoing it, Grace,' he said. 'It can't be that bad.'

Mother blew up. 'What do you mean, can't be that bad? It's all right for you, I do all the fucking work, and what do you do?'

Uh-oh, I thought. I'm getting out of here. I muttered something and whizzed to the front room. I'd keep myself busy there, tidying up, while Mother and Don had a set-to.

It was sinking in, now, about leaving here. I looked round the room. Mother had done it up really well. It looked like an advert in a magazine, with thick rugs and plush curtains, as well as the settee and extra armchairs, a couple of coffee tables and the trendy cocktail cabinet. And the radiogram, of course.

The room never seemed crowded even when there were a dozen or so people in it.

As I dusted around, I wondered how Mother was going to manage if the new house was much smaller than this one. Her business had really taken off when the Hodges had left and she could use the upstairs rooms. 'A little gold mine, Tess,' she'd said to me more than once. Well, I knew Mother had her head screwed on all right, she was good with money. She'd think of something. And there was the baby coming, too. I was thrilled at the thought. Mother would have her hands full, that was certain, and I'd be able to help all round. That was something to look forward to, even if I did have a bit of a pang at leaving this place, the only home I'd ever known.

'We're off to look at this shit-hole the council want to put us in,' Mother told me a couple of days later. 'Get the kids their tea.'

'Grace,' Don said. 'You don't know it'll be a shit-hole—'

Mother cut in. 'Oh no? Just you wait and see.'

The house was a bus ride away, and it was a couple of hours before they came back. Mother was looking grim.

'Told you!' she snapped to no one in particular. 'Shit-hole.'

Don was exasperated. 'It's not that bad, Grace. It's got a living room and three bedrooms. The kitchen's big enough, and at least there's a proper bathroom.'

Mother snorted. 'Yeah, living room and three bedrooms – you could fit them all in one of these rooms.' And she looked round the big front room, with its high ceiling and large sash window.

She was getting into her stride. 'And it has to be in a dead-end road. Fucking cul-de-sac. Quiet as the grave there – everyone'll know our business. Nosy parkers everywhere.'

Don was getting annoyed. 'Well, nothing you can say or do will make any difference, will it, Grace? The council own this place, they can do what they like with it and you just have to bloody well lump it.'

'I don't have to bloody well like it!'

Now Don tried a bit of the old flannel. 'Well, knowing you, Grace, you'll make a go of it. You'll think of something, you always do.' He was saying just what I'd thought.

That seemed to get through. Sitting on one of the red plush armchairs, she nodded thoughtfully. 'Yeah. The kids can stay in one room, Barbara can work out of another . . . It'll take a bit more organising . . .'

Mother took me round to the house before we moved in. It had been empty for a while and was very grubby, so we were going to clean it up. We filled a bag with scrubbing brushes, Vim and other stuff, and walked to the bus stop. Mother was still in a bad mood, so I didn't dare say anything.

At first sight, the house didn't look much. It was a semi, quite old-fashioned, with small windows and a plain front door; a patch of garden in front, with just weeds growing. Inside was every bit as disappointing. I wouldn't say the rooms were small, they were poky. How were we all going to fit in? There'd be Mother and Don and us five kids, and the new baby, not forgetting Barbara, who'd go on living with us. As for Mother's parties – well, they'd have to be scaled down, no question.

Still, it's what we were lumbered with, so we'd have to make the best of it, I thought. I did the heavy cleaning, scrubbing floors and cleaning the sinks and the bath. With

Mother in her condition, she shouldn't overdo things. I said this to her, and she laughed.

'I'm always fucking overdoing things,' she said. But she did take the odd break, sitting on the stairs and having a smoke. Those stairs struck me as very narrow and steep. The little boys had better be careful here. The only good thing about the house, as far as I could see, was the bathroom. As Don said, it was a proper bathroom, not like the bath we had, in the scullery with its wooden lid. And no more boiling up water in the copper and ladling it out with a jug.

'What's that for?' I asked Mother, pointing at a large white metal box on the bathroom wall, with a pipe that swung out over the bath.

'That's a geyser. Heats the water.'

I was impressed. 'That'll make things easier,' I said.

'Yeah, till I get the gas bill.'

We worked on till Mother was satisfied the house was clean enough, then packed up our cleaning stuff. When we were leaving, Mother shutting the front door, we heard a voice calling.

'Coo-ee! Grace!'

We looked round, and there at the next-door gate was an old lady, waving at us. 'It is Grace, isn't it? I thought I recognised you.' She was on the short side, rather plump, with a cloud of pure white hair and a very wrinkled face.

Mother looked puzzled for a moment, then obviously the penny dropped. 'Edith!' she said. 'I didn't know you lived in this neck of the woods.'

'I've been here for years, dear. And now we're going to be neighbours!'

Mother smiled, but to me the smile didn't ring true. She didn't seem really pleased.

The old lady was rattling on. 'And is this Tess? My goodness, how she's grown.'

I smiled politely. I was used to people saying things like that.

After a bit more chit-chat, Mother said, 'Well, Edith, we'd better be going. Got a lot to do, you know.'

'Of course, dear. Let me know when you're moving in – you'll be at sixes and sevens, I dare say, so I'll bring round tea and some of my cakes.'

'Lovely.'

Then with more smiles and waves, me and Mother were walking back to the bus stop.

'She seems nice,' I said.

'She is,' said Mother, in a flat voice. 'As far as I know. I've seen her about Surrey Street for years. I didn't realise she lived here, though.'

I was puzzled. 'Is there something wrong with her?'

'Not with her.' Mother looked grim. 'It's her son.'

'Her son?'

'Wally.'

Wally. Light dawned.

'You mean that horrible man who comes round, the one who looks like Bluto and always stinks of booze?'

'That's the one. A nasty piece of work.'

We were at the bus stop now, and Mother leaned against it.

'All we need,' she said. 'Having that bastard next door.'

'You mean he goes round to see his mum a lot?'

'He'll be bloody well living there now,' said Mother.

This was really bad news. Wally had been off the scene for a while, and from what everybody said I gathered he was in real trouble. His wife had kicked him out, but Wally had gone round to her place and attacked her, raped her. His wife went to the police – that must have taken a lot of bottle. There was a new law just come in that meant a man couldn't rape his wife and get away with it, what the police called a domestic. Wally was found guilty, and went to prison, but there'd been an appeal and he got off. I thought of him staring right down my blouse, and shuddered. He was bad enough at the best of times. What would he be like now?

Anyway, I had to put off that thought for a while. We'd been given four weeks' notice to quit, so there was a lot to do, sorting stuff out. And getting rid of furniture. As Mother said, you can't put a quart in a pint pot, so the plush three-piece suite had to go, along with the bigger armchairs. We'd already got rid of the big old bed all of us kids used to share. We'd been in two small doubles for a while, us girls in one, the boys in the other. Those beds would just about fit in our new bedroom, with only enough space for a small chest of drawers. Life in our new home was going to be very cramped.

Meanwhile, 'Make the best of a bad job,' Mother declared. She was on the phone a lot, drumming up business, and for the next few weeks it was like Piccadilly Circus, as Bunny said. 'You'd know about that,' said Don. Men and girls traipsing up and down the stairs at all times. And Mother went on having parties, right up to the day before we left. The big front room looked a bit bare, but there was still somewhere to sit. Mother had bought a new three-piece suite, what she called cottage style, which looked quite smart. The settee and chairs had arms of polished wood, and they were upholstered with thick material in a blue and green pattern.

As Mother poured the drinks, she said, 'We're going out with a bang.' And everybody laughed.

So this last night was the same as usual. The party went with a swing, and every so often a man would come over to Mother and say goodbye, very polite. I knew what that meant. Before they left the house they'd be going upstairs with a girl, so Mother would know what was what, and who was with who. Later the girl would come back into the living room, then another man would say goodbye to Mother, and so it went. Mother never wrote anything down, as far as I could tell. She kept everything in her head.

Then it was moving day. One of Barbara's regular punters drove a big lorry, and we piled everything into it. Mother, Don and Barbara sat in the lorry, while I took the kids there by bus. By the time we arrived, Mother was organising everything. The front room looked quite nice already, and beds were being put back together upstairs. Going in and out with stuff from the lorry, I was keeping an eye out for Wally, but I only saw Edith. She was all smiles, and as she'd promised kept us supplied with tea and cakes. She mentioned that Wally was staying up north for a week or two. I heard her say to Mother, 'It's his wife's fault. I never liked her.' I remembered Mother saying to me that Edith just couldn't see what he was really like. 'She thinks the sun shines out of his arse – and I know for a fact he taps her for money, and knocks her around.' I couldn't understand that, her not seeing through him.

At last we were unpacked. Not counting that horrible time in Beulah Heights, this was the first night I hadn't slept in our old home, and it did feel strange. The next day was a Sunday, so we could have a bit of a rest, then it was back to work and school as usual. Us kids all had to go to school by bus now, as it was too far to walk. I didn't mind. It made a change. It just meant I had to get the kids up earlier.

We'd been there for about a week when I came home from school to see an ambulance in the road, right outside our house. I stood stock still for a moment, my heart thudding. Was it one of us? I hurried up the road, just as our front door opened, and two ambulance men came out with someone on a stretcher. It was Mother!

'Mum!' I cried. 'What's happened?'

Don was by her side.

'You go in, Tess, look after the kids. The baby's coming a bit early, that's all.'

I looked at Mother's face. Her eyes were tight shut, she was frowning, and very pale. She was breathing in short bursts.

'Go on, Tess,' said Don, pushing me towards the door. 'I'll be back later.'

I walked indoors, and saw the others sitting huddled in the front room. Everyone was quiet except Andy. He was sniffling.

'Don't worry,' I said. 'Mum's going to be all right. Who wants some tea?'

As I cut the sandwiches, I tried not to worry. I knew Mother was strong, but she had been working very hard. Had she overdone it? Was that why the baby was early? It wasn't due for another couple of months.

I couldn't wait for Don to get home.

'How is she?' I asked him the minute he opened the front door.

'Dunno yet. They're doing all they can. I'll go back tomorrow.'

I don't know how I got through the next day. I couldn't concentrate at school, and teachers had to say, 'Pay attention, Sandra!' more than once.

Then we got through the next day, and the next. When I came home from school, Don said, 'I'm just going to fetch your mammy. You wait here with the kids.'

That must mean Mother had had the baby, so why did he look so glum?

An hour or so later, we heard a car stop outside the house. I opened the door, and saw it was a taxi. Don helped Mother out, and I felt my heart would burst with joy that she was home again. But where was the baby?

Questions later, I thought. I'll put the kettle on.

When I came back from the kitchen, Mother was sitting in one of the cottage armchairs, Don hovering around her. The kids were piled on to the settee, gazing at her.

Mother sighed, and looked round at us. Her face was fixed, I couldn't tell what she was thinking.

'I had a baby boy,' she said. 'Your brother. We called him Maxwell.'

A boy! I'd hoped it would be a boy. This was exciting. 'Where is he, where is he?' I wanted to know straight away.

'In Croydon cemetery.'

What!

'Or he will be in a day or two,' she added.

We were all quiet. The only noise was the coal burning in the hearth.

Then Andy started sniffling again, and Mother levered herself up. Don went to help her but she shook off his arm. 'I'm going for a lie-down,' she said.

As she made her way up the narrow stairs, clutching the rail, I glanced over at Don. I'd never seen tears in a grown man's eyes before.

*   *   *

Mother was poorly for a few more days. I tried asking Don what had happened to the baby, what was wrong with him, but he brushed me off. 'Just too soon,' he said, turning his head away. And that was it.

Mother didn't talk much about the baby, though one day she said, 'I'm off to the cemetery.' She didn't ask anyone to go with her.

We were all feeling low. It was such an awful shame. And it was around now, of all times, that Wally had to put in an appearance.

It was a Saturday afternoon. I was coming back from the bagwash, carrying two full pillowcases. I was just wondering whether to use the line in the little back garden to air them, because there was never enough room on the old wooden clothes horse. I wished we could have one of those sheilas that Mother's friend Kitty had, a rack you could pull up and down. That kept the laundry out of the way. I wasn't taking Kitty's daughter Rosemary to school any more as we were too far away, but I'd kept in touch with Jenny, the girl who lived in the next-door flat, and was looking forward to going out with her again some day soon.

All this was going through my head when I realised Mother and Don were in the front garden, face to face with a big man on the other side of the fence. I stopped at the gate. You couldn't mistake Wally. He was saying, 'Well, this is all very handy, Grace, ain't it? A knocking shop on me own doorstep.' He laughed, but in an ugly way.

'You—' Don started, but Mother broke in.

'Yeah, Wally, we're neighbours now, and I want to keep things friendly. I don't want us to fall out.'

I remembered Mother saying how you had to handle Wally with kid gloves, soft-soap him so he wouldn't lose his rag. 'On a knife-edge, that bastard,' she said. 'You don't want to set him off on one.'

Now Wally just stood there grinning, great beefy arms folded across his chest. 'No, Grace, we don't wanna do that.'

'Look, Wally, you've had a hard time and I'm sorry for it. But we just want to go on without any trouble.'

But Wally was looking at me. 'Well, well, if it isn't little ginger nut,' he said. 'Not so little now!'

'Tess, take the washing indoors.' Mother's voice was sharp.

I hurried up the path, keeping my eyes straight ahead. I emptied the bags on to the kitchen table and started sorting out the washing. I heard the front door slam, followed by Don's voice.

'I'll have him, the fucking bastard. I'll swing for him.'

'No, you won't.' Mother's voice was still smooth. 'Remember, you don't tangle with him. He's a nutter. He'll stop at nothing if he's pushed.'

As it happened, it wasn't long before he was pushed, and Mother's life was on the line.

16

Warning Shots

I knew Mother was back to her old self when she walloped me one evening. I'd been out with Jenny again, and as usual wherever she went, boys appeared like magic. I so envied the way she didn't have to do anything, just smile and be pretty. We'd been to a dance in a local hall, and a couple of soldiers were chatting her up. One of them drew the short straw and was stuck with me. He was nice, though, didn't try anything, and offered to walk me home.

'Not right for a young girl like you to be out on her own,' he said, and that was thoughtful. In fact I hadn't noticed the time, and I was running late. He didn't take my arm or hold my hand, though, just practically marched me back home. Not very romantic! We'd just turned the corner when the figure of a woman came flying towards us. It was Mother. Oh no, I thought. Is she going to make a scene?

'What do you mean keeping my daughter out till this time?' she yelled at the soldier, stabbing a finger at him.

Poor bloke. 'I was just—' he started to say, but Mother wasn't having any of it.

'I don't care what you were "just",' she snapped. 'Now clear off or you'll feel the weight of my hand.'

Honestly, he was about a foot taller than Mother, dressed in uniform, but he seemed to shrink.

'Sorry,' he mumbled, then he turned and ran. Actually ran, back down the street. The last I saw of him by the light of the streetlamps were the soles of his big black boots going up and down as he pounded the pavement.

Now it was my turn.

'You! In!'

And for the second time that evening I was marched along. When we were indoors, Mother clumped me over the head and shoulders. 'When I tell you to be back by ten I mean ten!'

Then it was straight to bed, with my ears ringing. I never liked being hit, of course, but this was more like the old mother, the one with vim and vigour. And again, she was protecting me, she was caring for me. If she didn't care, I reasoned, she'd take no notice of how late I was.

Lying there in the dark, I hoped her bad temper would work itself out by the morning. But by this time it had become obvious she had other reasons for being in a bad mood. As she'd feared, business wasn't going well in the new place. Things had to be very discreet in this neck of the woods. Of all the neighbours, only old Edith next door had been friendly. The others seemed pretty stuck-up, and Mother didn't want them getting wind of her business. Barbara worked some of the time in the house, with carefully timed visitors, but Mother was sending her out more often. I supposed those visits included the dress designer and the old actor, and I thanked God it wasn't me. At the same time, I'd forced myself not to worry in advance. If Mother was going to send me out again, I'd worry about it when I knew. I'm not saying I actually forgot what had happened, far from it, but I found I could lock those memories away and just get on with life.

In any case, I did have more interesting things to think about. I was growing up, nearly fourteen when we moved, and Kath had joined me at secondary school. It wouldn't be long before it was Jess's turn. The days of being locked in were past, and we were all grateful for that. Nobody had to use the chamber pot now, thank God. We could all use the toilet in the bathroom any time we liked, as long as we were quiet. Mother still kept us in line, of course, but it just wasn't physically possible for her to keep up the rod of iron in that small house. In that respect at least life was looking up.

A few weeks later, Barbara disappeared again. She'd never got over her infatuation with Mother, and her resentment of Don. It wasn't so easy for her and Don to avoid each other in this small house, and there was many a sarky comment, till one day Barbara flew off the handle again, upped and went.

'I'm going to my mum's!' she shouted.

'Fuck off then!' Don yelled back.

Mother shook her head. 'I don't know why you rise to her,' she said. 'You know what she's like.'

Don just grunted, and Mother added, 'Maybe the sea air'll do her good.'

'Sea air?' I asked.

'Oh, her mum lives on the coast, down Brighton way,' said Mother. 'Mad old bat, she is. Like the old woman who lives in a shoe – loads of kids.'

I remembered Barbara telling me ages ago that her mum and dad had turned her out of house and home, so these days they must be on speaking terms again.

'The old girl knows which side her bread's buttered,' Mother added. 'Got her on the game herself in the first place, didn't she?'

I expected Mother to be out of sorts, her main source of income going down the drain, but to my surprise she seemed quite perky.

The next day she said, 'We've got a visitor this evening, Tess. Remember Jean?'

I remembered Jean all right, the gorgeous blonde at one of Mother's parties who had men eating out of her hand. For some reason she chose to go about with boring Claude. Wasn't it something to do with drugs?

Mother answered my thought. 'Well,' she said, 'I was right – saw that coming. Claude has got her well and truly hooked on the stuff, poor cow. So she needs to be earning, doesn't she, and where is she going to get that sort of money?' She grinned. 'She doesn't have to look far, does she?'

So that was it. Barbara out one door and Jean in at another. I was sorry if Jean was in trouble, but, as Mother explained, she didn't have much option now she'd got mixed up with drugs.

'It's me or the streets, isn't it?' she said. 'Imagine that lovely girl slumming it out there. Up against the wall in the dark? I don't think so. She's got class, that one. I'll look after her. I'll have punters, quality punters, queuing up round the block.'

As she was in a good mood I dared to make a joke. 'That'll give the neighbours something to look at.'

'Neighbours!' Mother snorted. 'Fuck 'em.'

It was quiet at home that evening. The kids were all in bed by eight, and Don was working a late shift at the factory. Me and Mother tidied up after tea and watched a bit of telly, waiting for Jean. It turned out Claude was with her, and just as well. I don't think she could have got here on her own. As she came in, I looked up at her and had a shock. Same lovely face, but the eyes were different. They looked black, just a ring of sapphire blue showing. And she sat slumped in a chair, with none of her old sparkle and charm. She hardly spoke, and then just a mumble.

If that's what drugs do to you, I'll never touch them, I said to myself. Mother had always been very strongly against them: 'Bring nothing but trouble, your soul's not your own,' she'd say. She was against excess drink, too. Anything, it seemed, that meant you weren't in control and other people could take advantage.

I sat quietly in a corner while Mother and Claude talked.

'I didn't mean for this to happen, Grace,' said Claude. 'Lovely kid, but she kept having a go at me. "Just a bit more, Claude, just a bit more." You know the sort of thing. Well, if I could sub her I would, but I can't and someone's gotta pay up.'

'Well, she'll be in good hands here,' said Mother. 'You know that.'

Claude nodded. 'Yeah, better with someone she knows.'

They went on chatting, till suddenly there was a tremendous knocking at the front door, and we all jumped. Except for Jean, who barely moved.

'Who the hell is that?' said Mother, getting up.

Before she reached the door we could hear who it was.

'Come on, Gracie, open up!'

I could hear Mother groan before she opened the door and said, 'Wally! What brings you here?'

Sure enough, it was horrible Wally from next door, much the worse for wear. He was an ugly customer at the best of

times, and even worse when he was drunk. He lurched past
Mother into the front room, and stood swaying in front of the
fireplace. He caught sight of Jean and grinned, showing his
big yellow teeth.

'Ah, ain't that a sight for sore eyes,' he said, slurring his
words. 'Thought I saw you comin' in, you little beauty, and I
wasn't wrong, was I? Come on, gel, knickers off!'

Claude was on his feet now, poking Wally in the chest.
'What d'you think you're doing, you big bastard? You're bang
out of order, leave her alone.'

Wally staggered back, shaking his head. 'Whaddya mean?
She's on the game, ain't she?'

'Not for the likes of you!' Claude's face was grim.

Wally spluttered. 'Of all the fuckin' nerve . . . You wait till
I get my 'ands on you, you little cunt.' And he came at Claude,
swiping a big meaty arm in the air.

Claude dodged out of the way, while Mother tried to
intervene. 'Calm down, calm down,' she said, hovering round
the two of them. But it was no use. They'd both got their wind
up and they weren't about to stand down. They went head to
head, yelling abuse, making threats, the whole thing snowbal-
ling, till Claude put the tin lid on it.

'If I see you in the street I'll fucking run you down where
you stand.'

It flashed through my mind that Claude really must be
losing his rag – he loved his old Lanchester, kept it polished up
like new.

Now Wally went, 'Run me down? Run me down? You
couldn't run me down in a fuckin' tank. You ain't got the bottle.'

'Oh no?' Claude came back. 'You get out there and I'll
show you who's got bottle!'

This was crazy, but Mother couldn't stop the pair of them charging out through the door. She followed, while I stood in the doorway, my heart thudding at the sudden shock of it all.

Wally planted his legs apart in the middle of the road, crooking his fingers at Claude, beckoning. 'Come on, big boy, bring it on, bring it on,' he sneered, as Claude wrenched the car door open. This was a deliberate jibe, as Wally was at least six inches taller than Claude and built like a brick shithouse, as Mother said.

'Stop it, Claude,' cried Mother. 'He won't move, he'll let you do it! For fuck's sake don't listen to him!'

But Claude ignored her, and started revving the engine.

Now Mother dashed up the street and clutched Wally's arm. 'Don't do this, Wally, you don't know him. He'll run you down, he will. He won't stop!'

Wally shook her off. 'Get out of it, Gracie, this is between us.'

Then the car leaped forward, straight at Wally. As I watched in horror, at the last minute Mother flung herself in front of him, pushing him out of the way. The car smashed into her and sent her sprawling over the road.

'Mum!' I screamed, running like mad to her. Claude had slammed on the brakes and was getting out of the car.

I got to her first, and crouched over her. 'Mum, oh, Mum!'

The car had caught her on the side, and her arm stuck out at a strange angle. I could see blood pooling on the road. She was still conscious, thank God. 'Get an ambulance,' she hissed, her teeth clenched.

Before I could move, Claude was beside me saying, 'Grace, Grace, I'm so sorry—'

'No time for that,' Mother cut in. She was breathing in

short bursts, frowning heavily. She must have been in such pain. 'For Christ's sake get out of here before the Old Bill arrive, and take Jean with you. We don't want the dozy cow blabbing. I'll do the talking – got that?'

Claude nodded and I dashed back to the house, overtaking Wally. He seemed to have shrunk into himself, quiet now. As he went through the gate of his mother's house, I ran indoors to the phone. I dialled 999, thinking, Go on, go on! The dial was so slow, going round three times. Why wasn't it 111? That'd be quicker. I gabbled into the phone and gave our address. I was aware of Claude coming back into the room and shaking Jean. 'Come on, come on! We gotta go!' Then they were off.

By the time I went back to Mother, the street was empty. Obviously none of the neighbours had wanted to get involved, all their doors firmly shut.

I tried to comfort Mother as she lay there. It broke my heart to see her bleeding and in pain, but she wasn't giving in. 'Don't you forget, Tess,' she said, her eyes glittering, 'not a word. I'll tell the Old Bill it was hit and run, you know nothing, all right?'

I nodded. Of course Mother would take care of everything. Even when she'd been hurt, she was in control.

It didn't take the ambulance long to arrive, followed by a police car, then it was all systems go. I knew I couldn't go with her to the hospital, not with the other kids by themselves in the house. I'd tell Don when he came in. What a shock he was going to get.

While I sat indoors waiting for Don to come home, I thought it all over. Why had Mother risked her life for Wally? My blood ran cold as I thought how she might have been killed. She couldn't stand him, she didn't owe him any favours. What was going on? Then I remembered she'd mentioned the Old Bill. I knew that if Wally was hurt, even slightly, he'd be after Claude with a shotgun, no question. If he was killed, there'd be hell to pay. Either way the police would be on the case, nosing around . . . and getting too close to Mother's business for comfort. That must be it. A savvy woman, my mother. She looked ahead.

Mother was taken to hospital. The minute I finished telling Don what had happened, he was off to Casualty in a flash. I waited up for him, anxious to know how Mother was.

'Her arm's badly broken,' Don told me. 'She took a hell of a bash, and there's damage all down one side. But thank Christ it wasn't any worse.'

That was one thing we could agree on.

'She'll be kept in for quite a while,' he said, 'weeks most likely. You kids'll have to go away again. I spoke to the lady almoner at the hospital and she said she'd arrange it.'

My heart sank, the spectre of Beulah Heights rising up in my mind.

'But I'm fourteen,' I protested. I'd had my birthday a month or two back – not that you'd know it. Mother didn't make a fuss about birthdays. 'I can look after them.'

'No, you can't,' said Don. 'I'll manage Andy, like last time. I can change my shifts. But the rest of you will have to go into care. No arguing.'

I went to bed with a heavy heart, dreading what was to come. It was bad enough that Mother was hurt, bad enough that she was away from us. To crown it all, we were being farmed out God knew where.

In the event, just to show you never can tell, the new home couldn't have been more different from what I feared. Instead of looking like something that belonged in Transylvania, it was a couple of low-rise buildings, all clean and modern. And no boot-faced Mrs Danvers here, just a bunch of nice motherly ladies who looked after us and the other kids in the home. We had our own beds, even our own rooms, all very bright and tidy. The only drawback was being separated again, boys in one block, girls in another. Poor Buddy had to sleep by himself, but Kath and Jess left their rooms and came into bed with me. That was more like home.

A couple of things stick in my memory. We discovered toothbrushes here. Mother was very hot on personal hygiene, but for some reason never bothered about teeth. The ladies tut-tutted and showed us how to use them. That was a novelty. There was another new experience too. We were taken to the seaside for the day. We'd never seen the sea, and to be honest didn't know what to make of it. We wandered about on the sands — it was somewhere on the south coast, Jaywick I think — and had ice creams. That was the best bit. It was a hot day, and nobody had thought to warn me about the sun. It certainly never occurred to me. Typical ginger, I have very fair freckly skin, and the back of my neck and my shoulders got horribly burned. I remember thinking, Well, if that's a holiday, I don't think much of it!

The time passed without much more trouble, and there was the routine of school as well to keep us occupied. Of course we all missed Mother like mad. It was such a relief to get home, about three weeks later, and see her look alive again. She was pretty much an invalid, though. Her arm was still in a sling, and she found it difficult to walk. She spent most of the time in bed, but just knowing she was there made all the difference. I was happy to do most of the chores, now we were all together again.

In fact it was almost like Christmas for a while. The market boys dropped round, with presents of fruit and flowers for her. They even had treats for us, sweets and chocolates and little toys. We had other visitors, too, from the old days at our first house. There was my old heart-throb Teddy, and Big Joe, as well as a very sorry-looking Claude. No sign of Wally, thank goodness.

'You must be raking it in, Gracie,' said Bunny. 'All those little white envelopes.'

He'd popped in one afternoon, full of concern for his old friend. He perched on a chair beside her bed, looking like a leprechaun, while I handed round cups of tea.

I knew what Bunny meant. I'd heard more than one visitor say to her, 'You won't go short, Grace. Don't you worry.'

'Your mum's quite the heroine, Tessie, isn't she?' Bunny said to me. Then he turned back to Mother.

'Seriously, Gracie, you've done yourself a favour. You were always in with the boys – now they can't do enough for you.'

Mother grinned. The bruising round her face was nearly gone, I was glad to see.

'Hope it lasts,' she said.

'Oh, milk it, duckie,' said Bunny. 'Milk it for all it's worth.'

As it happened, Mother did make the most of it. 'We could be on to a good thing here, Tess,' she said. 'Blood money, that's what it is.' And of course, with no Barbara, we would have been feeling the pinch otherwise. At the same time, Mother didn't have to exaggerate all that much. She'd been pretty badly injured, after all.

Wally was lying low. Mother might have kept him, and Claude, out of trouble, but there was no getting away from it: he was a loose cannon – nobody knew what he'd do next. More trouble was looming for all of us from the big klutz next door, no question, and he would change the course of our lives. But before then, I had trouble enough of my own to deal with.

17

Dream and Despair

The first few weeks of Mother's convalescence were a happy time for me. She was steadily getting better, though she put on a bit of an act when the boys came round. She managed to look pale and exhausted, speaking only in a whisper.

'A right tragedy queen, that's me,' she said with a laugh, and we did have a good giggle over it. We knew it couldn't go on for ever, but as Bunny said, milk it while you can.

I had another reason to be cheerful. Things were looking up on the romance front. One day Mother told me to have the evening off. 'Treat yourself,' she said, slipping me a half-crown. I was delighted. I hadn't been to the pictures by myself for ages, but there was a film playing in town I was very keen to see. So off I went, full of the joys of spring. Only to have them dashed when I got there and saw it was only a bloody cowboy film playing, and I can't stand westerns. I'd forgotten it was the day the film changed. Still, I was here now, and any film was better than no film, and anyway I'd have money left over for chocolate.

It was during those old Pearl and Dean adverts that seemed to go on for ever. A pair of long legs suddenly appeared on the seat beside me. Next minute this boy had hauled himself over and was sitting at my side. 'All right?' he said with a huge grin.

I'd never seen him before, but by the light from the screen I could see he was very good-looking. So I grinned back and said, 'Yeah.'

He started chatting me up and before long his arm went round me, and by the time the big picture started we were snogging. No Tit-up Tess this time, though. He didn't try it on, and I didn't encourage him.

After the picture ended, he said, 'I'll walk you home.'

My heart lifted. No other boy I'd met at the pictures had offered to do that. When I had a good look at him in the foyer I was even happier. Tall, dark and handsome, all right. Black curls, sparkling brown eyes, gorgeous smile, fit body. And with a strong Irish accent that made his words sound musical. Touch of the blarney all right. I was thrilled. It was the first time I'd ever truly fancied a boy. He made my heart beat faster, and I wanted to be with him, close to him. Now I realised what the other girls meant when they talked about fancying someone.

We chatted on the way home, and he told me about himself. His name was Sean, and he was eighteen, just four years older than me, which seemed about right. He'd left his home and parents in Ireland to work over here, and he had a job in a local hotel, where he lived in. At our gate he kissed me again, and said, 'See you next Saturday?'

Try and stop me, I thought, and we made a date. He'd been very respectful and hadn't taken any liberties. I went indoors all happy and smiley.

When Mother saw me she said, 'You look like the cat that got the cream.'

'I've met a boy . . .' I murmured through a rosy glow.

I remember so well how I felt that night. Just then I believed I actually had a chance of being like the other girls, a teenager in love as the pop songs said. Well, a girl can dream . . .

It was a couple of days later. I'd been thinking about Sean, reliving our meeting and our kissing, wishing the time away till Saturday. I'd been chatting to Mother, full of myself, getting the tea ready in the kitchen, and at first didn't notice that she wasn't saying anything back, not even teasing me.

I stopped to draw breath and when I turned to her, sitting on one of the wooden chairs, my heart almost stopped. She'd been getting stronger, brighter, but now her face was closed, her mouth turned down. She usually sat upright, always keeping a straight back, but now she was slumping, as if all the stuffing had been knocked out of her.

'Mum? What's up? What's the matter?'

She said nothing, just turned her face away from me.

I felt a sinking sensation in my stomach. I asked again, 'Mum, what is it? Tell me!'

Now she turned her head to face me, and sighed heavily. 'Oh, Tess . . .' Her voice trailed away.

Now I was really worried. Was she ill? All my concern was for her.

She made an effort to sit up, cradling her bad arm in the other. 'Shut the door, will you?' she said.

I went over to the door and did as she asked, cutting off the noise of the telly the kids were watching in the front room.

I sat on the other side of the table, waiting, my heart thudding. I was nervous, my happy mood all gone like a puff of smoke. I'd realised by now that the only time Mother sat me down and looked serious, taking me into her confidence, was when she was in a jam, like when Barbara left and I had to fill in.

'It's like this,' she started. 'You know the business has gone down the drain since we came here. With Barbara, we just about kept afloat, but then she buggered off. If I hadn't been getting money from the boys, we would have gone under. As it is, that money's drying up now – I can't keep up my invalid act for ever. They're not stupid.'

No, I thought, they're not stupid.

Mother cut to the chase. 'It's bad enough forking out for all the usual stuff,' she said. 'You know Don's wages don't go anywhere. And now I've got a debt to pay. It's been hanging over my head for ages, and now I've got to cough up, or else.'

I couldn't think of anything to say.

She went on. 'You've been such a help, Tess, a real treasure. I know you'll understand. Can you do one last thing for me, as a special favour? One of our little secrets?'

I just sat there and looked at her. She didn't quite meet my eyes.

'One last time and that'll be it. You're such a good girl, Tess. You don't know how much it means to me to know I can rely on you.'

I swallowed hard. I couldn't bring myself to say anything – but what could I say? For all that my heart was sinking with dread, it didn't enter my head to refuse her. The way I see it now, it was like it had always been, the way she controlled me. Not just being scared of good hidings, but something much deeper, something that had entered the heart of me. All those years of wanting to please her, being in debt to her, longing for her approval and her love. And we'd been getting along so well recently, we were like a team. I couldn't possibly let her down.

I nodded, feeling the tears prick my eyes.

Mother must have been holding her breath, as she let it out with a 'Phew!'

She was all smiles. 'It won't be so bad,' she said. 'You'll see.'

Then I did think of something to say. 'What would happen if you didn't have the money?'

Mother's smile vanished. 'You don't want to know,' she said, frowning. 'There's some very nasty people out there, I can tell you.'

'Like Wally?' I asked.

'Worse than Wally,' Mother said. 'They really know how to hurt people. They do things.'

Hurt people? Do things? My blood ran cold. Nothing should hurt Mother, ever again.

She was smiling once more. 'So tell me about this boy . . .'

I took a sickie from school on Friday, the day before my date with Sean. At least I had that to look forward to. That was how to deal with the prospect of something bad, I'd learned. Don't agonise about it before it happens, just concentrate on something pleasant.

This time was different right from the start. I'd asked Mother, 'Are we getting a taxi?'

And she immediately said, 'Oh, I'm not going.'

'You're not going? You're not coming with me?' There were butterflies in my stomach already. They now started flapping their wings with a vengeance.

'I'm not really up to it, love,' said Mother, passing a hand over her forehead.

Did she mean it? Was she acting again? Surely not.

'Anyway,' she added, 'you're so grown up, you don't need me there.'

I wasn't so sure. Even though Mother had done her vanishing act at the critical time – 'Just popping out for some cigarettes' – at least she was somewhere near, she'd be coming back for me.

'Then how do I get there?' I asked, with a shake in my voice.

'Don't you worry. He's coming to pick you up and take you to his gaff.'

'Where does he live?' I really meant, How far away is it? How far away will I be from you?

'London – Kensington. Posh area, you know. You'll be getting the train there and back.'

So I had to travel with him too. At least while we were on public transport he couldn't do anything, could he? I sat down to wait, my heart in my mouth.

All too soon there was a knock on the door, and Mother was waving me off with her good arm as I walked down the street with this strange man.

'See you later,' she called after me.

When the man arrived I'd hardly looked at him. He didn't make much impression either way: he was a nondescript sort of man, tall, quite well dressed. He didn't speak as we walked to the station. As he bought the tickets I had a closer look at him, but there still wasn't a lot to remark on. Sandy-coloured hair, thinning on top, round glasses. Not a man you'd pick out in a crowd.

The journey to Victoria seemed endless. Part of me wished it really would go on for ever, while part of me wanted everything over and done with as soon as possible. I sat next to the window and he sat next to me. Again, he didn't speak, just looked at me. A couple of times he patted my knee, and pushed his leg against mine. I kept my eyes fixed on the window, hardly noticing the scenery going by. All kinds of thoughts were running through my mind, none of them good. Here I was alone with a stranger, going miles and miles away to goodness knows where for goodness knows what. What if he was taking me away and I'd never get home again?

Then there was the tube ride. I'd never been on a tube before and I found it frightening – noisy, smelly and crowded. I hated the thought of being underground, felt I was suffocating. I couldn't have been more relieved when we got out at Kensington and hit the fresh air – well, as fresh as London air can ever be. It was a short walk to his home. At least, I supposed it was where he lived. It was a small flat in a new block, and like him quite nondescript. The rooms I saw didn't look at all homely; they seemed just to have basic furniture. Nothing looked poor or shabby or dirty, just plain and kind of skimpy.

He showed me into a room that had a bed in it. There was nothing else to make it a bedroom, no wardrobe or chest of drawers or anything, but obviously enough for this man's purpose. And so I paid Mother's debt. That's what I kept thinking of, how I was saving her from being hurt. That, and that I would see Sean next day. Not long now.

He knew Mother wouldn't be calling for me, so he took his time. He told me to take off my clothes, one bit at a time, slowly. When I was naked, he touched me all over, rubbing, squeezing, pushing a finger in me till I cried out. He tried to get me to put my mouth over him, but somehow I found the strength to refuse, to jerk my head away when he forced it down. But he had his other amusements. After what seemed an eternity came the photographs, and I posed as he directed.

And then it was over. My hands were shaking as I put my clothes back on. He seemed quite matter-of-fact, locking the door behind us as we left. We took the chaotic tube again. I vowed then and there never to go on the tube again, and I haven't to this day. Next, we were on the train to Croydon. Again he didn't speak, just sat very close to me. I could feel his eyes on me, travelling up and down my body, so again I stared out of the window, my eyes blurred with tears so I couldn't see much. I felt sick to my stomach. At the time I didn't know the right word for what he did to me. I'd know it later. He defiled me.

There was another idea too, stirring in my mind. A seed of something. This is too much, I said to myself. Too much, even for Mother. She could never have known how bad it was going to be. Then I had a thought that shocked me with its suddenness. Did she know? Did she know exactly and still send me out with him? Was it arranged? No, I couldn't believe that she'd let this happen. But the doubt was there now, and my mind whirled round as fast as the train wheels.

We got out at West Croydon and walked along past the shops. It had started raining. Just as we got to Woolworths, he stopped and spoke.

'I'd like to get you a present,' he said, smiling. His teeth were small for a man. 'Pop in here and choose anything you want, anything at all.'

I didn't want any present, I wanted nothing from this man. Then I thought, Maybe I can get something for Mother. Among the mad mix of feelings churning around in my head

I felt a twinge of guilt, that I was doubting her. I was disloyal. I'd get her something to make up for it. So we went in and on a counter near the door I spotted some jewellery. They were just bringing out these sets, matching necklace, earrings and bracelet. Complete junk, of course, but pretty. I chose a yellow set for Mother; she liked yellow. I remember it cost 12s 6d in old money. I made a point of telling the man it was for my mother, because I didn't want him to think I wanted anything he could give me.

We walked the rest of the way in silence. When Mother opened the door I walked into the kitchen and sat down at the table. The kids must have all been in bed by now, and there was no sign of Don.

I heard Mother saying goodbye to the man, then she came into the kitchen. She shut the door and sat down at the table.

'All right?' she said.

What could I say? I just nodded, my throat tight. Then I said, 'I got you a present.'

'A present? Oh, Tess, you shouldn't have.'

She took the bag from me and glanced inside it. 'Lovely,' she said. 'You are kind. I won't forget this, you know. You've just about saved my life.'

Then I couldn't help it. I put my head down on the table and I broke down. My whole self started crying. Great heaving sobs, tears streaming from my eyes as if I could wash that man away, wash the memory away. I felt I was drowning in a deep pit.

Well, crying has to stop some time, and I gradually cried myself out. I couldn't look at Mother, but I knew she'd been sitting there the whole time.

When I grew quiet, and my breathing had settled down. I made an effort and lifted my head.

'Oh, Mum,' I said, 'it was awful. Awful. I'm not ever going to do that again.' As I said those words I knew I meant it. Come hell or high water, I'd never do it again, and Mother had to know. I'd been a little worm, and I was turning.

'Of course you won't, darling.' Mother's voice was low, soothing. 'Now I'll put the kettle on and make you a nice cup of tea.'

It didn't occur to me at the time, but later, when I'd had more experience of life and men, I wondered how Mother had known I wouldn't actually be raped. I think I've worked out why she made the 'no penetration' rule in the first place. There'd be evidence, physical evidence. Even if the man had used a condom, like with her girls, I might have been injured. Or so traumatised that I couldn't keep our little secret, then all hell would have broken loose. Even so, the man might have assured her he wouldn't go all the way, but how did she know? How could she believe him? Did she have something on him? Blackmail? After all, a man in the height of passion might not have the best memory in the world . . . That man in Kensington had a young virgin naked in his room. He, more than any of the other men, could have raped me, even killed me. As it is, I must have been lucky.

18

The Writing on the Wall

I hardly slept that night. I lay in bed with my back to Kath, holding myself rigid. I tried not to think of what had happened, but the memory kept sweeping back. I didn't have any more tears left to cry, though, so at least I didn't disturb the other kids.

Push it away, push it away, I kept telling myself. You got through the other times, nobody died, you'll get through this. You know you will. Mother said you'll never have to do it again, so it's over. If there was one thing I clung to, it was that – it was over. I was still trying to sort it out in my head, that I was going to stand my ground. If Mother ever changed her mind and said I had to go out, I'd say no.

The thought made me catch my breath. I don't think I'd ever disobeyed Mother in my whole life till then. I'd annoyed her, of course, was slow to do things or even done the wrong thing, but I'd never actually stood up to her and said, 'No, I won't.' I prayed I'd never lose my resolve. I think now that what gave me strength wasn't just the awfulness of what happened. It was the thought of Sean. As soon as we'd met, I knew he was going to mean a lot to me. If he ever found out what I'd done, he'd be disgusted, think I was dirty. I'd stick to my guns for him if not for me.

The other thought, though – that Mother might actually know what the men did – I couldn't get my head round. I'd understood why I had to help, that it was her business, that I was saving everyone's bacon. But could she really not have known what was on the menu for those punters? More doubts came crowding into my mind. Was there really no other way she could have raised money? Didn't the local boys see her right after she was knocked down? What did other hard-up mothers do?

I think of myself now as I was then, a teenager on the point of growing up, full of confusion. Desperate not to fall out with Mother, but desperate never to be exposed like that again . . . I had a glimmering of an idea how Mother worked on me. I realised that sometimes she was nice, sometimes she was nasty – and that she was nicest when I had to do something especially nasty. Or afterwards, like the morning after I'd gone to London.

'Out with your young man tonight, Tess?' she asked me as I got the breakfast ready. She looked and sounded cheery, as if she didn't have a care in the world.

I could only nod, and go on slicing the bread.

'Why don't I curl your hair up for you?' Mother went on. 'It always looks nice.'

She hadn't done that for ages, not since I'd first helped at one of her parties. Now I was torn. On the one hand I felt I couldn't just act normally with Mother. On the other hand, I was really looking forward to going out with Sean; he'd been the one bright spot on the horizon, and I wanted to look my best. In the end, vanity won.

'Yeah, thanks,' I said.

Later that day, as Mother rolled my damp hair in strips of rag, neither of us said anything about the previous day. Not the man calling for me, my trip to London and back, my outburst last night – nothing. We just chatted about this and that, nothing special. Though when I was dressed up and she'd combed out my curls, she did put her head on one side, and say, 'Well, if you don't look like a film star yourself!'

I knew that was just old flannel. Usually Mother was sarky about the way I looked, said I was no oil painting, what could anyone see in me? So she was obviously trying to butter me up. And sucker that I was, it worked. I couldn't help smiling at the thought. At the same time, though, I was a bundle of nerves, convinced that Sean wouldn't turn up. He could have been having me on, and then I'd be shown up as a fool in front of everyone. And behind this was the thought of Mother. What if she managed to put her oar in? What if Sean could disappear just as Victor had?

When Sean knocked on the door and I opened it, I was speechless with relief. I just beamed at him, thinking, Wow! He's here! He must think a lot of me if he's walked all the way from the middle of Croydon. He seemed pleased to see me again, and we walked hand in hand to the Odeon. I can't remember what the film was – a comedy, I think, maybe one of the St Trinian's. But it didn't matter. What did matter was that I was going out with a lovely boy, a breath of fresh air and very fanciable to boot. He really seemed to like me, and didn't take any liberties. I was in heaven. It wasn't too hard to put yesterday's hell behind me.

After that, me and Sean went on quite a few dates, usually to the pictures. I just couldn't think what he saw in me. He was so handsome, so kind, he could have had his pick of the girls. As for me, my slogan could have been, 'I might not be pretty, but I'm faithful!' So I kept my fingers crossed. He was great company, a wonderful talker, and I really felt alive with him. I made the best of our times together. He was so gorgeous, I could feel myself becoming something like aroused for the first time. Nothing more than petting in the back row, though.

We went out two or three times a week. Mother never tried to stop me, though I was on edge thinking she might. Maybe she was still keeping me sweet. In any case, after a few weeks she had something else to think about: Barbara suddenly turned up.

Nobody had heard from her for months. Of course I had been wishing with all my heart that she'd come back and let me off the hook. So when I came home from school one afternoon and there she was, sitting at the kitchen table with a fag and a cup of tea, I could say a friendly hello and mean it. As before, there weren't great ructions, and she seemed to slip back into our lives as if she'd never been away. She and Don were still pretty snappy with each other, but more than once I heard Mother keeping the peace.

'Look, the pair of you,' she'd say. 'We've got to make this work. We'll be up shit creek without a paddle if we don't.'

I gathered this meant Barbara going out to places more and more, rather than having punters visit the house. Mother was still nervous about any of the snotty neighbours cottoning on and squealing to the police. Meanwhile, I was keeping my guard up where Mother was concerned. Helping round the house as usual, of course, and seeing to the kids, running any errand she wanted. But just let her mention one word about little secrets . . . I'd grit my teeth and tell her straight, I swore I would.

As it happened, I never had to confront Mother. Somebody else came back into our lives and turned us all upside-down.

Wally.

Nobody knew where he'd been since the incident with Claude that had put Mother in hospital. And frankly, nobody cared. He'd managed to piss off everyone. 'You can't trust him, he's out of order,' everybody said. And I remembered how much Mother's girls had hated him when he visited them, he was too violent. Bad news all round. But as I say, he'd been lying low for months, so he was the last person we expected when one Sunday night there was a loud knock at the door. We were all having a quiet night in, watching telly, even Barbara. Now we jumped, as a voice outside roared, 'Open up! I know you're in there, yer fuckers!'

Don half rose from his armchair, but Mother said quickly, 'I'll get it.'

In an instant she was opening the door, trying a friendly approach. 'Wally!' she said. 'Long time no see.'

He barged straight past her and stood in the middle of the room, swaying. Drunk as usual. He glared round at us all.

'Kids, go upstairs,' said Mother sharply. The boys whizzed out, frightened by this apparition, closely followed by Kath and Jess. I was following them when to my horror Wally grabbed my arm.

'Not so fast,' he slurred. 'You an' me can 'ave a very nice time. That's what you're 'ere for, ain't it?' And he pushed his face close to mine, breathing stinking fumes over me, slobbering, pawing me.

My heart grew cold. What did he mean? Did he know what I'd done? Did everybody?

'What! What do you think you're doing, Wally?' yelled my mother, as shocked as I'd ever seen her. She tried to pull him off me, while Barbara – little Barbara – actually grabbed hold of his arm and said, 'She's just a kid, Wally. If you want some, have me.'

Wally looked her up and down, sneering. 'You? I don't want you. You're old meat. I want fresh meat.' And he turned back to me.

I was paralysed with fright. For an instant nobody said a word.

Then Don marched up to him and poked him in the chest. 'Leave her alone, you bastard!' he spat out. 'Leave us all alone. Get the fuck out of here if you know what's good for you!'

Wally staggered back, so astonished he looked almost funny. Then he looked not so funny. You could practically feel the menace coming off him in waves.

'You—' He jabbed a finger at Don. 'Outside. Now. I am gonna fuckin' do you, you little piece of dago shit.'

Don turned on his heel, out into the front garden, and Wally stumbled after him. They squared up. Mother, Barbara and I stood in the doorway, goggling, and fearful, to tell the truth. Don was just a little bloke, even if he was pretty fit, and next to him Wally looked like a giant, rough and tough. What chance could Don have?

But Don was a hero that night. He danced round Wally like a boxer, jabbing him with his fists, the old one-two, working so fast that Wally, slow-witted and slow-moving, could hardly touch him. Before long Wally was on his knees, shaking his head. He must have wondered what the hell had hit him.

The noise had brought our next-door neighbour out, old Edith. As usual, the other neighbours kept their front doors firmly shut. But Edith sailed to her son's rescue. 'Stop it, you!' she shouted at Don, all four foot ten of her.

Don stepped back, well satisfied. Edith was urging Wally to stand up, clucking over him like an old mother hen. He managed to get on his feet, staggering. He glared at Don.

'I'll 'ave you, you little prick. I'll 'ave you,' he said, his voice dripping with poison.

Then he shuffled through his mother's front gate, shaking off her protective arm. Her front door closed, and the drama was over.

Back indoors, Don said, 'I need a drink,' and for once Mother didn't object.

As for me, I marvelled at the man. David and Goliath, like out of the Bible. And he'd never even liked me! But I suppose it was more the whole family he was defending, not just me. I was still worried by what Wally had said, about that was what I was here for. Did he know something, or was he just chancing his arm? Whatever, we all knew we'd made an enemy that night.

The very next day, I'd been to the pictures after school with Sean, and he walked me home as usual. I was just telling him about the to-do the previous evening as we turned the corner. Then I could see something was up. There was a lorry parked outside our house, and heaps of stuff all over the pavement, lit up by the streetlamps. Odds and ends of furniture, along with bags and suitcases. Mother, Don and Barbara were busy running in and out of the lorry, filling it up. A man was helping them, and as I got closer I recognised him. He was Alf, Barbara's regular, the driver who'd helped us move from our old place. What the hell was going on?

As I came up to the gate Mother saw me and said, 'Hurry up, we haven't got much time.'

'What?'

'Don't stand there gawping – go inside and pack your things. And tell the kids to hurry up.'

'What?'

'You deaf or something? Come on – we're going.'

'Going where?'

'We're moving,' said Mother.

'Moving? Where?' I asked.

'Oh, for God's sake,' Mother snapped. Then she spoke in a softer voice. 'We're going to live at the seaside. You'll like that, won't you?'

'But why?' I asked. It had flashed into my mind that this was one of Mother's tricks, just to split up me and Sean. 'And how long are we going for?'

Mother had run out of patience. 'Never you mind why,' she said. 'Just get a move on.' Then she added, 'And we're not coming back.'

Sean's arm had tightened round my waist when Mother first spoke. Now he went up to her and said, 'Can I come with you?'

That stopped Mother.

'Come with us?'

'Yes,' said Sean. 'I want to be with Tess.'

He wanted to be with me! He'd drop everything and come with me? I forgot the shock of the news and my heart swelled with happiness.

Mother looked him up and down, and seemed to come to an instant decision. 'You can come if you like,' she said, 'but you'd better be quick about it.'

'Half an hour,' said Sean. 'Give me half an hour. I'll run back to the hotel, grab my stuff and tell them I'm off.'

And then he was pelting back down the street, my mother yelling after him, 'Half an hour, boy, not a second more!'

I pitched in with the rest of them, fetching and carrying, clearing out the house – though not of everything. 'Just stuff we can carry easily,' Mother ordered, ramming clothes into a pillowcase.

'What about the beds and chests of drawers?' I asked.

'Oh, bugger them. It's only furniture. If we don't get out of here soon we'll have coffins for furniture.'

What! Then I found out why it was panic stations. Mother had got a message on the grapevine that Wally was on the warpath, and was out scouting for a shotgun. 'And he'd use it all right,' said Mother.

Now I think Mother had guessed there'd be a showdown with Wally one day. She must have been planning our move for a while. At the time, I was thinking of nothing except that Sean wanted to be with me, saying over and over in my head, Come on, Sean, come on. Don't be late. Mother means it, she won't wait.

'He's late,' Mother declared. 'We'll go without him.'

'It's not been half an hour yet,' I cried. 'You said half an hour, it's only been twenty minutes!'

My heart was in my mouth, and I kept running up and down the street, hoping to see him coming. And I did. He just made it, gasping with the effort, clutching an old rucksack with all his worldly possessions.

'Come on! Come on, Sean!' I urged him.

A last look round the house, and the front door was slammed shut, the key posted in through the letterbox. A mad scramble into the lorry, Mother, Don and Barbara squashed into the front bench seat with Alf the driver, and the rest of us – Sean, me and the kids – wedged in at the back among all the stuff.

And in the best tradition of moonlight flits, we drove off through the night to a new life.

19

What Next?

'Put your foot down, Alf!'

Those were the last words I heard Mother say before the big back doors of the lorry clanged shut on us kids, along with Sean. Alf was obviously happy to oblige. We zoomed down our road, screeched round the corner and we were off. Maybe he felt like I did, like we were all in a film, and he saw himself as the getaway driver after a big bank job. It all seemed so unreal. That mad scramble to pack up our stuff, the dread that Wally would turn up any minute with a shooter, my anxiety that Sean would miss the boat – or rather lorry. One minute life was chugging along as normal, the next we were hightailing it out of town like a bat out of hell, us kids crammed together among all our belongings without so much as a chink of light to relieve the pitch dark.

If it was a film, I thought, me and Sean would be the romantic interest. As we sat against some piled-up bags, his arm round me, my head on his shoulder, we were young lovers eloping at the dead of night, getting away from anyone and everyone who would stand in our way. To me, at that time, it was like the outside world didn't exist. We were in a place of our own, where no one could get to us, our whole lives ahead of us. No matter that our magic carpet was a clapped-out old lorry and the kids were going, 'Ow!' every time it hit a bump in the road . . .

It's been all of fifty years since that moonlight flit, but I remember it all, how I felt, what I hoped. Like so much of what happened to me when I was young, it's burned into my mind – and at least this memory is a good one, a little patch of magic. Not like those other times, when Mother sent me out, or when she rejected me. All the time I've been going over and over my early life, combing through my childhood, I've been searching for clues, like some forensic scientist on telly, trying to piece together what happened, and why. And this means trying to understand Mother, to make sense of what she did, what she allowed to happen to me. I have a very good reason for this. I so wish she hadn't done it. With all my heart I wish things had been different, my life had been different. If I can get to grips with Mother, then maybe I can sort things out, let them rest.

Some people might say, when they look back over their lives, 'I've no regrets. I wouldn't change anything about my life.' I've heard them say it, usually with a joke along the lines of 'I'd still do all the bad things I did – but sooner!' Not me. I'm not proud of the life I've led. It's pointless saying it, I know, but I wish I could turn the clock back. I'd try to lead a decent life, an honest life, one where I wasn't used and where I didn't use anyone. Because I did go on to use people. I grew up in a brothel, and I ended up being a madam myself. I grew up with a mother who fenced bent gear, and I became a thief myself, hoisting from shops.

Is it any excuse to say I didn't have much of a chance? That when I was growing up, there could have been two signposts pointing to my later life, one marked 'Vice' and one marked 'Petty crime'? I hope so. I'd be easier in my mind now.

But that's all in hindsight, isn't it? At the time, I just took life as it came. Mother ruled the roost, what she said went, and that was it. I might have my small rebellion up my sleeve – that I would never, repeat never, be sent out to those men again – but for a long while I didn't know whether I'd have the strength to resist her. After all, she'd been my sun and my moon all my life. I loved her with the blindness of a child who needs a mother's love, and she'd ground into me the enormous debt I owed her – my very existence. And she'd shown me love back, or something like it, but only now and then, on her terms. Just when I felt I could feel secure with her, she slapped me away, threw me into despair. There's nothing like being kept on tenterhooks to keep your need sharp. It's like dying of thirst in the desert. You think your time is up, then someone dribbles water into your mouth. You revive, take heart, and are thankful to your rescuer. Then you go to take another drink, but they keep back the water. The water you need, to live. You're desperate, and then they relent and give you another dribble, and you're so grateful.

That set a pattern for the rest of my life. I always hoped for the best, but wasn't too surprised when I got the worst.

I'll say this for Mother – she was a real grafter. She didn't sit around moaning when things went wrong. She set to with a will. I realise now that leaving Croydon must have been a tremendous wrench, a leap into the unknown, but Mother rose to the challenge. She built a new life for us, of a sort.

That new life started with a familiar mix of up and down. The first night we spent in a small hotel, in what turned out to be Brighton. I'd heard of Brighton, but didn't know much about it – just that it had a reputation as a place for dirty weekends. People would snigger about it, talk about husbands and wives playing away. Us kids thought the hotel was very swish, a bed each and a cooked breakfast next morning. I heard Mother grumbling about Alf: 'Got an all-nighter for nothing!' she said. So she must have paid for a room for him and Barbara as well. The rest of us squeezed into a couple of other rooms, Don and the boys in one, Mother and us girls in the other. Sean was in with the boys, sleeping on the floor – no hanky-panky for us.

The next night, we were definitely slumming it. We drove off to Barbara's mother's place, which was in Seaford, a way up the coast. It was a big wooden house, so ramshackle it looked as if it would slide down a slope to the beach. Barbara's mother, Iris, was a caution. A tiny, dumpy woman, almost completely round, like an apple. And in fact she was always eating apples, chewing them with ill-fitting dentures that slipped up and down. She had jet-black hair that she curled with hot metal skewers. There was always a smell of burning about her.

'She's not the full shilling and no mistake,' said Mother. And I guess she was right. Iris didn't seem to be all there, despite the fact she had a brood of little kids. I remembered what Mother had said about the old woman who lived in a shoe. That was Iris all right: she never seemed to know what to do.

It was soon obvious that there was no question of staying in Seaford. 'Dead and alive hole,' said Mother. She'd been taking Barbara round and about, trying to hook punters, but no dice. And it was winter – no tourists around. Nothing for it but to take the train to Brighton and work the streets there. This was more successful, but what with the fares and the hotel bills, couldn't be a long-term solution. Meanwhile, the eight of us – Mother, Don, me and the kids as well as Sean – were squashed into one spare room, the family lying top to toe in a double bed and Sean dossing on the floor. It was bloody freezing, that January. We'd brought some blankets with us, but not enough. At one point we resorted to using another mattress on top of us for extra warmth.

God, that place was the pits. And the town itself was just as Mother said, dead and alive, nothing to do. After an uncomfortable couple of weeks, Mother had sorted things out. She'd got the basement flat of a big old house in Brighton town, drummed up custom for Barbara, sent Don off to get a job, arranged new schools for us kids. She was a dynamo when she had to be.

I was only at school for a few months, turning fifteen in May 1958 and leaving at the end of term. My heart wasn't in it; the only thing I really remember is feeling so proud when Sean came to meet me after school, and the other girls looking on and being jealous. That was such a novelty for me, and I made the most of it. At the back of my mind, I knew it couldn't last. Every day I expected Sean to leave me.

At least he never got to know about Mother's business. He was an honest boy, raised by strict Catholic parents, and I don't think he would have stayed around at all if he'd sussed it out. He wouldn't have noticed anything in our last place in Croydon, as Mother had to be very discreet. For all he knew, we lived on Don's wages, and had to do a moonlight because we were hard up and had got behind with the rent. And running away from a landlord didn't count as a sin! He didn't see anything of Mother's business in Brighton, either, as he soon got himself a job as a trainee chef in a hotel, and lived in. We met whenever we could, going to dances and the pictures, and saw ourselves as teenagers in love.

It was after I got a job myself that the crunch came.

I'd landed a job as a trainee hairdresser, in quite a classy salon. I'd always liked messing about with hair, and I was thrilled when I got it. I felt good about myself for the first time. It seemed a chance to strike out on my own, in a proper job, like other girls. It never crossed my mind that I'd ever be involved in Mother's business. I'd got used to the idea of it, sure, took the way of life for granted and had been friendly with a lot of her girls – they were usually perfectly nice. But I just knew I could never have anything to do with it.

The job paid peanuts, and out of my wages I was supposed to buy my own equipment, like combs and scissors and an overall. I asked Mother to help out, but she refused. 'You should be helping me out now you're earning,' was her way of looking at it.

Anyway, while I was eking out a living at the salon, I'd got friendly with other girls. In fact I was building up a social life of sorts. I seemed to make friends quite easily, always anxious to please, and I never minded making myself the butt of my own jokes. Fat and jolly going together. I got friendly with a girl called Dorothy, a smart blonde with a curvy figure. I was too naïve to realise it at the time, but she was what I'd later call loose. Not a pro, just a good-time girl. And through me she met Sean . . .

Well, I don't know how Sean had managed to keep himself in check with me; we did go in for pretty heavy petting, as it used to be called, though never anything like the full monty.

Oddly enough, I was tempted myself, but would never have dared take the plunge. Then one day I thought I'd surprise Sean after work and drop round to his room. When I knocked on the door he answered, and in an instant my dreams came tumbling down. He was just wearing underpants, and I could see beyond him that there was a blonde girl in his bed. Dorothy. Obviously any Catholic scruples only went so far.

'Tess, I can explain—' he started to say.

But I turned on my heel without a word and walked home. I was crushed, no doubt about it. But even as the tears sprang from my eyes I was thinking, I knew it. What else could I expect? No one would love me enough to stay with me for ever. I simply had to accept that people would let me down. I didn't deserve any better.

It didn't stop me trying again, though. Hope springs eternal, I suppose.

By now Mother was building up her business, and just like in Croydon we lived two lives. One ordinary and legit, with the younger kids going to school and Don and me working, the other on the wrong side of the law. Mother had recruited a couple of new girls – I say girls, but they were full-grown women. And in the case of Big Bertha, very full grown. She was enormous, fat as a barrel, and made me look like a sylph. She had a beautiful complexion, clear and glowing, and a mass of blonde hair coiled round her head in an elaborate pattern. The men liked her, and did she like them! She was especially partial to sailors. If anyone was going to Portsmouth, she'd say, 'Bring me back a matelot.' Man-mad, she was. Now and then Mother would grumble about her: 'She'll do it for nothing, that one.' Bertha always seemed to be knocking kids out – well, at least three. I know for a fact she had a couple of abortions, and from what I could gather, Mother had a hand in them. Really dodgy ground, there, and highly illegal in those days, of course. At the time I only heard whispers, but later Mother talked about her particular method, a strong douche with soapy water. It must have been so dangerous – Bertha was lucky to survive. But nothing seemed to slow her down.

I also heard something about those kids who survived. Apparently Bertha sold them to a woman who wanted them. I'd never heard the like. I knew children went into care, of course, were even adopted by new parents. But whoever heard of selling kids? I was learning how other people lived, all right.

The other recruit was Scotch Terry, with sandy colouring, as skinny as Bertha was fat and also a hit with the men, despite a jagged scar down one side of her face where a punter had glassed her. Mother had picked up both women in the Belvedere, a pub on the seafront very popular with working girls. And also, I was later to find out, gay men and women. In fact the whole of Brighton was quite a hotbed of what you could call underground life, people outside the mainstream of society. These were the bad old days, when homosexuality was still a crime – at least, for men. Brighton had a network of bars and clubs where gays of both sexes were welcome, could feel safe. This was a bonus for Bunny, Mother's camp old friend from Croydon, who came down a few months after us and got himself a room. Like before, he was always on hand to run errands for Mother. Talking of old friends, Ruby and Betty followed us too, and soon Mother was organising Ruby's work.

One of Mother's new friends was called Bobbie, a small, smart woman in her fifties, with a face like leather. She must have spent a lot of time in the sun. She was living nearby with an Irishman called Billy, and one day they came round with his brother, Pat. He reminded me of my old heart-throb Teddy, tall, dark and handsome, and when he asked me out, I was thrilled. It was soon after I'd lost Sean, and there's nothing like a new boyfriend for cheering a girl up! The trouble was, Pat was married, and he was too old for me. He tried it on, and I wasn't having any. There was one kind of satisfaction, though, for me. When he brought me home, we passed a couple snogging on a corner. The bloke glanced at me – and it was Sean.

'Tess?' he said. He looked stunned, as if to say, 'You're out with another feller!' The girl with him, Dorothy of course, tugged at his sleeve. She obviously didn't like him paying attention to me. And I felt like a little bit of pride was restored to me.

Funnily enough, not long afterwards I got a Valentine's card from Sean. He wrote that he'd joined the Army, in the Catering Corps, he was sorry things hadn't worked out, he wished me well, all that sort of thing. And I really didn't have much of a pang. I must simply have grown out of him, got over him. But he was a lovely boy, and I'll never forget him.

On the work front, I'd had to leave the salon. I just couldn't manage on my wages, what with having to buy my own equipment, and Mother was forever urging me to bring back stuff for her – anything. Lacquer, curlers, whatever. She meant nicking, and I couldn't bring myself to do it. Not yet. I was realising that no matter what I did, Mother thought I owed it to her to get stuff, if not for herself, then to sell on. She was obviously up to her old fencing tricks again. Bobbie was a shoplifter, it turned out, and Mother was only too happy to find a good home for the proceeds.

It was the same for me in my next job, in a shoe shop, but I didn't see how I could smuggle out pairs of shoes, even if I wanted to. I would have been terrified of being caught, anyway. I think I was still hoping for that ordinary life, like other girls, having a regular job and doing regular things. I wanted to be a normal teenager, and the late fifties was a great time to be a teenager. Rock'n'roll, fab clothes . . . With my first week's wages from the shoe shop, I put down a deposit on a Dansette record player, and bought a gorgeous petticoat with layers of stiff net to make a skirt stick out. I thought it was the bee's knees.

At least I managed to keep some of my wages – Mother took most of them every week. I accepted this, not that I had much choice, but by now I was sixteen and wanted more independence. I thought back to Jenny, the girl in Croydon who was living by herself at my age, and I envied her. I would have so liked to do my own thing, not to be accountable to Mother for everything – like any other teenager, I suppose. Anyway, it wasn't likely that I could afford a place of my own. Even if I could, I suspected that Mother would track me down and bring me back. It was as if she thought she owned me.

As it happened, I did manage to break away from her, but I didn't do it on my own. I met a man called Ronnie, who was a friend of Mother's friend Bobbie. I didn't know at the time that what they had in common was shoplifting. The road to petty crime was getting closer . . .

Ronnie was about ten years older than me, short and tubby with a round serious face and black greasy hair combed straight back. He had an air of Al Capone about him, but when I got to know him I realised he was a really nice bloke, kind and thoughtful. He was forever bringing me gifts, little bottles of perfume, a necklace, that sort of thing. Mother prickled when he came round. Maybe she thought I was going to fall for him and get away from her. The very first time he visited us in our flat, I had a present for him. By now I'd changed jobs again and was working in a bakery. Those were the days when you could leave one job and just walk into another. Anyway, this particular evening, I brought back some leftover cream cakes as I knew he liked them. I didn't nick them. We were allowed to take the leftovers home rather than letting them go off.

Mother was in the room when I gave Ronnie the cakes, and you would have thought a bomb had gone off.

'Cakes? Fucking cakes! What are you giving him cakes for? You never bring anything back to me, you selfish cunt. Where's my cakes?'

She was raging. Ronnie was stunned, and offered her the box. She struck it out of his hand and stomped out of the room, giving me a glare that could burn me to a crisp.

'What was all that about?' asked Ronnie, shaking his head.

'Oh, that's just Mother,' I said. I hoped it didn't put him off me, having a mother like that. Though his own mother was in prison, for shoplifting, so he couldn't really say much about mine.

Me and Ronnie had been going steady for months by the time his mother came out of prison. He took me round to his parents' place in town. His father was a lovely man, relaxed and good-humoured. I took to him straight away. But his mother was a different matter. She was distinctly cold to me, looked me up and down like I was muck.

'What's your mum got against me?' I asked Ronnie as he walked me home.

He shrugged, and grinned. 'Thinks you're not good enough for me,' he said.

I was a bit miffed, to tell the truth. Who did she think she was to look down on me? She'd been in prison, I hadn't. Later, I realised that she must have known I wasn't right for Ronnie. She was a shrewd woman, who loved her son. I bet she saw that I wasn't as keen on him as he was on me. And being born and bred in Brighton, she must have known a lot of people who by now would be up to speed on Mother and her games. A jailbird would look down on a brothel-keeper.

But Ronnie's mother didn't come between us. Though I didn't love him, I liked him a lot; he was good company. And he seemed to love me. Well, that was irresistible, of course.

He was the first man I went all the way with, in his flat one evening. And to be honest, I could have done without it. I was still a virgin, and being entered sexually was awful. Not that it hurt, particularly, but I hated feeling exposed, vulnerable. My mind flashed back to the time I'd been naked with that man in London, and I felt sick. I insisted the light was out. I'd enjoyed snogging in the past, but now the whole thing struck me as a nasty, dirty business, with no pleasure. Why did people make such a fuss about it?

But Ronnie seemed keen. It was all right for him, I suppose. I wondered how working girls could put up with this, having sex with a string of men. Torture. I'd rather die.

When Ronnie was insistent, I tried to put him off with a hand job, but now and then he had his way. It was the price I paid for being with him, I supposed. You have to do things you don't like if you want to be loved. And when he asked me to live with him, I saw it as a way of leaving home. By now, Mother's business was flourishing. It was like the good-time days in our first home in Croydon, and when the ground floor in the house became vacant, she rented that as well. I hated it, more and more girls, more and more men, all about sex, horrible sex. The whole business made me ill, and I couldn't wait to move in with Ronnie.

Mother objected at first, but I stuck to my guns.

'All right then, but I want you round here once a day,' she ordered.

I don't think she was that bothered for my welfare. It was more a case of keeping tabs on me. And she gave me shopping lists for Ronnie: 'Tell him to get me this, get me that,' she'd say. It had dawned on me by now what Ronnie did for a living, and I kicked myself for not realising straight away. It didn't shock me. Lots of people I knew were hoisting. It was just a way of getting by.

Ronnie was very skilled, and he brought in quite a lot of money.

'No need for you to work, Tess,' he told me. 'I'll look after you.'

What a luxury! He must really love me, I thought. The least I can do is keep the flat nice, cook him tasty meals. We settled down into a shared life, and the only cloud was the sex. I got the hang of it, and went through the motions. Lay back and thought of England, studying the ceiling. I was learning that sex meant a lot to men, they'd do anything for it. No wonder Mother's business was booming! I still couldn't see anything in it myself.

Then one day our life fell apart. I was cleaning the flat when there was a knock at the door. Police. They barged in and searched the place, while I stood gaping at them. It turned out that Ronnie had been nicked. He'd been working the shops in Portsmouth with Bobbie and Billy, and they'd all been caught, with a lot of stolen gear on them. This was terrible. I knew the risks Ronnie ran, but somehow I thought he'd never get caught. He himself was always quite philosophical. 'Goes with the job,' he'd say, and I suppose with his mother getting caught, he'd take it in his stride.

The upshot was, he was sentenced to six months inside, while Bobbie and Billy got nine months each. I left court with my mind in turmoil. I was sorry Ronnie had to go to prison, a horrible place, but I was worried for me too. What was I going to do? How could I afford the rent on Ronnie's flat while he was inside?

'Come back here, of course,' said Mother.

But I wouldn't, at least at first. I'd managed to get a bit of independence, and I liked it. I liked it as much as I didn't like being in a house with all that sex going on. So I went out and got another job, waitressing this time, in a little café in a side street. The pay wasn't much, but I thought if I worked hard and got tips, then I might be able to make ends meet.

As it happened, I couldn't. It was a losing battle, so I crept home with my tail between my legs. At least Mother didn't say, 'I told you so.' She just expected me to earn my keep looking after the kids, doing the housework. I didn't mind, but when I mentioned that I'd love to get the latest hit single – I think it was Pat Boone and 'Love Letters in the Sand' – she looked thoughtful.

'If you want to earn some dosh for yourself,' she said, 'I could put you on to Val.'

It turned out Val was a hoister, who needed someone to help her: act as lookout, that sort of thing. So Val and me teamed up. She looked more like the popular image of a cheap tart than a hoister – bleached blonde hair and a hard face. And she was tight, very tight, with money. People used to say, 'If she found a razor she'd cut her throat rather than waste it.' But she was good to work with, she gave me confidence – which was just as well, as I was terrified of being caught. Then again, if I could be useful and earn a few bob for myself, better get on with it. I didn't want people to think I was a coward, not any daughter of Mother's. So I'd keep an eye out when she was in a shop, and now and then we'd use the old identical-bag trick. We each had the same shopping bag, and Val would fill hers with nicked stuff. I'd wander over to her as if I didn't know her, casually put my bag down on the floor, and pick up her full bag. She'd stroll off with my empty one, so if anyone was suspicious they wouldn't find anything on her. These were the days before security cameras and all that paraphernalia, but I must say my heart was in my mouth till we met up down the street and swapped bags again.

We usually stuck to Brighton town, sometimes branching out to Hove or Portslade. Val would give me my cut – as much as a tenner on a good day. I found I had plenty for new clothes and records, as well as going to the pictures at the weekend. I started nicking stuff for myself, just little things like a packet of hankies or stockings. I was getting used to nice things.

Not much more than three years in Brighton, and I'd learned a thing or two. Nobody would stay with me for ever. Sex was horrible. Menial jobs weren't worth the effort – all that work for tuppence-ha'penny. Better to team up with a hoister and get good money. Working girls could get good money too, but Ronnie's mother was right: hoisting was a far cry from being on the game. It might be Mother's business, but I'd never descend to that level.

Around this time, Mother learned something too: get on the wrong side of little Barbara one time too many, and she'll grass you up.

I'd always thought Mother was invincible, that she could get away with anything, but even her wings were about to be clipped. The brothel-keeper was about to be a jailbird as well.

20

Freedom and Love

'I'll kill her, I'll fucking kill her!' Mother hissed through gritted teeth, her hands clenched, steam practically coming out of her ears. Another minute, I thought, and she'll explode.

Me and Don were visiting Mother in Holloway. I was still reeling from the shock of her being banged up in the first place. But in Brighton she hadn't managed to get in with the Old Bill. She wasn't paying sweeteners so she had no warnings. Even so, I thought she'd get round the judge when she came to court, what with her gift of the gab. But no. She was convicted of 'procuring' and sent to prison for six months.

It turned out that Barbara had been nicked for soliciting on the seafront, and had made a statement to the police implicating Mother. She and Mother had had another set-to just before this. Barbara had the hump, and was obviously getting her own back. What happened to her, I never knew. I don't even know if she was prosecuted herself, or whether she got off on account of landing Mother in it. After being with us for years, she dropped off the radar and we never heard from her again. Just as well, or Mother might have carried out her murderous threat. At least the trail didn't lead back to our flat, for some reason. If the law had known Mother was running a full-blown brothel, what's more with young kids living on the premises . . . well, good job it didn't.

As we said goodbye to Mother in the airless visiting room, I said, 'I hope you'll be all right, Mum.'

She shrugged. 'Got no choice, have I?' she said. 'I'll be all right. Just toe the line, do my bird and get out.'

She suddenly grinned. 'Remember what I've always said – you can't beat the law, you just flannel 'em.'

I did remember. One of her favourite flannels was exaggerating the rank of any policeman who might be sniffing around. 'Ooh, Inspector,' she'd say to a lowly constable. I don't know if anybody was ever fooled, but it amused Mother.

On the train back down from London, me and Don sat quietly, lost in our own thoughts. He must have been worrying about Mother, and how to cope without her money coming in. Of course, in her absence the brothel side of things would evaporate. I had a sudden image of Don among all the girls, with Mother away. He'd just go round shagging them! For free. As Mother said, he had no head for business. So there'd be just his money coming in, and the family allowance for the kids. It occurred to me that I might step up the shoplifting, just for what we needed. I'd be looking after my brothers and sisters in Mother's place – well, at least, the younger ones.

Kath had left school too by now, and was fulfilling her childhood dream of working with animals, helping out at a local vet's. I'm glad one of us got our dream. It didn't look like I'd be training for the ballet any time soon, and Jess sure wasn't destined to be a nun! In fact nobody knew what Jess wanted, least of all herself. She just kind of drifted round the place. She'd always been a Dolly Daydream, as Mother called her (when she wasn't calling her Boss-Eyed Bastard – Jess had a cast in one eye), and she seemed to have even less backbone than me. She was terrified of Mother, and tried to make herself small every time Mother was in the room. Jess had always made up stories, and had a feel for the dramatic. But as she grew up, she seemed to get lost in her stories, and if you weren't charitable you'd call them lies.

I must have got soft, living with Ronnie, because I found all the housework heavy going, especially washing the laundry by hand. But it was good to be back with the kids, and we all made the best of it.

The best of it for me, it didn't take me long to realise, was being without Mother for the first time in my life. I had to write to her regularly, of course, but I wasn't at her beck and call. I didn't have to report daily. It's not till something stops that you realise what an effect it's been having on you, and, to tell the truth, I felt free.

Sure enough, I did do the odd bit of shoplifting, when the kids were at school, either with Val or by myself. I'd got more confident now, though nothing like Val. Usually it'd be for everyday things, stuff we needed round the house, but now and then I fancied a new sweater or something, so I nicked that as well. Looking back, I realise that I would never have called myself a thief at the time. Thieves were burglars who broke into houses, or robbers who held up shopkeepers with guns. I'd never have classed myself with those criminals. Funny how you can square things in your own mind. As Mother said, nobody's hurt. And now I could feel more justified, as money was tight.

I managed to keep up a social life too, when I wasn't needed at home. This was the great age of the coffee bar, and I loved it. People buzzing, music playing – pubs and bars and clubs came later. One thing starting up now in earnest was the drugs. I knew something about them, in fact had been scared off years ago when I saw how the lovely girl Jean had fallen apart through them. But everywhere around me people were knocking back pills – Hayley Mills, they called them. Speed, black bombers, coffin lids; the only pills I ever took were slimming pills, part of my lifelong struggle with my weight. No good, though – they made me sick. When I moaned about it to a girl I knew, she immediately said, 'I'll have them.' There was something in the pills that could give you a buzz, if you knew how.

I'd got to know a whole bunch of people round town. It didn't dawn on me for quite a while that there wasn't a single straight one among them. And when I say straight, I don't mean the opposite of gay. I mean people with regular jobs, who got their money legit. Everyone I knew was either on the game or involved in one scam or another – shoplifting like me, or fencing bent gear. Ducking and diving, bobbing and weaving. And I saw nothing strange in it. In fact I was in my element, what had become my element. A crazy world. Those dreams of a 'normal' life were long gone. I had been friends with some straight people, like the girls in the hair-dressing salon, but it was difficult to keep up a conversation. 'Does your mum work? What does she do?' And like in Croydon, I could never invite anyone back home. It was easier to go with the flow, stick with your own.

In the event, Mother was let out after four months, for good behaviour. 'I'm a good girl, I am.' She grinned. She'd played the game, worked the system. And early in her stretch she'd had the brass face to try to include me in one of her schemes.

On my second visit, we were sitting at a table opposite each other, and several screws were standing round the room. After the usual greetings, Mother leaned forward and murmured, 'Look at that screw over there,' and she jerked her head sideways. 'What do you think of her, eh?'

Think of her? I didn't think anything of her.

'Looks nice enough, I suppose,' I managed. 'Why?'

Mother's voice dropped, and her eyes bored into mine. 'She likes you,' she said. 'Saw you when you came the first time. She'd like to get to know you.'

Again, I could only say, 'Why?'

Mother sighed. 'Oh, for Christ's sake, you dipstick, she fancies you, doesn't she?'

'Does she?'

'Yes, she does.' Mother was hissing now. 'She fancies you, she wants to have a drink with you.'

'Why?'

I thought Mother's eyes would pop out. 'You know what I'm talking about, don't kid me. She's a fucking lezzie. You play ball, and there'll be perks for me.'

What! So that was her game. I was gobsmacked. This time I really hadn't expected anything like this. Full of surprises, Mother. She was only setting me up, practically pimping me. It obviously made no difference what sex a potential punter was. I was wiser now, though. I realised that Mother would not only have wanted me to be nice to the screw, but would have blackmailed her afterwards. Well, I was having none of it, any more than I would have gone with another man.

'Oh, no, Mum,' I said quickly. 'I couldn't do anything like that.'

'No?'

'No.'

And she could see I meant it.

She leaned back in her chair, one eyebrow raised. 'So that's the lie of the land, is it? You won't put yourself out to help your poor old mother when she's banged up. You don't think it's fucking hard enough in nick without you stopping me getting a few home comforts?'

I shifted uncomfortably. I hated it when Mother did this.

She shrugged. 'All right, have it your own way. Never mind about me. So you don't love your old mum like you used to. After all,' she said, twisting the knife a bit deeper, 'it's only because of you kids I'm in here in the first place. Getting food on the table.' Another big sigh, then, 'Suit yourself.'

And she turned her head aside, wouldn't look at me. I crept out miserably. Mother could send you on a guilt trip, all right.

That ploy might have failed, but Mother had obviously had better luck in other directions. She had a fund of stories, all about her scams, which became more and more embroidered. Eventually you'd have thought the entire prison was eating out of her hand and she was the governor. In fact, she had a kind of swagger about her now. She'd always had a straight back, held her head high, but it was like she was double cocky after prison. As if it made her a hard nut – harder than she was already.

With renewed energy, Mother set to rebuilding her business. Says a lot about the reforming nature of prison, doesn't it? She never seemed to think that she might be a marked woman – she never lacked confidence. She got back in touch with her girls and their old punters, and went out recruiting for more. One time she brought back a girl who was to become one of my particular friends. Gina was a gorgeous girl with a cloud of auburn hair. She always spoke with a French accent, so I suppose she was French, but nobody ever knew much about her background. It was obvious she was nobody's fool, though – a very canny girl. She came to live with us, just like Barbara had, and introduced me to her friend Lana, who lived just across the road. She was a tall, leggy blonde from Manchester, a lively girl, great fun.

Gina and Lana went around a lot together, and started to include me too. It turned out that they were hoisters as well, only on a bigger scale than me. In fact they had a lot more bottle than me. I'd go out with them, but hang back as they casually walked through one of the little boutiques that were springing up everywhere, and practically strip it. Often the people in these boutiques were complete amateurs – or off their head on something, conked out at the back of the shop.

The girls were more worldly than me, too. They took me to clubs and bars in town, and that was a whole new ball game. Very glamorous, like in a film. I'd always wanted to go to a nightclub, and they were more exciting than the pubs Ronnie had taken me to. A special favourite was the Stage Door, run by a woman called Babs – a great character, a real laugh, Queen of the Clubs, in fact. 'This is really living!' I'd say to myself. Sometimes boys would chat me up, but nobody made much of an impression. I wrote regularly to Ronnie in prison, trying to sound cheerful, but to be honest I wasn't missing him much.

My sister Jess took to joining us on our jaunts round the shops when she wasn't at school. There was never any question of Kath teaming up with us. She'd always been straight as a die. I used to tease her, call her Queen Victoria. And by now she'd met the young man who was to become her husband. A steady, regular life was on the cards for her, and that was just what she wanted. But Jess, like me, had no scruples when it came to hoisting, and also like me she had the knack. The four of us made a great team. Mother was pleased. I didn't know at the time that Jess was getting a taste for something else. She'd come with us to bars and clubs, too, looking older than her years, and the drugs found a happy target in her.

Meanwhile, at home she was as much under Mother's thumb as I was, much to Gina's astonishment. Of course, Gina worked for Mother, she was valuable to her, so she never got the rough edge of Mother's tongue. One particular night sums up Mother's continuing power over us kids.

Me and Jess had been out clubbing with Gina, and forgot the time. When we got home, through the basement door, Mother was up waiting for us, looking like an angry wife in a cartoon. All she needed was a rolling pin.

'What time do you call this?' she barked.

'I call it half past one,' said Gina cheerfully, and made to go past Mother.

Mother blew up. 'I will not have my house treated like a hotel! Coming back at all hours, making me wait up. Well, I tell you, if you want to be up all night you can stay up all night. You'll stay sitting down here all night. Got that?'

Me and Jess looked at each other. Instantly crushed. Gina was bewildered. 'What—' she started to say, but Mother cut her off.

'You too, while you live under my roof.' And she swept out.

We all sat down, not saying anything. The minutes ticked by, then Gina stood up. 'Oh, this is ridiculous!' she said. 'I'm going to bed.'

In the doorway she looked round at me and Jess. 'You're not staying down here, are you?' she asked.

Me and Jess nodded miserably.

Gina was astonished. 'You're mad,' she said. 'Why don't you just go to bed?'

'We've got to stay here,' I mumbled.

Gina shook her head. 'I don't get it,' she said. 'You're not little kids.' And she went out of the door. We heard her footsteps going upstairs to her room on the ground floor.

No, we weren't little kids, but we'd had a lifetime of Mother telling us what to do. She didn't hit us any more, except for the odd slap, but the insistence, the fear, had gone deep. I know it sounds mad, but me and Jess sat there all night, only dozing off after a while. We didn't dare disobey Mother. With me it was a reflex action anyway. And as far as Jess was concerned, it was the fear. More than once she'd said, 'If Dracula was on one side of the room, and Mother was coming at me from the other side, I'd run to Dracula. "Take me, Dracula!"' Allowing for Jess's dramatic bent, this was fair comment.

With the business building up again in the flat, I was keen to get away. Ronnie was coming out of prison in a couple of months, and though I wanted to get away from home, I wasn't keen on living with him again. He was a nice man, and I did like him, but I just couldn't stand the sex. I'd resorted to all kinds of ploys to get out of it. Encouraging him to get drunk, the old headache routine . . . I know I wasn't fair to Ronnie, who deserved a loving partner. But for all I thought I was grown-up, as far as love and sex were concerned I was just a dumb, ignorant fool.

As I was to find out before long, when my world turned upside-down.

'You can come and stay with me, if you like.' Linda was an Irish girl I'd met, friendly and outgoing. Good company.

'Will there be room for me?' I asked. I knew she was very keen on men, and often talked about bringing them home. She wasn't on the game, or at least only when she had bills to pay. Mostly she was just a good-time girl. I wouldn't want to be in the way, and I felt uncomfortable at the thought of being in the same room as her having sex.

'Oh, yeah,' said Linda. 'Don't you be worryin'. It's a big room, and there's a little alcove thing, with a curtain. You'll be grand there.'

But how could I tell Mother? She'd let me go and live with Ronnie because she had a use for him, he would get gear for her. But if I moved in with Linda, what would be in it for her? It wasn't as if Linda would turn tricks to oblige her. As it happened, Mother herself opened the door for me.

I'd planned to go to the pictures, but Mother wanted me to stay in for some reason. I tried protesting – 'But, Mum –' and she blew up as usual.

'How many more times do I have to tell you that while you're under my roof, you'll do as I say? If you don't like it, you can fuck off out of it – go on, there's the door, what are you waiting for?'

I saw my chance.

'Okay,' I said, 'if you say so.'

I whizzed off to fling a few things into a bag, and nerved myself to walk back past Mother. She was scowling, for once lost for words.

Then she tried to save face. 'Have it your own way, then. See if I care – but you'd better be round here once a day if you know what's good for you.'

'Fine by me,' I said. I knew she'd want me to keep supplying her with gear.

And I was off.

But as I feared, it was awkward sharing the room. When Linda brought a man back, I could hear everything, them going at it hammer and tongs. I'd lie there in my narrow little bed in the alcove, thinking, How can she do it? How can she possibly like it? What's all the fuss about?

And then I found out.

I'd gone to a coffee bar with Linda, who was meeting a man she fancied. 'Why don't you pick up a feller and bring him back?' she said.

'Oh, no, I can't do that. I don't want to go to bed with anyone. I don't like it. And even if I did, I don't know anyone.'

'Sure you can,' Linda said. 'Wait and see.'

And in the coffee bar she introduced me to a man, who was sitting at a table by himself.

'Hi, John,' she said, 'this is Tess. Tess, this is John. We're having a little get-together this evening, John – want to come back with us?'

I gathered she knew him slightly, and though he seemed a bit taken aback, he said yes, fine, readily enough. I think he thought it was a party, or anyway drinks. I was nervous. I wasn't used to this idea of hopping into bed with a man I'd only just met. Maybe we could simply talk.

And we did talk. He told me about himself, but quietly, not in a showing-off sort of way. He was a travelling insurance agent, working the south coast. He told funny stories about his customers, and I began to relax. It helped that he was very good-looking, to my eyes at least. He had dark hair swept back, a strong chin, he was well-dressed. When I saw *The Man from UNCLE* on telly a few years later, I looked at Robert Vaughn as Napoleon Solo and thought, That's John!

He was charming, no doubt about it. Maybe it was Linda and her feller having it off that encouraged him, but before I knew it we were squeezed into my bed behind the curtain. I didn't know what to think. I probably wasn't thinking, to be honest. Just aware of an excitement and a physical attraction I'd never felt before.

Of course I was sexually inexperienced. He wasn't, not by a long chalk. He knew his way around, all right. Talk about the earth moving! I thought I'd died and gone to heaven. I thought my heart would burst, my body was on fire. Yes! Yes!

At last I knew what sex could be like, should be like. Not a mechanical plugging away with me lying there like a lump, but mutual pleasure – ecstasy. Nothing like an orgasm to make you change your mind!

He left early, about six o'clock. I stayed in bed for hours, dozing, waking up, on cloud nine. I'd met my dreamboat. I could still smell him. I was utterly in love. I never knew life could be this good.

When I got up, around midday, there was no sign of the other man. Linda was grinning at me, though.

'All right, all right,' I said, sheepish. 'Don't take the mick. I know now, don't I?'

*   *   *

John didn't say anything when he left about seeing me again. But he must! I thought. That night I went back to the coffee bar, dressed in my best, hoping – praying – he'd be there. He did come in, with a bunch of friends. He caught my eye and just nodded at me. My heart was racing. I'd never had a one-night stand before. Was this going to be it? I didn't know what to do, so I hung back, talking to people I knew, pretending to be interested.

At the end of the night, with the place closing, he walked over to me and said, 'All right?'

I nodded, and he walked back with me.

I'm not ashamed to say I was like a bitch on heat, wanting more and more. And he was all over me like a rash. When we quietened down, he started talking.

'I have to tell you,' he said. 'I'm married. With two kids.'

I couldn't say anything. I wasn't surprised.

'I don't love my wife,' he went on. 'I only married her because I got her pregnant and I couldn't just ditch her.'

I found myself thinking, It doesn't matter. It doesn't matter at all. I don't care. It's you I want, I don't care about anyone else.

After that night we saw each other as much as possible. Sometimes we had a whole weekend together, and that was bliss. We hardly left the bed, we couldn't have enough of each other. The inhibitions I'd had with Ronnie had fallen away, though I still had to have the light off, always self-conscious about my body.

I hadn't told Ronnie I was with a new man, I didn't have the bottle. I just kept writing to him as usual. That was why he knew where to find me when he came out of jail.

It was early one morning. John was still in bed with me. Much to my delight he was staying the whole night. For once,

Linda was alone in her bed. There was a ring at the front door, and after a while one of the other tenants answered it. I heard voices.

'It's Ronnie!' I gasped, shocked rigid. 'John, don't say anything!'

Then came the knock on our door and I opened it a crack, peering round.

'Tess, I'm back!' said Ronnie, beaming from ear to ear.

I had to think quickly.

'Ronnie, what a surprise. Sorry I'm in a state, I'm not very well. Do you mind not coming in?'

His face fell, and I felt mean.

'Let's meet tonight,' I said. 'I'll be better then.'

Ronnie was frowning, but what could he do?

'Okay then,' he said. 'See you at the Belvedere at seven.'

Thank God for that. Put off the evil hour when I had to tell him it was all over. In the event, he was upset, and angry too. We had quite a row about it. But I don't think he was broken-hearted. Within a month he was going out with another girl, a nice girl much more suitable than me, and he ended up marrying her. I was truly glad he'd found happiness – he deserved it.

For a few months more I was walking on air. I didn't know and I didn't care what tales John told his wife: working late, staying with a friend . . . Usually he'd get home in the early hours of the morning, or even later. He never seemed to want to leave me. He'd drag himself out of bed, get dressed, I'd ask for one more kiss and we were at it again.

That first intensity couldn't last, of course. After some months, I began to suspect the shine was wearing off for John.

It wasn't for me, but I thought I could tell John was cooling off. It's a funny thing, but through me his life had changed. He'd been rather quiet, but now he met lots of other girls, and they liked him. He was good company, and they obviously found him attractive. And some of those girls were lookers, and here was me, fat and plain and ginger . . . A dreadful jealousy began creeping into my heart.

When I talked about John to Gina, she shook her head. 'He is a charmer, yes,' she said in her soft French accent, 'but you should watch that one.' She could see which way the wind blew. At first I only suspected, and it drove me mad. Having found love, I was desperate not to lose it – absolutely desperate. I hadn't felt so anxious since the times Mother would blank me, throw me off balance. It was like with Sean, only a thousand times worse. Nobody was ever going to stay with me – why should they?

At the time my mind was in a ferment. I wouldn't have been able then to think things through, to wonder why I was so anxious, why I was so convinced love wouldn't last. I had very little self-awareness – and even less self-esteem. All I could do was the very thing guaranteed to annoy this love of my life: challenge him, quiz him. Where have you been? Why are you late? Another woman's perfume on him, her lipstick on his collar . . .

I think John was essentially an easy-going man, and that was part of his charm. But even he couldn't put up with my jealousy for long. I'd go further than words: if he seemed to be brushing me off, I'd go for him, pound him with my fists. More than once I actually took off one of my shoes and hit him with the stiletto heel. Then he'd lose his rag, quite understandably, and we'd have a fight. He'd punch me to the ground and rage at me, something like hate in his eyes. That was terrible. I could take the pain, but not the hate.

What the hell was going on? I look back now and can hardly recognise that mad woman. I know you can never excuse a man for hitting a woman, but to be honest I was a red rag to a bull. In fact I never heard of John ever hitting anyone else before he met me. He wasn't like Mother's old enemy Wally, known for being rough towards women just for the kick of it. So it must have been me. Yes, John did have an eye for the ladies, he was a womaniser at heart, so I had just cause to be jealous – but I couldn't deal with it.

It took me a long, long time to see this black hole in my mind for what it was. I'd never been confident about myself in my whole life. If I was a building, I'd be one with no foundations, just shifting sands. Someone who had grown up with a proper sense of her own worth would never have badgered John the way I did. She would have had more pride. Mind you, someone who'd grown up straight might have stayed away from married men in the first place . . .

Still, I wasn't a puppet. I bet other people have overcome dodgy childhoods and gone on to lead decent lives. It was obviously beyond me. Meanwhile, when we weren't fighting, me and John were loving. We always made up in the end, couldn't keep our hands off each other.

There was never the slightest question of him keeping me and I wouldn't expect it. He had a family to support, after all. Linda wasn't asking much for the use of the room, but I had to pay her something, so I was keeping up the hoisting. Sometimes by myself, sometimes with Gina and Lana, or Jess, or all three. Usually it was easier to work as a team, one keeping lookout while the others lifted. It depended on the shop and the staff.

Me and John had been together, after a fashion, for about a year when I was lifting by myself and I got careless. I nicked a packet of stockings, priced 12s 6d. The price turned out high for me – I was caught red-handed and found myself up before the bench. My turn for prison.

21

The Worst and the Best

No wonder they call it going down. I felt like I was falling into a bottomless pit as I stood in the dock and heard the sentence from the bench.

'Three months.'

I was trembling. 'Please,' I whispered, 'please don't send me to prison.'

But in no time I was bundled off and out of the court into a prison van bound for Holloway. I knew Mother had been in court, but I didn't have a chance to see her. When I was out on bail and told her I'd been caught, she said, 'Oh, for fuck's sake, you silly cow, they've got you bang to rights. You're bound to go down.' She reckoned I was for it as it wasn't a first offence. After I met Val I was in a shop by myself and tried lifting something, just a trinket, and was spotted in the act by the shop owner. He called the police and I was hauled off to the station and given a good talking-to. I kept saying sorry, I don't know what came over me, I'll never do it again. In the end they didn't press charges but I had a formal caution. Fat lot of notice I took of it.

Mother did offer words of wisdom. 'Just keep your head down, and your nose clean. You'll get through it.' Well, I thought, you should know.

I had to face it. I'd done the crime, so I'd do my time, as the saying goes. And it served me right, of course. I stole and was caught, and this was my punishment. I knew I was risking prison every time I hoisted — hadn't I seen it happen to Ronnie? And it's not like I hadn't had that warning myself.

I really should have learned my lesson. I didn't have the toughness you need to cope with the fall-out. Take Gina. She'd been nicked three or four times before I met her, and to hear her talk, you'd think she just brushed it off, didn't let it affect her. But me, I was a quivering wreck. For a start, anybody in authority always intimidated me, whether they wore a uniform or not. To be in court, with all that formality — I felt like a wriggling worm. And to be locked up! I'd visited Mother when she was there, of course, and found the whole place relentlessly grim.

As the prison doors clanged shut, I was put into the system with the other new arrivals. First to a reception area, a sort of holding room, where we were strip-searched and told to have a bath. That was humiliating, being naked at all, let alone in front of strangers, and having your body examined. We were given a uniform and our own clothes were packed away till we were released. Once we'd put on the uniform — a dress and cardigan, underwear (including what I'd call granny knickers) and heavy shoes — we were taken to our cells. My cell was the same as everybody else's, I suppose. It was like a small boxroom, with a single bed, a washstand and a table and chair. A tiny window was a reminder of the outside world, while the chamber pot reminded me of the bad old days at home when we were locked in.

In fact the whole experience of being locked in made me feel the same as I did when I was a kid, as if I was buried alive. I felt I couldn't breathe. That night I cried myself to sleep. How the hell had I got here? I asked myself over and over again. I knew the answer, of course, and it was all my fault.

The following day set the pattern. Bell to get up at 7.30, then half an hour to wash, dress and make the bed before we were unlocked. Next, emptying the slops – disgusting. Then the routine of meal, work, exercise, meal, work, exercise . . . till we were locked in after tea until eight the next morning. The worst thing was the smell and the dirt. I'd never imagined a place where women lived being so dirty. What made it worse was having the slop bucket. I heard what some girls did at night when they wanted a poo but couldn't face being in the cell all night with the stink (I sympathised with that). They'd wrap the poo in newspaper, making little parcels. Then they'd poke out the glass in the window and push the packets through. Imagine a heap of those on the ground in the morning!

After the initial fright, I tried to pull myself together. At least I didn't mind being told what to do. Just like school, I did as I was told and kept my head down. One thing singled me out from the other girls on the wing, which was called YP for Young Prisoners. As well as seeing the doctor, we all had a session with the prison psychiatrist. A first for me, but I've never been averse to talking about myself. Anyway, five minutes was it for the other girls, but the shrink called me back every day. It was Mother he wanted to know about, never mind me! That didn't surprise me, though I was a bit embarrassed to be singled out. He seemed to be fascinated, and made a lot of notes. For all I know, some of her story has gone into a medical book.

I got on with the other girls, on the whole. I found the butch lesbians a bit off-putting, with their cropped haircuts and tattoos, and rolled-down stockings that looked like socks. I'd nothing against lesbians as such, of course. I'd been around them all my life, even if I didn't realise at first. It was their underlying aggression that made me feel uneasy, but they didn't bother me.

One new girl in particular caused a stir: Christine Keeler. She'd been all over the papers, in the thick of the notorious Profumo affair – disgraced ministers, sex scandals, Russian spies, all that sort of thing. Our wing governor was against her joining us. We heard her shouting the odds to someone: 'I won't have my girls corrupted by a prostitute!' Apparently anyone in for vice wasn't supposed to mix with young offenders. The thing was, though, Christine was actually in for perjury, not anything to do with vice, so she did qualify for the wing, and was put in the cell next to mine. And to tell the truth, some of the girls there had done a lot worse than her, like GBH.

Me and Christine chatted now and then, and I found her nice and quiet and friendly, not at all as the papers had portrayed her. No change there, then. She was certainly very pretty, with lovely hair. I trimmed the ends for her, in my capacity as unofficial hairdresser.

Then my time in Holloway was up. I was only going to be there for a week, while I was assessed, and I couldn't wait to get out of there. Counted off the days. I don't know what the prison is like now, but when I was there it was grim. I was assigned to an open prison called Hill Hall, in Essex, and that was a totally different kettle of fish, thank God. It was a big old country house, with lovely grounds and dormitories instead of cells. Not a holiday camp, of course, but much more relaxed and encouraging.

Not that I could appreciate my new surroundings for long. After a couple of weeks or so I was feeling really ill, could hardly eat. What I did manage to get down I usually threw up, and it's not as if the food was especially horrible. Not bad, in fact. I realised my periods had stopped. Could I be pregnant? Me and John certainly hadn't planned anything, but accidents happen . . .

I saw the prison doctor, who examined me but said I wasn't pregnant.

'It's the shock,' he told me.

I wasn't convinced, but there was nothing for it but to drag myself through the days and weeks of my sentence. I was put to work in the gardens, but couldn't do much, barely pull weeds. At least John wrote to me, and sent me flowers, and managed to visit me once, which cheered me up a lot. It showed he still cared. I didn't say anything about possibly being pregnant. I didn't want to worry him. Anyway, he was full of the fact that his wife had left him, taken the children back to her mother, so I could join him in their flat. I was over the moon, a dream come true. At that time I didn't think about her, or what she must have thought about me. I just thought of me and John being together all the time. Now I'd think, Homewrecker.

Towards the end of my sentence I'd lost so much weight that I passed out in the garden one morning. But next day I was out of there and back to normal life. Or so I thought.

I settled in the flat, which was at the other end of town. Quite a walk to get to see Mother every day; that was still her arrangement, and I didn't think of letting her down. Anyway,

John was out at work a lot of the day, so I might as well visit her.

I'd become more and more convinced I was pregnant, and went to my doctor. A test proved me right. I was at least four months gone, and I didn't know how to react. On the one hand I'd always loved babies, and was delighted I was expecting – though hoping that my weight loss hadn't harmed it. On the other hand, what would John say? Would he be pleased or angry? Would he think I'd tried to trap him?

I nerved myself to tell him, and I couldn't read his face. He looked away. I think he was shocked. I couldn't bear the suspense, so I challenged him.

'What do you say?' I asked him anxiously.

He shook his head. 'Four months, you say? Too late to get rid of it?'

I was crushed. Get rid of it. So that was what he would have wanted. For myself, I thanked God it was too late.

'Yeah, the doctor said too late.'

'Not a lot to say, then, is there?'

And he went out. Not a happy event for him, obviously.

It was now that our relationship, which had been turbulent enough, started to get rockier. I'd always been madly jealous of him, even when maybe there'd been no reason. Now the sickness had worn off and I could eat again, I was getting fatter and fatter, and I knew that was a turn-off for John. I convinced myself he was seeing other women, and we were rowing more than ever, without the making-up afterwards.

The crux came when I was eight months gone, feeling like a hippo waddling round the place. Who could fancy me like this? John was late back one evening and I was working myself up into a frenzy of worry and suspicion. Then he came in, calling out, 'I've brought Little Eddie back for a drink.' Eddie was a colleague of his, a little gay bloke and nice enough.

I took one look at John and saw a pink smudge on the side of his face.

'That's lipstick!' I shouted, pointing at him. 'Who is she? Who've you been playing around with, you bastard?'

John tried to calm me down. 'You're imagining things,' he said, 'nothing's happened.'

But I wouldn't leave it. I felt he'd done the dirty and my heart was breaking as I kept screaming abuse at him. Then that wasn't enough. I took off one of my shoes and flung it right at his face. That did it. He drew back his arm and gave me one punch between my eyes, smashing my nose. Then he punched me again and again, till I fell to the floor. He kicked me in the belly. 'My baby!' I thought, and curled up on my side to protect it, choking on the blood pouring from my nose. Now John was kicking me in the back, again and again. Through the mist of pain I could hear Eddie shouting.

'For God's sake, John, stop it – you'll kill her!'

That's the last thing I heard before I passed out.

When I came to, I was lying on the bed. John was hopping up and down, panicking like mad. There was no sign of Eddie.

'Tess, Tess, are you all right? Oh, God, I don't know what came over me . . .'

All I could think of was the baby. I cradled my belly, and could feel movement. I wasn't passing any blood as far as I could tell. All the pain was coming from my head. I couldn't cry, I could hardly breathe.

When I could get up and make my way to the bathroom, I squinted at myself in the mirror. My face was caked in blood, my lips were split and swollen to twice their size, my nose was smashed. A broken head to match my broken heart. The pain was fierce, but I kept repeating to myself, The baby's okay, the baby's okay.

I didn't go to hospital, though that would have been the sensible thing to do.

'What would you tell them?' John asked. I could see he was anxious. Not so much about me, I could tell that. He was worried that the police might get involved. After all, beating up a woman who's eight months pregnant isn't exactly your usual domestic.

What could I do? At heart I knew it was my own fault, goading him like that, making him lose his rag. On the other hand, I really loved him, but I knew he was cheating . . . what a nightmare, what a life to bring a baby into.

I patched up my face as best I could, and rested in the flat. After three days, my brother Buddy called round. I wouldn't answer the door. He called out, 'Mum wants to know where you are, why you haven't been round.'

'Just tell her I've got flu,' I said. I was surprised she'd waited that long to find out why I wasn't paying my daily visits. I didn't dare let her see me like this. I knew what she felt about other people hurting her kids, and I didn't want her having a go at John.

I knew she wouldn't be satisfied for long, though, and after another three days decided to go round and see her before she came to me herself. I didn't look quite so bad; the swelling had gone down a bit. My eyes were black and blue, though, so I put on a pair of dark glasses.

Mother sat in the front room of the flat staring at me, frowning. 'Why are you wearing those bloody silly glasses indoors?' she wanted to know.

'I've hurt my eye,' I said. 'I don't like the light.'

Before I could blink, she'd whipped off the glasses and was staring down at my damaged face.

'Who did this?' she said in a deadly quiet voice.

When I didn't answer she said, 'It's that fucker John, isn't it? Isn't it?'

I lowered my eyes and nodded my head. No point trying to hoodwink Mother.

Well, she went apeshit. Completely lost it. Stormed round the room effing and blinding, reading the riot act to John as if he was there. I just curled up in my chair, misery washing over me.

As it happened, John guessed I'd be visiting Mother, and called for me later that day after work. A rash thing to do. When Mother saw who it was at the door, she dashed into the kitchen, and stormed out brandishing an axe of all things. John took one look and belted back the way he came. I swear Mother followed him for 200 yards, screeching her head off.

Never one to do things by halves, Mother made some phone calls when she came back in.

'I've put the boys on to him,' she told me.

Oh, no. I knew what she meant. She'd called in a favour and got a couple of heavies on to John. She'd done that to other people before, the last time just a few weeks earlier. One of Mother's working girls got into a fight at a party. A bloke kicked her downstairs and his girlfriend beat her up. The girl complained to Mother, and she made the phone call. A heavy was down next day, and left the bloke badly broken up and the girl with her teeth smashed in. Serious stuff. Mother knew some frightening people. John could be crippled for life, even killed.

I begged her, pleaded with her, to call it off. Whatever had happened, I still loved him, didn't want him to come to harm.

'You're a fool to yourself,' snapped Mother.

'But he's the father of my baby,' I said, weeping. I think that swayed her, and she promised to cancel the contract. John never knew how lucky he was.

I think John realised he'd been out of order, that he could have killed me, and for the next month he behaved himself. I could convince myself that everything would be all right again, roses round the door. Then came the highlight of my life. Nothing so important happened before, nothing so important happened after. I gave birth to a beautiful, healthy baby girl.

When the midwife put her into my arms I just cradled her, gazing at her. I couldn't take it in at first. This lovely little baby, absolutely perfect in every way, was mine, and she needed me. Something moved deep within my heart, and tears came to my eyes. For the first time in my life, tears of joy. I looked into her clear, bright eyes and made a solemn promise. In my heart I told her everything I would have wanted to hear from my mother.

I love you. I will always love you. I will always be there for you. You will have a life of love.

22

Life Changes

That was it. Whatever happened to me, I'd move heaven and earth to make sure my baby grew up happy and secure, kept safe from harm. It's the greatest joy of my life that my daughter grew up to be a lovely, caring woman, with a fine, hard-working husband, blessed with beautiful, clever children. What's more, she's always been respectable and honest, leading a decent life. She wasn't going to follow my path, no way. I wouldn't wish that on anyone, let alone my beloved daughter.

My path was to take me from one doomed relationship to another, to prison again, to a life in the vice trade, from Brighton to London and back again. It wasn't all gloom – there were some good times, and I mixed with a lot of great characters, mostly on the wrong side of the law. But the worst times came about because of my need for love. I've done a lot of thinking over the years, and I keep going back to when I was a kid, when I never felt confident, never felt secure. I'm no shrink, but I reckon there must be a connection. And that means Mother.

It was only when I became a mother myself that it hit me full in the face, just what my mother had done to me. When I first saw my precious newborn, the rush of love was immediate, pure and passionate. I didn't have to think about it. I knew in my bones that I would look after her, care for her in every way I could, come hell or high water. And I know this is right, it's natural, it's the way a mother should feel.

What about my mother, then? When she had her babies, did she feel that overwhelming love? If she did, I can only say it couldn't have lasted. Looking back, I realise us kids took second place in her life, after what she wanted. What she wanted most of all, of course, was money, and she did anything and everything to get it. If it meant locking us away for hours on end, and hurting us to keep us in line, so be it. Much worse things have happened to people, I know that. But how could she bring herself to send me out to those men? She must have known what they'd do. And she couldn't be sure they'd stick to any limits she set.

There's a word for what she did to me. Grooming. Working on my impressionable young mind, brainwashing me until doing what she wanted was second nature. Playing mind games till I didn't know where I was with her, just knew I was desperate for her to love me. I might hate what other people did to me, but pleasing Mother was paramount. God help me, she could even make me feel privileged in the process.

What happened to me was a violation, even if I wasn't actually raped. The thought of that happening to my own daughter fills me with absolute horror, it's unspeakable. But long before the physical abuse started, Mother had made sure I was damaged in my mind. Fucked-up, in short. I could have run away, I could have told someone . . . but I didn't, I couldn't. I've no way of knowing whether she did it deliberately, singled me out for a cash cow as soon as I started to develop. I don't want to believe she was that cold-hearted. Maybe she just saw an opportunity – she always had an eye on the main chance – and didn't waste any time thinking about it. Shut her mind, counted the money.

If I'm looking at my upbringing to puzzle out what made me the way I am, maybe I should look at Mother's too, what I know of it. The violence, which made thrashings a way of life. The poverty – they'd have to be poor with seventeen kids in the family. Maybe that set off her obsession with money. I've often wondered how someone brought up so strictly by Victorian parents could have slid so easily, so naturally, into a life of vice and petty crime. Perhaps it was the war, which loosened a lot of morals. She must have started in the black market, at least . . .

But I could speculate till the cows come home, and I'll probably be no nearer knowing what made her the way she was. I do know I shouldn't blame Mother for all my faults. She wasn't there twisting my arm when I made bad choices in life. But I like to think that if I'd had a different upbringing, where I was happy and secure, I wouldn't have had such a low opinion of myself, would have learned early on to stand up for myself, and expect other people to treat me with respect. And if I hadn't grown up in a brothel, where crime was as natural as breathing, maybe I wouldn't have lived a life in vice, and become a thief myself.

Fat chance.

John had had to let the flat go as he couldn't keep up with the rent, and took a bedsit in an old house for the three of us. He adored our daughter, who we called Angie; she was always his darling little girl. But things between him and me didn't improve. For a while after the birth, as I lost weight and he fancied me again, we were close. I'd wake up in the morning and look at him as he slept, and think how much I loved him, thanked God he was still here. But then he went back to screwing around. So while I loved him with my heart, my head told me to get out now while I had a chance.

'He'll pay you back for his wife and kids leaving,' my mother said. 'You wait. He'll blame you.'

I think she was right. When I had a go at him and fights blew up, it was the hate in his eyes that was destroying me rather than his fists.

So why didn't I leave him? Why does any woman stay with a man who beats her? Sensible, well-adjusted people who've never been in that position can't understand. To them, it's simple. But all I can say is that I clung to John for so long despite everything because I did love him, I loved him deeply. Maybe all the stronger because he was the first man I'd ever loved – and, as it happens, the last. And after all, when he was angry, it was my fault, I'd driven him to it by my jealousy. I convinced myself that if I loved him with all my heart and went on loving him come what may, he'd have to love me back.

Underneath all this was my conviction that I didn't really deserve him, or anyone. I was worthless, and shouldn't expect people to stay with me. At least the beatings were a sign of attention. One day, when Angie was about three months old, I found myself saying to Gina, 'I'm worried about John. He hasn't hit me for weeks. He can't love me any more.'

Now I look back and can hardly believe I could think like that. Any attention, no matter how painful, is better than none. How pathetic is that? On a more practical note, how would I cope with a baby on my own? As it was, money was tight. I was getting social security as an unmarried mother (keeping quiet about John), and that paid the rent, but of course John had to support his wife and children. So back I went shoplifting, telling myself it was only for necessities.

Meanwhile, Mother wasn't on my back so much. She and John had hated each other on sight, and she kept away. She still expected me to go round to her, though. She always wanted to know what I was up to. I thought she'd love to see Angie, and she did make all the right noises when she first saw her – 'lovely baby' – but she wasn't exactly a doting grandma. She was far too busy with her own life, running Gina as her regular girl and any others she could get into her clutches. Gina worked out of the clubs, like most girls did in those days. There wasn't a lot of street walking. She'd pick up a punter and bring him back, then go out again. And of course Mother would be fencing bent gear – a right female Fagin.

When Angie was about a year old, I fell pregnant again. John hit the roof, and insisted I had an abortion. He'd leave me if I didn't. I told myself it would be impossible to have another baby in the bedsit, though my heart was heavy. I would have loved another baby. Anyway, John took me to a doctor in London, while we left Angie with a friend. It cost us a hundred quid, a hell of a lot of money he had to scrape up from everywhere. But I didn't want to go the knitting-needle route at home, or try my mother's soap-water douche. I wanted a proper doctor. He injected something into me, and by the time we got home I was in labour. I lost the baby, or what would have been a baby, in a bucket.

I cried and cried, but tears were no use. I had a living baby to look after. I was desperately unhappy, though, and started to put on a lot of weight. John took the mickey, and played away more than ever, but he didn't stay out of my bed. With the result that six months later I was pregnant again. Another abortion. God knows where he got the money. I was too miserable to care. When I recovered I went out shoplifting more than ever, pushing Angie in the pram.

John warned me. 'You're gonna get caught again one day. Pack it in.'

Easy for him to say, but I wanted things for Angie. I'd got pretty proficient by now.

As I was big, I had an advantage in that a large, loose-fitting coat didn't look odd on me. Plenty of room to stash a pile of dresses complete with hangers that I'd quietly swept off a rail. Three either side, held under my arms, and a casual stroll out of the door . . .

Meanwhile, I managed to get us a new flat, bigger and much nicer than our bedsit. It was on the ground floor of a big old house, one of the many in Brighton, and we settled in quite happily. Then, a thunderbolt. Mother and Don moved into the basement flat below us, complete with my brothers and meal-ticket Gina. Kath and Jess were sharing flats with friends by now. I don't know how Mother worked it, but one morning she knocked on our door and said with a grin, 'Hello. I'm your new neighbour.' She'd always wanted to keep tabs on me, and this time she was on the spot. John was furious, but he couldn't do anything. Funnily enough, by now me and Don weren't enemies. He'd been diagnosed with Parkinson's disease, and he was turning into a frail old man. I felt sorry for him, and he seemed to like talking to me. Mother was more impatient. She cared for him, sure, but he got on her nerves. When she lost her rag, Don would creep upstairs.

One time we were talking, Don said, 'John does love you, you know.'

'Funny way of showing it,' I grumped.

'Oh, he may not even know it, but he does. And you will leave him, Tess, he won't leave you, and you will break his heart.'

I could only laugh. 'Don't be silly, Don. I won't ever leave John, I love him too much.'

'You will,' Don said quietly, 'and he will chase you all over town.'

Hell would freeze over first, I thought.

He went on, 'You've always underestimated yourself. You've got a lot going for you. Your beauty comes from within.'

Bollocks, I thought. What's he going on about? But I wouldn't argue with a man who was just a shadow of his former self.

One day I decided to go back to Croydon, my old stamping ground, for a bit of hoisting. It had a lot of new shops now, with rich pickings. I had a good day, but at last knockings I was caught red-handed. I was sent down again, and this time prison really hurt. Not because I had a longer stretch, twelve months, but because I'd be parted from Angie.

My last look at Angie's little face stayed with me the whole time I was banged up in Holloway. I knew she was being well looked after, staying with John's mother in Brighton. She was a lovely woman, generous and kind. At first she'd been suspicious of me, blamed me for the break-up of her son's marriage, but over the years she'd softened, and I was delighted Angie had one dependable nan, one who wouldn't fly off the handle at the slightest excuse. I used to wish she was my mother.

In the event I served eight months. I soon got used to the routine again, and just got through one day at a time. John's mother wrote to me regularly about how Angie was getting on. I yearned to see her, but she was three by now. I didn't want her having any memory of her mum in a place like this. She thought I was poorly, in hospital. John wrote too, and sent flowers, and visited every month, so that was good. Mother's letters always had a shot at John and his bits of stuff. Then she started telling me that John was bringing the same girl back to the flat every night, a very good-looking bit of stuff. She could hear the bedsprings, they were going at it hammer and tongs, she couldn't get any sleep. She had to bang on the ceiling to shut them up.

This choked me. I knew he was always chasing other women, but this was too much. I'd sit in my cell imagining them making love in the way we did, and I worked myself into such a state I thought I'd break down.

When John visited me, I had a go at him.

'You can't believe your mother,' he protested. 'You know what a vicious old cow she is, and she's always had it in for me.'

Whether that was true or not, there was a change in my heart. By the time I left prison, I was hardened towards John. I remembered Don's words, the last I ever heard from him. He'd died a few months into my sentence, and I was glad the governor let me out to go to the funeral to pay my respects. Mother had him cremated. 'He was always cold when he was alive,' she cracked, 'now he can have a warm.' But I know that was her way of covering up her emotions. She'd see tears as a sign of weakness.

Now I was thinking, How strange, if Don of all people, who'd disliked me most of my life, could see something in me that I couldn't myself. For I knew now that I couldn't stand it any more, and I was going to tell John so.

Something else had changed for me while I was in prison, something that took me by surprise. Having been round lesbians much of my life, and not thinking anything in particular about them, I found myself for the first time being attracted to one. She was called Steve, big and butch, and like me she'd been assigned to work in the jam factory. One day when no one was looking she pulled me to her and kissed me full on the lips. I was shocked, and pushed her away. But that kiss had kindled something, and it wasn't just because I'd had no sex for months. I liked it.

Me and Steve fell to talking when we were together, and I liked her more and more. She was kind, encouraging, made me feel good. I realise that's a common thread in my life. If someone shows they like me, I'm pathetically grateful. Anyway, we grew quite close, flirty, sending each other little messages written on toilet paper, though unlike the other lesbians we didn't actually have sex.

So there were two shake-ups for me during that time in prison. First, I'd changed my attitude to John. It was inevitable that we'd part some time soon. Second, it seemed I swung both ways. As it happened, my affairs after John were always to be with women, and I was to find out that when it comes to cruelty, there's no difference between the sexes.

Just as I came out of prison, Mother was going in. Holloway should have had a revolving door specially for us. She'd been nicked for dealing in illegal pills, and couldn't wriggle out of it. The drugs scene wasn't really for her. She should have stuck with what she knew. Anyway, she got six months.

For me and John, things went on much the same as before, only he was nicer to me. I knew he was still seeing his girlfriend, but I didn't care. When I wasn't looking after Angie, I was thinking about Steve, and getting my head round this new way of feeling. So when I met Jean, the idea of falling in love with a woman wasn't as strange as it would have been.

I met Jean through her girlfriend, Millie, a sparky little woman who looked a bit like Barbara Windsor and worked as a nightclub hostess. Millie knew John and sympathised with me. 'He'd fuck a tree if it had a skirt on,' she said. She had a daughter the same age as Angie, and sometimes we'd babysit for each other. One day I took Angie round to Millie's, and bumped into Jean, also blonde, but tall and slim. She was friendly, quietly spoken, and seemed to be a nice girl. I immediately felt at ease with her, and she seemed to like my company all right.

Before long, I realised that every time I saw her, Jean was courting me – me! She treated me like a queen, always complimenting me, telling me how beautiful I was, how desirable, giving me sweet little gifts. For the first time in my life I was hearing everything I'd always wanted to hear from someone. And I fell, hook, line and sinker, plunged into a gay world that was every bit as crazy and dramatic as the straight one.

'Millie's left me.' It was Jean on the phone, sounding miserable. I'd already heard that Millie had gone off with another girl, and I sympathised. 'Why don't you bring Angie round here?' Jean went on. 'I'll cook us a meal and maybe you can cheer me up – you're good at that, Tess.'

Why not? John was away working that weekend, and I knew he'd taken his girlfriend with him. If I'm honest, something in my mind was thinking, What's sauce for the goose . . .

Jean wined and dined me, Angie safe asleep in the next room. Before long, we were making love, and it was intoxicating, a revelation. She could read me like a book. At last we fell asleep, exhausted from love-making. Then all of a sudden I was jerked awake by shouting and screaming. What the hell was going on?

It was Millie. She'd gone crazy, standing over Jean on the bed and pumping her arm up and down. She was stabbing Jean! Jean was pushing her back and then they were rolling around on the floor like mad things. I had one thought: I'm out of here. I grabbed my clothes and dived into the next room. I phoned for a cab and dressed quickly, relieved that Angie was still sleeping peacefully despite the racket. Then we were away, heading for home and safety. As the cab whizzed along in the early hours of the morning, I wondered what on earth I'd got myself into.

Jean came round the next day, full of apologies. She hadn't been badly hurt – fortunately Millie's knife was more decorative than practical.

'I don't know how she heard,' said Jean. 'Someone must have seen you coming in, and she was jealous as hell.'

'But she left you!' I protested.

'I know, but it doesn't make any difference. She never dreamed I'd get you. You're quite a catch, you know, Tess.'

And despite everything, I was pleased as Punch, really proud. Of course, everybody knew how much I'd loved John, and I was never one for sleeping around, so maybe it was a feather in Jean's cap to win me over. And she was like a drug to me. Quite apart from the fact that she was a nice girl and sex was great, it was the way she treated me that really hooked me. By everything she said and did, she made me feel secure in her love. I'd been alarmed to find out she was on the game – I hated to think of her with punters in case she was enjoying it. 'No chance,' she said. She had an old sugar daddy too, a bank manager called Bob, who was like a permanent punter and very generous with it, so she earned a good whack. She asked me to come and live with her, bringing Angie of course.

Meanwhile, as I grew distant towards John, getting up the courage to tell him I was leaving him, he seemed to want to get closer. How ironic is that? Things came to a head when one day he took my arm and said out of the blue, 'Marry me, Tess.'

What? My head reeled, just as part of my mind thought how much I'd longed to hear those words in the past. Now, they meant nothing. I knew John would never change, he would always put me through the mill. I can still see the incredulity on his face when I shook my head.

It was painful all round, I can't deny it, leaving someone you thought you loved with all your heart. And I did love him, I know I did. I was just learning to love myself a little bit at last, or at least not hate myself so much. But John was never going to take it lying down. He was jealous, madly jealous, and things were going to get bad.

*   *   *

I hadn't been living with Jean long before she asked me to visit Bob with her, just for a social evening. She'd been drinking – and this was her one flaw. I've never been one for booze or drugs, but Jean often knocked back too much whisky. I guess it's one way of handling life, but it was a big worry. I asked her, 'Is it me driving you to it?'

And she said, 'No. I drive myself.'

This particular evening, I didn't want her to be on her own in such a state, so I did go with her, leaving Angie with a good friend of mine. Jean got there all right, but then passed out. Bob, a tall, thin, grey man, helped me to lay her down on the settee, then all of a sudden there was a thunderous knock on the door. Bob answered it – and a fist smashed right into his face. It was John. He must have followed me and Jean. As Bob crumpled to the floor and I stood frozen with shock, John strode over to Jean. He dragged her up and punched her round the head. Then he flung her on the floor, kicking her, going for the head again. I was screaming at him by now, 'Stop! Stop!' I could hear bones cracking. Nightmare. He was killing her.

I dashed to the phone and dialled 999. I yelled into the phone for ambulance and police. By now Bob had got to his feet, and between us we managed to pull John off Jean.

When I saw Jean in hospital the next morning, she was so badly beaten and disfigured I couldn't recognise her. This was way beyond anything John had dished out to me, and he had to pay for it. He was charged, and tried. One thing I remember is the tone of the judge's voice, very sneery and superior, as if he was talking about a lower form of life. In his summing up he called me 'a woman of no great virtue . . .'

So the changes in my life had brought more jealousy, more violence, more pain – and now my character was smeared across the papers for all the world to see. I was crushed, though more worried about what would happen to Angie. The judge had implied she might be in danger, and it took me a while to convince the Welfare she was healthy and safe, a normal little girl.

John wasn't sent down but put on probation, and ordered to stay away from me and Jean. Dramas apart – what my mother always called 'murders' even if nobody died – Jean and I went on to live happily together like an old married couple, both looking after Angie. Jean had insisted I gave up the shoplifting. 'I couldn't bear to lose you,' she said, and I was touched. We eventually got a nice flat in a big old house, the middle two floors. Before long Mother managed to get the basement flat here too, and involved herself in our lives. It turned out she knew the landlord – he was one of Gina's regular punters.

Jean managed her business herself. Very discreet, high-class clients and only by appointment, and never when Angie was at home. There was no need for Mother to stick her oar in. Anyway, after Don died she wasn't the big madam running the show any more. The boys had flown the nest by now as well, and Mother lived alone. She relied on her pension and hand-outs from Jean, who was very generous to us all. Mother would still needle her, though. She didn't like anyone being close to me. I just wanted Mother to shut up and go out to bingo.

After we'd been together about seven years, life took a bad turn. Jean's drinking got steadily worse, and though she never hurt me physically she could say spiteful things. Sex stopped. I thought it was because I'd got so fat. I was a size 20 by now. Our old closeness was fading, though I still loved her. Then

Jean met a couple of boys who were dealing in bent gear. Before long she was buying loads of stuff off them in the flat – jewellery, furs, stereos: expensive stuff. At one point there was a telly in every room. I begged her to stop, but she was taking no notice of me at all now. She was drunk every night and I despaired.

The inevitable happened. Early one morning there was a knock at the door. Half a dozen cops barged in and turned the place upside-down. The boys had been caught and grassed up Jean. I was arrested along with her, but released after a couple of hours. Jean had told them I was completely innocent.

She got eighteen months. I left the court feeling empty. Would we ever have a life together again?

I was with Jean's sister Carol and her girlfriend Jackie the day Jean was sentenced. They had a plan. They'd move in with me and Carol would take over from her sister. She was a very pretty blonde, and had been working as a stripper in London. She just oozed sex, so this line of work was right up her street. Carol was the original dizzy blonde, a bit dumb but kind-hearted and fun. She was straight-talking, never pretended to be anything she wasn't.

Jackie was the butch one of the couple. In those days the difference was much more marked than it is now, when unisex is the thing. Butch and fem, it was, the masculine and the feminine. Jackie did all the housework, and we all settled down. My contribution was to answer the phone, make appointments for Carol. At that time, I remember, it was £10.50 for hand relief, £15.50 for intercourse, £15.50 for French (oral) and £25 for French and intercourse. There wasn't any kinky sex, we never had a call for it. I used to get £5.50 for every punter she did, and believe me the girl was busy. Some days I would have £50 or more, a lot of money at the time.

Jean was moved to Styal Open Prison, up in Cheshire. I used to visit her every month. I lived for those visits, I missed her so much. But on my sixth visit she was distant, wouldn't look me in the eye. The Dear John letter that arrived soon after shouldn't have been such a shock. I was gutted, couldn't stop crying. I heard Carol tell Jackie that Jean was in love with a girl called Sylvia. If it wasn't for Angie, I swear I'd have topped myself.

I thought I was the lowest I could be, but no. There was another step down.

23

The Road to Hell

It was Christmas, my first without Jean for seven years. Carol and Jackie had gone to London so it was me and Angie and Mother in the house. The phone was ringing non-stop. Some men can't wait to get away from their families at Christmas, so it's a busy time for working girls. Mother was answering the phone as I was too depressed. I'd been drinking Scotch and Coke, though I'd never been one for the booze. It was Jean's favourite tipple.

By late evening Angie was in bed. After putting the phone down for the umpteenth time, Mother turned to me and said, 'I don't know why you don't do these punters, Tess.'

What! I couldn't believe my ears. 'Oh, no, I couldn't.'

'Why not?' asked Mother, calm as you like. 'Who are you saving yourself for? Jean? She doesn't want it, she's made that quite clear.'

Mother warmed up. 'Anyway, maybe if you did it and saved up, when Jean comes home you two could go away on holiday together. She couldn't refuse you once you'd made that sacrifice for her. That would really prove to her how much you loved her. She was good to you all those years, now it's your turn to prove how much you love her.'

Jean couldn't refuse me . . . Mother had a point. And just then I didn't give a damn.

'Book the next one who calls,' I said, and a big grin spread over Mother's face.

Then the deed was done. I was a prostitute. No going back. Once you've done it you can't un-prostitute yourself. And Mother was my pimp.

I was careful, though, only to work when Angie was at school – most men don't mind what time it is. No way was her life going to change as mine had.

Meanwhile I was still hoping for a real relationship in my life. I met Marti in a nightclub. She was a big girl with dark hair and blue eyes. She came back to the flat and that night we made love. The earth didn't move, but I was glad of the closeness, something to fill my empty heart.

Marti worked in a garage, and didn't know my line of work.

'Why don't you tell her?' said Mother.

'Not yet,' I said. I hardly wanted to admit it to myself, let alone someone I'd just met.

Within a week Marti moved in, and I still didn't tell her. A couple of days later I came in from shopping and Marti was sitting in the kitchen, crying. Mother was standing beside her.

'Tess, how could you do it?' Marti said between sobs. So Mother had beaten me to it. 'You've got to stop, you've—'

Mother broke in. 'Don't be a fool, Marti, don't stop her working. You'll get a new car and won't want for much.'

Straight to the point, Mother. Think what you can get out of something. Always practical. It was like the time we heard bad news about my sister Jess. She'd been off the radar for quite a while, well in with the druggy set. I'd hear the odd snippet now and again. The last I heard, she was living in a flat with some guy, then he buggered off and an old pro had moved in to help with the rent. She was called Slaggy Pat, and her name said it all. She was rough-looking, none too clean. She'd been around for years, mostly working the pubs, and it showed.

One dinnertime the phone rang, and it was Slaggy Pat. I recognised her croaky voice.

'It's Jess,' she said. 'She's taken an overdose.'

And the poor girl was dead. She'd left us all for the drugs, now the drugs had taken her. A lost soul, Jess, alone at the end. There were many tears for her, even from Mother.

But I won't forget what she said to Slaggy Pat the very next day. We were in Jess's flat, packing up her few possessions. 'If you're staying here, you'll have to earn your keep. Get some cards out and bring the punters in. I've got a funeral to pay for.'

I liked living with Marti, but I couldn't get over Jean. I heard stories about her when she was out of nick, sleeping with this girl and that, even one called Mary who was a heroin addict. I was livid. She'd left me for a junkie! I always blamed myself, though. If only I'd been better looking . . . if only this, if only that.

Meanwhile, I'd given up the game. Every time I did a punter it felt like a little bit more of my soul was chipped out. Even my old ploy of concentrating on something else didn't work. The idea of a legit job was a non-starter. Who'd employ me with my lack of skills? That's what I said to myself at the time, though of course now I know it was just an excuse. An honest woman would do anything to support herself and her child – scrub floors, anything. I can truly say I took it for granted that the only course for me was shoplifting again. Even the threat of prison and being parted from Angie didn't stop me. Mother thought I was mad giving up the paying punters, but it wasn't her who had to have men inside her.

Mother had a new job too. Somehow she'd wangled her way into running a charity shop in the town. In no time she was creaming off the good stuff that people donated, and using the shop to flog bent gear. One day I was in there, looking at a pile of records. I was going through them one by one, saying to myself, 'Got that one, got that one, oh, that's a good record, oh, but I've got it already.' Then I got to the last one and it had a label on it. 'To Tess from Marti'. The whole pile of records was mine. Mum swore she hadn't taken them, and it was no use arguing. It wouldn't be the first time that something of mine found its way into her possession.

Life with Marti jogged along, and I grew to love her. But history repeated itself, and after six years she left me. One night she didn't come home and I had a gut feeling. I was in a real state. What was I doing wrong? No one would ever want to live with me for ever, I thought. No till death do us part for me.

Marti left me for another woman, naturally enough. But that woman was a close friend of my sister Kath, and she was married with four kids. I'd never known the like. All four of us saw a lot of each other and I didn't pick up any clues. Marti must have been cheating on me behind my back, while this woman, Maggie, sat in my kitchen drinking tea, pretending to be friendly while planning to run off with my lover. What's more, Maggie did a Sophie's Choice with her kids. Calmly selected two to take with her, and left the other two with her husband. How anybody could do that beats me. People in my game get a lot of stick for what we do, we're supposed to be the scum of the earth, but here was a respectable married woman, a mother, pillar of the community, betraying her kids. I'd never sink so low.

As for Marti, I thought I'd done everything I could for her – I'd been good to her, hadn't I? Clothes and jewellery, plus a new car. How could she betray me? I felt unwanted and really ugly. It was then I realised that my three relationships – with John, Jean and Marti – had something in common. Apart from the first few months with each of them, I'd never felt loved or secure. I wanted love so much yet I managed to drive it away. I remembered all the times my mother had told me I was fat and ugly and no one would want me. She was right.

I was so desperate that I went on to make the biggest mistake of my life. A mistake that dragged me down to the lowest pit.

It was a year after Marti left. I was in my late thirties by now. Angie was a teenager, and she'd grown into a delightful girl. Like me she'd gone into hairdressing, but unlike me she stayed the course and became very good at it. I had no secrets from her. When I thought she was old enough, I'd told her about my life (though not about being sent out to men), and nothing seemed to faze her.

'I love you just the way you are,' she said, and I could have cried.

She was a popular girl, and her friends were always in and out of our home. Very different from my childhood! That was only one of the ways I was determined her life would be as different from mine as possible. All her friends knew I was gay, but it didn't seem to matter. They liked coming round our place.

Though I loved being so close to Angie, and had a bunch of good friends, I still yearned for that someone special. And one night in a club I thought I'd found her.

A friend of mine, Shirley, introduced me to someone called Chris Cave. At first sight I thought she was a gay boy, short and tubby with a fleshy face, a faint moustache and a goatee beard. But there was something odd about this person, and I soon found out what.

Chris had had a sex change, but not a full one. She'd had her breasts and womb removed, and she was taking hormone pills to make her facial hair grow and to lower her voice.

'I didn't go any further,' she told me. 'I couldn't have made it stand to attention.'

We got talking and it turned out she knew people I knew. I didn't fancy her one bit, but she held a certain fascination for me. She was staying at Shirley's for the weekend and we met again the next day. Chris seemed okay, so when she dropped by and asked if she could meet me the following weekend, I said, 'Yeah, why not?'

My Angie didn't like Chris one bit. 'There's something wrong there,' she told me. I wish I'd listened to her, but I was lonely, and that makes you vulnerable, makes you ignore warning signs.

Chris lived in London, and we arranged she'd come back down the following Friday for the weekend. On the Wednesday before, I received the biggest bunch of red roses you ever saw. They were gorgeous. The card read: 'Can't wait to see you again. Until Friday. Love, Cavey.'

It was that easy. That's all it took, one big bunch of red roses. When she arrived on that Friday I insisted she stayed with me, and that night we made love. Not altogether my cup of tea, the way she did it, but any attention is better than none.

Mother caught sight of us as we were going out next morning, and saved up her comments for when Chris had left on the Sunday.

'What are you doing with a bloke?' she asked. 'He wasn't a punter, was he?'

'No, she's a girl.'

'A girl? Bloody awful-looking one. She should do something about that facial hair.'

'She's a lesbian. She's had a sex change.'

'Oh, God, no. This time you've really gone off your head. I've seen you with some funny people but this one takes the cake. She's awful. How could you sleep with that?'

'Well, as you keep telling me, Mum, I'm no oil painting myself, so we should get on fine. Maybe this one won't leave me.'

'I bet she won't,' said Mother. 'No other cunt would have her.'

To which I could only say, 'Good.'

Chris and Mother didn't ever get on. In fact they hated each other. Chris was very strong-willed, and I thought it might do Mother good if someone stood up to her for a change.

Mother would have approved of Chris's business sense, though. She told me she made her money renting her flat out to a working girl for five hundred quid a week, while she herself lived in a council house.

'How much?' I asked, incredulous.

'That's cheap,' Chris said. 'The girls in London earn five hundred to a thousand every day.'

And Chris was free with her money, wining and dining and giving me presents. 'You don't put your hand in your pocket when you're with me,' she said. 'I'm the man here and I'll take care of you.'

Take care of me. I was thrilled, and the first few months were great. Chris treated me like a lady, praising me all the time and telling me not to keep putting myself down. She said I was a good-looking woman, very sexy in bed. I went up to her house a couple of times. It was a mess: dirty, poorly furnished, holes in grubby carpets and curtains. For all the money Chris was getting, she wasn't putting it into the house.

It wasn't long before I found out where the money went. I should have known. Chris was a drunk. She drank vodka and orange, doubles. The story of my life. I was destined to meet drinkers.

Chris wanted me to move to London but I wasn't sure. I loved Brighton, and anyway Angie was here. Chris said she would consider moving to Brighton but I knew she never would. Brighton was too tame for Chris.

Meanwhile I'd joined forces with another friend of mine called Jill, and we were shoplifting on a grand scale. We had a buyer, who took all our gear for a third of the price. So whatever we got we could sell. On a shopping exhibition to Crawley we got nicked. We'd been going back to Jill's car with the gear each time, and it was full. We were loaded. Six dustbin bags full of stolen gear, plus leather and suede coats, all in all about two thousand quid's worth. This time I'd well and truly got it. Holloway next stop.

While we were waiting for court, Chris said, 'Don't worry. If you go to prison I will wait for you. In fact I'll speak up for you in court if you let me.'

And she did. Everyone thought she was a man, Mr Christopher Cave. She told the court she loved me and wanted to marry me. She said she would take me away from Brighton and they believed her. I believed her. At long last someone really loved me.

The judge put me on a six-month deferred sentence on condition I went to live with Mr Cave, a man who seemed very much in love with me and would protect me.

So that's what happened. I had no choice. I went to London to live with Chris for six months. At last she'd got her own way.

We were the opposite of compatible in the home. I'm very clean and organised, Chris was a slob. I was constantly cleaning up after her, and started to feel like a slave. She said I could do up the house as I wanted, but didn't come up with the readies. If I mentioned money she grew angry, and I couldn't bear that. Chris insisted on going out every night and my savings were slowly dwindling away. Apart from anything else, I was paying the rent on my flat in Brighton. Angie was now sharing it with her boyfriend, but neither of them had much money.

'Better get a job,' said Chris. 'Go on the game again.'

Not that again. 'I'm too old,' I said.

'Not for kinks. There's more money in kinks than anything else. I know someone who'll give you work.'

I'd heard of kinks, of course, but wasn't sure what it involved.

'It's easy,' said Chris. 'You'll soon get the hang of it. Take domination – all you have to do is tell the punter what to do, he's your slave and you're the madam.'

There was more. Heavy domination, where you treated the punter like he was less than an animal. Made him eat dog food. Kicked him now and again, then made him beg. There was bed bondage, what she called tied and teased: you tied the punter to the bed then sexually teased him. Heavy bondage was another matter. You tied the guy until he couldn't move, then carried out his fantasy. It might be rubber and leather – either you or he, or both of you, wore it. Then there was caning, heavy or mild, and whipping. Some punters wanted it hard, they really wanted to be hurt. Water sports meant you peed on them. All these services started at sixty to a hundred quid. More unusual services such as anal sex started at £150.

God, I thought, things have changed out there. We never did these services in Brighton. I told Chris some of these services I wouldn't, couldn't do.

Chris took me to her friend, Lindi St Claire, known as Miss Whiplash. Lindi was a big, busty blonde. I could see she was surprised when she saw me. I wasn't the usual type she had seen Chris with. Lindi said to Chris, 'Well, your tastes have improved.' And, God help me, I was flattered. Lindi showed me around her gaff, a big house in Earl's Court. There were four phones ringing all the time, and the maid answered them one after another.

Lindi used the basement for working in. There were a number of rooms down there, all done out differently, rubber, leather, whatever, and racks of costumes and uniforms. What boggled me was the dungeon. I'd never seen anything like it. Racks you could stretch a man on, thumb screws, leg irons, armour with nails inside, hoods and masks and I don't know what. In the middle of the dungeon was a big wheel, with cards all around it describing different forms of punishment and torture. The idea was to strap a man spreadeagled on the wheel, then spin it. Whatever card the wheel stopped on would be the man's punishment.

I thought I knew a lot about what men wanted, but this was something else.

'You'll make plenty of money,' Chris said.

I thought, I'll have to, the way you spend it.

I started work next day and bluffed my way through. I couldn't believe it: these men were paying all this money to be hurt and degraded. At least no real sex was involved, just hand relief. At first I felt very awkward, and had to keep reminding myself that the men wanted this, they were paying good money for it and no one was forcing them. I did get the hang of it and earned lots of money, but there was always something that needed paying with Chris.

After about a month she objected to the money I paid Lindi for working in her flat, £100 a day. Why pay Lindi when she could have it? So I was soon working for Chris, and realising just what sort of a person she was. A ponce in every way.

Taking drugs, too. One night I caught her in the bathroom upstairs injecting herself with something. I grabbed the needle and threw it down the toilet. Chris looked at me, her face twisted. She gave me one punch and I hit the floor. She punched like a man, then she started kicking me along the landing and down the stairs. She kept kicking me until I was outside on the pavement.

Even John had never beat me so much. I was stunned in my mind as well as my body.

I had to leave. Next morning I was packing my clothes, still aching all over, when Chris came in and saw me.

'What are you doing?' she asked.

'I'm leaving you,' I said. 'I can't live like this. I hate drugs. I lost my sister down to drugs.'

Right away Chris started throwing my clothes across the room, then she locked the door. 'You're going nowhere,' she said.

'You can't keep me here,' I said.

'Oh, can't I? I'll phone the police and tell them you've broken bail. You've got to live with me, remember? They'll drag you back to jail.'

She was right. I still had two months to go. I couldn't face the thought of prison, though if I could have known what was coming I'd have gone for a nice safe cell.

Then Chris worked the soft soap on me. 'Please, Tess, don't leave me. I love you. I'm sorry I lost my temper. I won't do it again.'

I'm easily fooled. By the time the two months were up and I could have got out of her clutches, I was well and truly hooked. She frightened me to death. She was a sadist, treated me like dirt, abusing me physically and mentally, then being nice again. Meanwhile I was abusing paying punters in the flat. What an insane world.

Why didn't I leave? I didn't even love her the way I loved John, but something else was at work here. It was as if I'd been conditioned to obey, and in the face of a strong-willed person I couldn't fight. Again I thought I must deserve it. I took everything she dished out.

Me and Chris had been together, if you can call it that, for about five years when she took herself off for a break in Spain, living it up on my money. While she was away, I had a phone call from my sister Kath in Brighton.

'Mum's taken a turn for the worse,' she told me.

Mother had been ill for some time, with cancer. She'd had one operation but the cancer had returned. Nothing else to be done. I hadn't seen much of Mother while I was in London, going down just a few times a year, and of course when she was in hospital and convalescing. For the first time I didn't have her shadow hanging over me, even if my life was far from what I wanted it to be.

Now Kath was saying, 'The doctors think she should go into the hospice tomorrow.' That was sooner than we'd thought.

I met Kath in Mother's flat. Mother was lying in bed in the front room, looking sunken and exhausted. She recognised me, though. 'Took your time, didn't you?' she managed to say.

Me and Kath went into the kitchen to warm up some soup for Mother, talking between ourselves.

'Oh, Kath,' I said. 'She looks bad. She hasn't got long, has she?'

There was nothing wrong with Mother's ears. She could hear us talking, even if she couldn't make out the words. She always hated people talking when she couldn't hear them properly – she'd think they were talking about her, plotting and planning. They had secrets like she had secrets. She especially didn't like me and Kath talking together. She probably thought we were ganging up on her. And even now that thought must have been uppermost in her mind, as suddenly we heard her call out, in a hoarse, rasping voice.

'Tess!'

I stopped what I was doing and dashed into the front room, only to find Mother lying rigid, her eyes glassy, her mouth lopsided.

'Stroke,' said Kath behind me. 'She's had a stroke. I'll call the ambulance.'

Mother was taken to the local hospital, and made comfortable. I stood there looking at the wreck of the woman who had dominated my life. Pity welled up in me, though my eyes were dry.

I sat close to her, and looked into her eyes, which were watering, their fierce bright blue now faded.

'Can you hear me, Mum?' I asked.

Her eyelids flickered, there was the slightest nod of her head, though she couldn't speak.

I kept my voice low, but clear. 'Mum, I'm going back to London tonight, but do you want me to come down? Give up London and look after you? Is that what you really want?'

For a moment there was no response, then the trace of a smile moved on her lopsided mouth, and her eyes looked brighter. Again, that slightest of nods. Even the colour in her cheeks came back and for a moment she looked young again.

'Right. I'll just go back and pick up my stuff, and I'll be back down tomorrow. Don't you worry.'

I kissed her forehead, and I swear there was another look on that familiar face. A ghost of a smirk and a touch of the old 'I've won!'

Yeah, I thought, you've still got it, haven't you?

I was as good as my word, back down the next day with my gear. All the family was there that evening, standing round the bed. We took it in turns to sit with her, hold her hand, stroke her forehead. Then we left her, saying our farewells, telling her we'd be back in the morning.

An hour later, we had the phone call. Mother had died quietly. After a tumultuous life, she'd just slipped away. No more pretence, no more crying wolf, no more lipstick on her leg to be wiped off. This was real.

We all cried, but my tears were partly for me, for my guilt. I'd left her when I should have looked after her. I'd never done enough to please her, and now it was too late. For all that she did to me, got me into, she was still my mother, and it was a kind of love that I felt for her, mixed with a lot of regrets.

But she'd wanted me to be with her again, at the end. Maybe she really loved me. And after the stroke she'd never spoken again, so her last word on this earth was my name.

When Mother was alive she always told me, 'When I die, I'll come back and haunt you.' And somehow I never doubted her. After the funeral I almost expected her to walk into the room and say, 'Right, that's taught you all a lesson. Maybe now you'll remember you have a mother.'

I realise now that she did haunt me, but in my mind.

Chris came hightailing it back from Spain when she heard the news.

'I knew you'd need me,' she said.

Actually she was sniffing around for money, but Mother left very little, just enough to cover the funeral. I wanted to keep something of her near me, so I'd taken her wedding ring, and wore it on a chain round my neck.

I went back to London, and really couldn't face doing kinks again. I brought in Deaf Julie to do the business, a girl Chris had known, while I was the maid. It was around this time that the flat was raided. We got wind there was a watch on, and had time to bundle the evidence out of the flat. When the police arrived I was sitting there innocently knitting. We were all arrested, me, Julie and Chris, and next thing we're up in court on counts of running a disorderly house. By a stroke of luck we had a brilliant barrister who spotted a loophole in the law and we got off.

The press had been sniffing around as there was a whiff of scandal about the case. Some high-ranking politician had been caught in flagrante, dressed in women's clothing getting spanked. One paper called me Madam Sandra, and had me opening the door in red thigh-length boots and a red basque, kicking a man on a chain. Laughable, a total fabrication – never trust the press!

As for the man . . . he might have been a politician, but I couldn't possibly comment.

The whole thing was a farce, but nerve-racking all the same.

'You could do with a break,' said Chris in one of her sober moments. 'Let's go back to Spain.'

We stayed with a friend of Chris's, Anita, who'd fled from London after being charged with running a disorderly house. For the first couple of days it was all right, like a holiday, but Chris was taking more and more cocaine. She was off her head most nights, picking fights with me.

One night when we were coming back from a bar with Anita it all got too much for me. I snapped. 'I can't stand this,' I said. 'I'm leaving you.'

Next moment Chris's fist crashed into my face, and I was sent reeling. She grabbed the chain round my neck and pulled it so hard it broke. The ring rolled away on the pavement.

'That's my mum's ring!' I cried, scrabbling on the ground.

I could hear Chris and Anita laughing, and then I felt the most searing pain in the pit of my back where Chris had kicked me. My back had never been strong since John had beaten me when I was pregnant, and all I could do was lie on the ground, curled up. Chris kicked me again, and again, and Anita joined in. It seemed to go on for ever. Then it stopped.

I heard Chris's voice. 'That's where you belong, you fat slag, in the gutter. Why don't you do us all a favour and crawl into some hole and die?' Then she made a noise in her throat and gobbed on me. She was laughing again as she walked off with Anita.

When I could move, I looked for the ring. But I couldn't find it.

I didn't think I could sink any lower. But I did.

I spent the night in a cheap hotel, in agony, and took the next plane home. I went to hospital, and found I had three cracked ribs. Unfortunately that wasn't Chris's last leaving present.

I stayed in my Brighton flat with Angie, and when I was stronger went back to London. I had to hang on to the flat, to keep the money coming in. Julie had buggered off after the court case, and I brought in Juicy Lucy to work the gaff. She had six kids by six different fathers who were all in prison, so she had to get the money in.

I heard Chris had come back from Spain, and told myself that if she came calling I'd be strong and tell her to leave. Meanwhile I kept the door bolted.

She did call, early one morning. She came crashing through the front room window and before I knew it I was knocked senseless. When I woke up I was lying on the bed in the spare room, my head spinning. Chris came in holding a small glass. 'Take this,' she ordered, and I mechanically swallowed the liquid in the glass.

After that it was like I was in a different dimension, out of my head. I don't remember much about that time except I had terrible, dark, mad dreams. I pieced it all together later. Chris was giving me a drug, some kind of strong sedative, and keeping me locked in the spare room out of the way so she could work Juicy Lucy and take all the profit.

It was Angie who saved me. By now she was pregnant with her first child, and she was worried that she hadn't heard from me for a couple of weeks. She sent her boyfriend James to look for me, and, bless him, he wouldn't take no for an answer. He insisted on searching the flat, and found me huddled on the bed, a stinking, bedraggled scarecrow wandering in her wits.

Not that I knew it then, but the nightmare was over.

24

After the Storm

Once you've hit rock bottom, the only way is up . . . Not that it seemed like it at the time. I was a wreck, in mind as well as body. I gradually got my strength back, but my head was all over the place. I felt the lowest of the low, scum of the earth. I hated what had happened to me, I hated myself for letting it happen, I hated what I'd become. I kept breaking down in tears. To tell the truth, I felt like ending it all. As before, it was only the thought of Angie that kept me going. That, and the baby she was carrying. But what sort of grandmother would I be?

Angie tried to cheer me up, bless her, talking about the baby, telling me I'd be a great nan. But when did I ever listen to advice? When I was shacked up with someone and having a terrible time, my friends all meant well. They'd shake their heads, saying, 'Why do you let it happen, Tess? You're always so strong. Why don't you stand up for yourself?' Which was all very well, seeing as how I prided myself on being loud and confident in public, life and soul, all that sort of thing. But inside, the real Tess was having none of it. I'd walk over hot coals to protect my daughter, but I didn't have whatever it took to protect myself from someone once they'd got their hooks into me.

It all comes back to Mother. How could she have made such a doormat of me that I couldn't resist her even when I was grown-up? I realise more and more that sending me out to men was only the most obvious sign of the way she treated me, manipulated me. I was hers to command, like an object, a possession. And while she had a strong right arm and often used it to hit me, the lasting damage was what she said to me, how she used words to persuade me, scare me, give me false reassurance. In short, betray me. 'Sticks and stones may break my bones but names will never hurt me': don't you believe it. Words, calculated and cruel, can worm their way into the heart of you, and stay there. Sticks and stones hurt your bones, true. But bones mend. Words can break your soul, and what cure is there for that?

When I'd recovered enough to drive, I started giving Angie a lift to the hairdressing salon where she worked. And in the unpredictable, freaky way that things can happen in life, it was one of these trips that changed my life again.

It was the day after the Great Storm of October 1987. I'd dropped Angie at work, and was driving back to our flat, being careful of debris in the road, when I accidentally cut up the car behind me. Much blaring of horns, so I stopped and got out to check for any damage.

'Tess!'

Instead of road rage, it was a smiling welcome from the other driver, who'd also got out.

I recognised her straight away. Her name was Carol, and I'd known her for years in a friendly acquaintance sort of way. She didn't mix with my crowd, who as a result always said she was stuck-up, but I'd always found her interesting and easy to talk to. Very fanciable too – slim and stylish, like the young Suzie Quatro. She was quite the entrepreneur, Carol. I knew she dealt in property, and had also built up a successful business in America, breeding pedigree dogs.

We chatted for a while, catching up. Carol might not get involved in the local scene but she knew everybody.

'Cavey's gone, then?' she asked.

I could only say, 'Don't go there . . .'

Then I had a thought. 'I'm going back up to London soon, to sort out the flat,' I said. 'Why don't you pop up for a weekend?'

'Great,' she said. 'I'd love to.'

And that's the way my life wasn't only changed, it was saved.

By the New Year, me and Carol were a couple. I was as stunned as I was chuffed – I'd never dreamed she would go for someone like me. If I said that to her, she'd say, 'Someone like what? Don't do yourself down.' Don had said something like that years ago.

It was Carol's idea for me to join her in Wales for a while, to rest and sort myself out. She'd been renovating an ancient cottage, and it was nearly ready. I was happy to go. I just waited for Angie to have her baby first.

Seeing Angie with her new baby, a little girl as beautiful as her mother, I thought my heart would burst with happiness. I knew she would love that baby just as much as I loved her. And of course I loved the baby too – being a grandmother was wonderful. Angie was talking about getting married late in the year. She and James were in no hurry. So when I could see she was settled with the baby, I was ready to go, and come back later to help with the wedding.

I let out the London flat and stayed in Wales, in the wilds of Carmarthenshire, for six months. The peace and quiet did me a world of good, and I loved being so close to Carol. I must confess, though, that I'm a town girl through and through, and couldn't wait to get back to the hustle and bustle of Brighton. Still, I'd had time to think about things. I thought back over my life, and talked about it long into the night with Carol. Her head's screwed on all right, unlike mine, and she has a lot of insight into human nature. She gets things in perspective, untangles mixed-up feelings, very down-to-earth. In fact it was her idea for me to write my life story.

'Get it down on paper,' she said. 'It'll clear your mind, sort out how you feel about your mother and everything.'

I wasn't sure if anything would clear my head, short of Dyno-Rod, but thought I'd give it a go one day. Meanwhile I resolved never to screw up my life again.

More immediately, there was Angie's wedding to think about. I wanted to give her the best wedding ever. It'd be my pride and pleasure to give her a day she'd remember for the rest of her life. Small matter of the readies, though. Carol had been urging me to give up the London flat. She'd had some dealings with the vice world herself, working in a massage parlour when she was younger, so she wasn't snooty about it. She just felt I was mixed up in the low-rent end.

'I'll only get enough for Angie's wedding,' I said.

I decided to let the London flat go, and start a business in Brighton. A small business, but, I like to think, perfectly formed. At least, to start with.

I had a couple of girls at a time, working two or three days each – a job share, no less, just like an office job. And in fact the prostitution business is a business like any other in most respects. Supply and demand, competition, customer satisfaction . . . I looked after my girls, made sure they were healthy, and insisted on condoms. All through my life in the business I made it a policy never to take on a girl who wasn't already on the game. I'd never be the one to get a girl started. More than once I turned a girl away, urged her not to go down that road, find anything else. I've been many things in my life, but I've never been cruel, never deliberately hurt a person. I've tried to keep up standards of my own.

I never took my own advice, of course, so I might sound like a hypocrite. And it's true that while I paid lip service to the idea of getting out, in truth I never made much effort. After all, it was what I knew, what I was used to. I was good at it, being the madam of my own little brothel. And it paid, it paid big-time. The amount of money in vice would boggle your mind. It didn't take very long for me to rack up the ten grand for Angie's big day, a day that went like a dream.

Soon after the wedding, Carol treated me to a holiday in America. We went to Disneyworld and had a fabulous time, really memorable. Oddly enough, it was because of this holiday that I had what seemed like a message sent to me by my mother from beyond the grave.

When I'd been to Spain, I just needed a one-year passport that you could get at the post office. To go to America I had to have the full ten-year job, and for this I needed my birth certificate. I'd never seen this in my life, so I had to go back to Croydon and ask at the births and deaths place for a copy. The clerk couldn't find it at first. There was nothing in the name of Sandra Doreen Rebecca Joy Stevens. After I'd waited ages, she found it – but minus the Sandra. Apparently my real given name was Doreen Rebecca Joy Stevens. I'd gone through school and prison as Sandra and the name had never existed! God knows what Mother was playing at. Something to keep secret, maybe. She'd been dead for years, and now I had a little reminder of her old games.

By now, it was clear that me and Carol were committed to each other. She sold her cottage in Wales, and made a good profit. We set up home together in Brighton and Carol looked around for a business proposition. As I say, she didn't turn her nose up at vice, she just didn't like anything sleazy. She had her eye on a sauna parlour. She wasn't the first to set one up in Brighton, but she was the first to have planning permission for it, unlikely as it sounds. A very determined woman – no bureaucracy will get her down. And her business, Venus Health Studio, was high-end all right, de luxe relaxation and massage.

Meanwhile, I was getting uneasy in my business. The girls in town were changing. More and more foreign girls were coming in, Russian and eastern Europeans mostly, and it was just like what happens in a legal business. When there's a glut, the customer can pick and choose, and drive down the price. And punters started demanding services my girls weren't prepared to supply: anal sex, and French without a condom. Yet many more girls were prepared to do anything. 'Right, if I don't get it here, I know where I can get it,' a punter would say. And off he'd go.

Those poor girls, often promised a proper job, only to be raped and forced to service a whole string of men by ruthless pimps. Often the girls are on drugs, and once a girl's hooked, that's it. She's so desperate, she'll do anything, absolutely anything, risking her health and her life twenty, thirty times a day just to get enough for a fix.

If people think that there's no distinctions in vice, they're wrong. They might say my business was criminal and immoral, but I must say this for it: I worked in the sex trade, not the slave trade.

I closed down my business, and with Carol set up a sauna parlour called Kittens. It was fabulous, and we flourished for a while, till a greedy landlord and increasing rent put the kibosh on it. It seemed the right time to close the door on that whole way of life anyway. I was in my mid-fifties, ready to retire, so to speak. Carol's younger than me, and always active. She keeps up the property investment – she was doing up houses and selling them for a healthy profit long before any of those shows on telly. She's a talented potter too, and our home displays a lot of her work. We live with a boisterous Airedale called Dexter, and as I'm writing this he's whining to be let out.

It took me years to get around to taking up Carol's suggestion and writing about my life. Going over and over it, I've returned time and again to that biggest influence on my life, my mother, trying to distance myself from her, to see her clearly without all the confusion and hurt and guilt. It's my firm belief that it was the way she treated me when I was a little kid that marked me for life. Other people might have had the strength of character to get over it, but I didn't. I suppose if I'd been strong, Mother wouldn't have been able to work on me in the first place. Even now I'm so anxious to please people that I put on a jolly act so they'll hang around and want to be my friend.

Mother used to say, 'Yeah, you think you're so fucking popular, don't you? But you're so fucking stupid. You think people are laughing at your jokes, but really they're laughing at you.'

That'd get me every time, even when I was grown-up.

Carol knows me better than anyone else in my life. It's as if the real me is Doreen, and only Carol knows her, and loves her for what she is. 'I always knew you were putting on an act,' she says, 'laughing at yourself before anyone else had the chance. You must believe you're a special person in your own right.'

That always gives me heart, for a while. It's just that at night, when I can't sleep, the old memories come back to the surface, and in my head I talk to my long-dead mother. 'I know what you did, Mum, and when. I might have a bash at why, too – the money. But what I don't know, I've never known since I had my Angie, is how you could do it.'

Nothing's more important than bringing up a child to be loved and secure. Get it wrong, and the child could well suffer for the rest of its life, as I know to my cost.

Carol's a great one for not putting up with any bad stuff. Her advice is, 'For God's sake let it go. You can't change the past, just come to terms with it. Don't let it ruin the rest of your life.'

She's right, of course she is. And I'm trying. Every day I count my blessings. My loving daughter and her family, and Carol – my wonderful Caz – and a great bunch of friends. I'm much better off than many another pensioner in the country. I'm loved, I know I am, and I cling to that. It's what I was looking for my whole life, and I mustn't let the past stand in its way.